# The Roman Catholic Church in Colonial Latin America

*Borzoi Books* on Latin America

*General Editor*
LEWIS HANKE
*University of Massachusetts, Amherst*

# The Roman Catholic Church in Colonial Latin America

———◆———

EDITED WITH AN INTRODUCTION
BY

## Richard E. Greenleaf

*Tulane University*

❧

*Alfred A. Knopf* / *New York*

THIS IS A BORZOI BOOK
PUBLISHED BY ALFRED A. KNOPF, INC.

———•••———

Library of Congress Catalog Card Number: 71–130774

Standard Book Number: 394–30290–7

Manufactured in the United States

First Edition
9  8  7  6  5  4  3  2  1

# Acknowledgments

Many people have contributed to the ideas and the format of this volume. My interest in Latin-American Church history was nourished for many years by Professor France V. Scholes, who encouraged me and shared his vast knowledge of the field. Professor Eleanor Burnham Adams, to whom this volume is dedicated, has been my mentor and scholarly associate for over a decade; her own scholarly contributions to the field have been an inspiration. The Reverend Fathers of the Academy of American Franciscan History, especially Antonine Tibesar and Mathias Kieman, have been a guiding influence on this Protestant whose field is Spanish colonial Church history. Professor Lewis U. Hanke, general editor of the Borzoi Books on Latin America, has unfailingly given excellent advice and direction. Father Jerome Jacobsen, editor of *Mid-America: An Historical Review,* was most helpful in securing appropriate excerpts on the work of the Jesuits in the New World. Finally, the cooperation of individual authors of selections included in this volume is gratefully acknowledged. My secretary, Mrs. Patricia Núñez Martínez, contributed materially to the preparation of the manuscript.

Richard E. Greenleaf

# Contents

# Introduction

The historian faces a difficult problem when he tries to construct a general account of the Roman Catholic Church in colonial Latin America. Clarence Haring, Charles Gibson, and Antonine Tibesar have undertaken this task so skillfully that their writings constitute primary references for those seeking authoritative information.[1] In this volume the editor has gathered essays which show that the Church functioned as a political and economic institution and as the social and intellectual catalyst of conquest and colonization in Hispanic America between 1492 and 1810.

> Spain transmitted to America her culture, and in large measure her political ascendancy, through the instrumentality of the Church. . . . The Church defended the divine sanctity of kings; the crown upheld the ecumenical authority of the Roman Catholic Church.[2]

Haring's statement supports the view that the Catholic Church in Spanish America was more than a religious institution; it was also an instrument of conquest, colonization, and governance of native peoples and colonists in the New World.

The Spanish monarchy and its Portuguese counterpart exercised vast supervisory powers over the colonial Church under the aegis of the Patronato Real, which included in

---

[1] Clarence H. Haring, "The Church in America," in *The Spanish Empire in America* (New York: Oxford University Press, 1952), pp. 179–208; Charles Gibson, "Church," in *Spain in America* (New York: Harper & Row, 1966), pp. 68–89; Antonine Tibesar, editor and contributor, "The Church in Latin America," *The New Catholic Encyclopedia* (New York: McGraw-Hill, 1967), Vol. 8, pp. 448–469.

[2] Haring, *op. cit.*, p. 179.

theory the right of presentation of every ecclesiastical officer
in the Indies, collection of the tithe, approval of all Church
literature before it was circulated, delineation of geographical boundaries of Church jurisdictions, and so forth.[3] Viceroys acted as vice-patrons and thus ensured close association
of political and religious functions in colonial administration. The obvious political character of Church activities
in the New World conditioned the institutional development of Roman Catholicism, determined its goals, and chan-
neled its activities:

> In effect, the Church in Spanish America was to be-
> come a bureau of the royal government dependent on
> the royal Council of the Indies for personnel, di-
> rectives, and finances—for everything, that is, save
> doctrine. And so the King found it very convenient
> to assign to his Church in Spanish America those areas
> of public administration that the state was either un-
> able or unwilling to administer: education, culture,
> and social welfare. The cooperation of the state was
> generous and often very enlightened, and the work
> performed by the Church benefited enormously from
> this cooperation. Yet, it also meant that for the
> Church the political element was to be in Spanish
> America even more pervasive than in Spain itself.[4]

The influence of politics in colonial religion was so per-
vasive that some scholars have wondered whether the Patronato Real was a benign influence or a retrogressive agent:

> The American Church became in fact a national
> church, living within the orbit not of the Roman

[3] See William Eugene Shiels, *King and Church: The Rise
and Fall of the Patronato Real* (Chicago: Loyola University
Press, 1961).
[4] Tibesar, *op. cit.*, p. 449.

Papacy but of the Council of the Indies, and attached
to Rome by very tenuous bonds.[5]

Against this background, Selection 1 discusses the guiding
principles of institutional development of colonial religion
from the reign of Ferdinand and Isabella until the independence movements.

During the first century of its existence, the Latin-American Church was concerned with building an institutional
framework appropriate for its mission in the New World.
Crucial to institutional development was the formulation of
mission techniques so that the variegated group of American Indians could be absorbed into Iberian religion and
culture. By the end of the sixteenth century the Spanish
monarchy had delimited the functions and areas of responsibility of diocesan and missionary clergy. The vast hierar-
chical apparatus of bishoprics and archbishoprics established
in the sixteenth century was expanded during two succes-
sive centuries to include supervision of the spiritual welfare
of both the Indian populations and the Spanish colonists.[6]

The conversion of the Indian and his integration into
Spanish culture raised some fundamental philosophical and
theological questions for both the clergy and the colonist.
Whether the native was rational enough to become a Eu-
ropeanized Catholic and whether he was entitled to protection of the universal fatherhood of God and the brother-
hood of man, and therefore to equal protection under Spanish law, generated heated controversies. Selection 2 describes the development of Spanish Renaissance humanist
thought in the Empire and the conflict between Christian
humanism and Spanish materialism in colonization policy.

---

[5] Haring, *op. cit.*, p. 182; see also Tibesar, *op. cit.*, pp. 449–
450, 455.
[6] See the excellent maps employed by Tibesar, *op. cit.*, pp.
465–467, to show the administrative development of the Church
in Mexico, Caribbean America, and South America.

Selection 3 tells how a Mexican bishop applied Renaissance humanist ideas to the specific problems of converting and teaching the Indian, and Selection 4 deals primarily with the theories of just war which some Spaniards tried to use to justify exploitation of the native populations. Selection 5 examines the special problems of Franciscan missionaries in Peru, where the friars organized Indian *doctrinas,* or quasi-parishes.

The greatest administrative problem facing the Church in the sixteenth-century was that of alleviating conflict between missionary clergy and bishops over jurisdiction, power to administer the sacraments in Indian parishes, and line of authority to the king. Because there were not enough secular priests to undertake the spiritual conquest of America, the regular clergy were granted special faculties ordinarily reserved for their diocesan colleagues. By virtue of the papal bull *Exponi nobis* of 1522, known in the Spanish world as the *Omnimoda,* prelates of the order clergy were granted the right to exercise most episcopal powers in areas where there were no bishops or where the bishop's see was two-days' travel from the monastic establishment.[7] Thus the regular clergy received a status of virtual autonomy in missionary affairs—subject to the Pope and the king rather than suffragan to any episcopal authority.

As the bishops assumed their sees in the sixteenth century, the prelates were loath to relinquish their extraordinary faculties. Bishops were confirmed and expanded in their powers by the Council of Trent (1545–1563) which revamped and clarified dogma and practice and decreed that only clergy subject to episcopal authority could administer the sacraments. Scholarly religious prelates in the New World made a strong case for excluding bishops from

---

[7] See Richard E. Greenleaf, *Zumárraga and the Mexican Inquisition 1536–1543* (Washington, D.C.: Academy of American Franciscan History, 1962), pp. 8–11 for workings of the *Omnimoda.*

America, contending that the missionary clergy had already organized the spiritual conquest and that the king was Royal Vicar in the Empire.[8] The monarchy vacillated in determining the jurisdictional issues; it suspended the Trentine dicta in 1567 and then called a junta, or council, in 1568. At this council it was decided that the bishop rather than the Pope would henceforth delegate powers to the regular clergy. In 1574 these mandates were incorporated into the famous *Ordenanza de Patronazgo,* which heralded the victory of the bishops.[9] But actual implementation of the order was delayed for decades; in some areas its dictates were never carried out.

The policies of Philip II in dealing with the conflict between the regular and the secular clergy often appear more political than religious. By confusing authority and responsibility in the Empire, he was able to teach bishops and prelates alike that the monarchy was the supreme religious authority. Selection 6 deals with the conflict between the regular and the secular clergy in light of the king's policies. The Portuguese kings, who exercised royal patronage in Brazil, encountered many of the same problems there. On the whole, however, the Church in Brazil in the sixteenth century was freer of political controls than was the Church in the Spanish colonies. The part played by the Jesuits in the Counter Reformation and their commitment to the prerogatives of the monarchy probably made strict supervision unnecessary. Perhaps the greatest Portuguese Jesuit missionary in the early colony was Manuel da Nóbrega. His organization of the missions of Brazil is the subject of Selection 7.

---

[8] Arthur Ennis, *Fray Alonso de la Vera Cruz, O.S.A.* (*1507–1584*) (Louvain, Belgium: Imprimerie E. Warny, 1957), pp. 101–103, 106–107, 144–148, has illuminating data on the Royal Vicariate.

[9] See Robert C. Padden, "The Ordenanza de Patronazgo, 1574: An Interpretative Essay," *The Americas: A Quarterly Review of Inter-American Cultural History,* 12 (1956), 333–354.

The history of religious achievement in sixteenth-century Latin America is largely the story of individual churchmen. The seventeenth century, which has been called the Baroque age of Latin-American culture, was an era of increasing refinement of existing institutions. As the Church organized daily activities to a greater degree, colonial society entered a stage of petrifaction. The rigid and complex institutional framework which resulted was accompanied by a Baroque mentality that is aptly described by Irving A. Leonard:

> a tendency to shift from content to form, from ideas to details, to give new sanctions to dogmas, to avoid issues, and to substitute subtlety of language for subtlety of thought; it served to repress rather than to liberate the human spirit, and to divert by spectacles, by overstatement, and by excessive ornamentation.[1]

But the social and intellectual milieu was far from ossified, and there was a surprising viability within religious institutions and Spanish Catholic culture, especially in those areas where European Catholicism had to accommodate itself to American reality. In Selection 8, Professor Leonard tells of an archbishop of the period who became viceroy of New Spain; here we get a picture of the private as well as the ceremonial side of seventeenth-century religious life.

The reluctance of the Spanish Church to allow those born in the colonies to become members of the hierarchy in the New World was evident from their staffing of the ten archdioceses and thirty-eight dioceses in Spanish America. Friar Antonine Tibesar's calculations reveal that in Mexico during the entire colonial period only 32 of the 171 bishops and archbishops were Mexican, and in South America only 64 of the 535 bishops and archbishops were American-

---

[1] Irving A. Leonard, *Baroque Times in Old Mexico* (Ann Arbor: University of Michigan Press, 1959), p. 28.

born.[2] In general, native-born and American-born priests had little prospect of rising to high positions in the diocesan clergy. This circumstance created a hiatus between the higher clergy and the priesthood and had grave consequences for the Church. It is no surprise that the lower clergy supported the colonial struggles for independence, while the bishops, for the most part, remained staunchly royalist.

A similar situation prevailed within the ranks of the regular clergy as a struggle developed between the creole friars and their Spanish brethren for control of the various religious orders in America. Selection 9 examines the details of the conflict in seventeenth-century Peru and the attempt to solve it by forced alternation in office of Spanish and creole prelates. Jurisdictional conflict between the regular and the secular clergy continued throughout the seventeenth century despite the 1574 pronouncement of Philip II awarding the real power in the colonial Church to the bishops. The legal crisis in the Jesuit missions sparked by the jurisdictional conflict is the theme of Selection 10.

Portugal stood in constant danger of losing control of her Brazilian empire during the seventeenth century. The invasion of the Dutch in 1624, the sorry state of the colonial economy, and the critical decline in missionary endeavor combined to bring the colony to the brink of disaster. More than any other man, the Jesuit António Vieira devised ways to alleviate Brazil's pressing problems. He led the fight to abolish Indian slavery and to humanize Indian labor institutions. He showed technical competence in his efforts to stimulate economic growth. Surprisingly tolerant toward the Jews, he proposed to use their capital and business acumen to help stabilize the colony.[3] His project for the

---

[2] Tibesar, *op. cit.*, p. 451.
[3] Charles R. Boxer, *A Great Luso-Brazilian Figure: Padre António Vieira, S.J. 1608-1697* (London: The Hispanic and Luso-Brazilian Councils, 1957).

founding of the Brazil Company in 1649, discussed in Selection 11, saved Brazil from continued Dutch domination.

While the major viceregal centers of the Spanish and Portuguese Empires struggled with tensions and crises during this middle century of the colonial era, some of the remote jurisdictions remained tranquil, safely living in the neo-medieval "long siesta of the seventeenth century." [4] The University of Cordova in the Bishopric of Tucumán was a case study in the survival of medievalism. A traditionalist curricula prepared the student, especially the budding theologian, for his role in the Aristotelian scheme of things. Prototype of the provincial university, the Cordova school epitomized the cultural time lag between most small educational foundations and the viceregal centers. Selection 12 tells how this university was founded during the seventeenth century and how its courses of study were established.

The primary agency that sought to protect Spanish Catholic culture and Roman Catholic dogma in America was the Holy Office of the Inquisition. Founded in the West Indies as early as 1517, the Holy Office of the Inquisition was under the control of bishops as ecclesiastical judges ordinary; where there were no bishops, monastic prelates performed inquistorial functions. This arrangement lasted until 1569 when Philip II founded two Tribunals of the Holy Office of the Inquisition in Mexico City and Lima, both suffragan to the Council of the Supreme and General Inquisition in Spain. A third court was established in New Granada in 1610. An episcopal-type Inquisition had operated in Brazil since 1531.[5] During the sixteenth century, the Holy Office was preoccupied with three large problems: Reformation heresies in the New World; the incursions of corsairs, or privateers; and the insincerity of Judaizantes (Jews who converted to Catholicism but practiced their old

---

[4] Leonard, *op. cit.*, p. 52.

[5] See Richard E. Greenleaf, "The Inquisition in Latin America," *The New Catholic Encyclopedia* (New York: McGraw-Hill, 1967), Vol. 8, pp. 462–464.

religion in private) and unorthodox conduct among the recently converted Indian population.[6]

Even though Philip II withheld from the new Tribunals of the Holy Office jurisdiction over Indians, the Inquisition continued to deal with the perplexing problem of enforcing Indian orthodoxy in the seventeenth century and the bishops contrived an entire branch of the Provisorate, or Vicar General's office, to investigate Indian heresy. Unfortunately, the investigations of bishops and Inquisitors were necessary, for in many areas of the Empire Christianity and the native religion had combined and created a religion that was Catholic in form but pagan in practice. During the seventeenth century many pastors discovered recurrent idolatry and religious syncretism among their flocks, and the provincial clergy had to devise ways to extirpate heresy and reeducate the Indian in true Christianity.[7] Selection 13 reveals the extent of the problem in Oaxaca in New Spain.

During the century after the Bourbons came to the Spanish throne in 1700, the Church became more of an instrument of regalism than it had been during the two preceding centuries of Hapsburg patronage. Gallican ideas, which supported a national church free of papal supervision, blended with eighteenth-century Josephinism, which upheld state-directed religion and Church reforms effected by the government. The Bourbon monarchs did enact changes in religious conditions:

> increase in parishes, demarcation of dioceses, better remuneration of clergy, the reorganization of theological studies, were directed in the first place by reasons

---

[6] See Richard E. Greenleaf, *The Mexican Inquisition of the Sixteenth Century* (Albuquerque: University of New Mexico Press, 1969).

[7] Richard E. Greenleaf, "The Inquisition and the Indians of New Spain: A Study in Jurisdictional Confusion," *The Americas: A Quarterly Review of Inter-American Cultural History*, 22 (1965), 138–166.

of state: pastoral care was held to be inseparable from the safety of the State.[8]

State-directed reform entrenched the view of Bourbon kings of Spain that the Patronato Real was not a series of papal concessions to the state but rather an affirmation of the power inherent in sovereignty. Thus it was easy to understand why Charles III (1759–1788) would not tolerate clerical disobedience and why he was suspicious of any religious order, such as the Jesuits, that functioned as "a state within a state." It is often alleged that Bourbon interference in Church affairs caused faith to be weakened in the eighteenth century. Whether or not the Church declined in moral stature during the last century of the colonization is a controversial topic; broadly based archival studies are needed to test many of the current generalizations.

It is true that the state ruled with a heavy hand. Between 1752 and 1767 the order clergy were divested of their Indian parishes, an action which culminated in the uncompromising expulsion of the Jesuits in 1767.[9] It is also true that Charles III and his colleagues made Spanish Catholic culture more secular as they embraced philosophical eclecticism and some of the new political and economic ideas of the Enlightenment. But the extent of Enlightenment influence in any given area of the Empire is hard to determine. Certainly members of the clergy were the most avid propagators of the new political and social philosophies, but as Mario Góngora has explained:

Only a small, but influential, number of the clergy adhered to the principles of the Enlightenment; the majority continued to be faithful to the Scholastic training that prevailed in the 17th century and at the

---

[8] F. Maass, "Josephinism," *The New Catholic Encyclopedia* (New York: McGraw-Hill, 1967), Vol. 7, p. 1118.

[9] See the excellent analysis of Magnus Mörner, *The Expulsion of the Jesuits from Latin America* (New York: Knopf, 1965).

beginning of the 18th. It was a case of an intellectual elite within a more passive group.[1]

Selected 14 probes these different attitudes of clergy toward the ideas of the Enlightenment.

Perhaps the staunchest foe of the doctrines of the Age of Science and the Age of Reason was the Holy Office of the Inquisition. Almost any source will regard the eighteenth-century Holy Office as a decadent, moribund institution, largely because it had become a political instrument. More serious study of source material is needed before this interpretation can be allowed to stand; the Holy Office had, in fact, always been a political instrument in the Spanish Empire. The failure of Charles III and his ministers to assign to the Inquisition its proper place in the task of preserving political and religious orthodoxy is one of the themes of Selection 15.

The decline of clerical morality in the late colonial period has often been linked with the growing wealth of the Church. But was this the case? To the archivist who investigates the documentary sources, it would appear that there was as much immorality among the clergy during the sixteenth century as at the end of the colonial period.[2] But

---

[1] "Church and Enlightenment in Latin America," *The New Catholic Encyclopedia*, Vol. 8, pp. 440–441; see also John Tate Lanning, "The Church and the Enlightenment in the Universities," *The Americas: A Quarterly Review of Inter-American Cultural History*, 15 (1959), 333–349.

[2] Inquisition archives in Mexico, Peru, and Spain are good sources for the study of the morality of the clergy, since most breeches of conduct and discipline were handled by the Holy Office. While contemporary sources testify to the worldliness of the clergy in most areas of the Empire, many of the generalizations about immorality and corruption in Peru are quoted from Jorge Juan and Antonio de Ulloa's *Noticias Secretas de América* (London: Bany, 1826). After a celebrated dialogue on the veracity of the *Noticias* (see Lewis U. Hanke, "Dos Palabras on Antonio de Ulloa and the *Noticias Secretas*," *Hispanic American Historical Review*, 16 (1936), pp. 479–514). Luis Merino, in his *Estudio Crítico Sobre las "Noticias Secretas de América" y el*

how should immorality be interpreted—in a stuffily self-righteous way or as a reflection of the morals of the society in which the clergy ministered? Church historians have yet to formulate criteria for evaluation of this controversial topic.

The wealth of the Church at the end of the colonial era needs serious study. Generalizations abound, but statistics are fragmentary. Whether the Church was an economic burden to the Spanish colonies is a question frequently asked. What the clergy accomplished in philanthropy, education, and hospitals is sometimes overlooked. In Selection 16, Clarence Haring gives a fair appraisal of the controversy over Church wealth. More-detailed information on the sources of Church income and the resources of charitable institutions known as *Cofradías* (confraternities), and estimates of disbursements as well as of possessions and income, await primary research by competent scholars. Friar Antonine Tibesar declares:

> Only when the necessary preliminary studies have been done can it be determined if the Church in Spanish America remained faithful to the vast responsibility thrust upon it by the reluctance of the state to care for education and charity and by the generous gifts of the faithful.[3]

One archival study done to assess the role of the nunneries in the economy of New Spain is extracted in Selection 17. Students of Inquisition finance tend to question the familiar generalization that the Holy Office prosecuted heretics in order to line its pockets. Until detailed analyses of many hundreds of volumes of Inquisition account books prove

---

*Clero Colonial (1720–1765)* (Madrid: Instituto Santo Toribio de Mogrovejo, 1956), pronounced them to be lacking in perspective with a tendency toward rhetorical exaggeration. Future studies may revise Juan and Ulloa, either documenting the charges of immorality or placing them in more accurate perspective.

[3] Tibesar, *op. cit.*, p. 460.

the contrary, Haring's remark that it would be difficult to sustain these charges must be allowed to stand, as must his judgment that "there is certainly no clear evidence that the economic backwardness of the colonies can be ascribed to the Inquisition." [4]

In Brazil during the last century of Portuguese domination, the keynote of administration was reform. An enlightened prime minister, the Marquis de Pombal, had set the pattern for the clergy to follow. Although Brazilian economic and social planners remained within the confines of liberal orthodoxy, they expounded many Enlightenment theories of environmentalism, education, and the natural laws of economics. Ideas and techniques of nascent capitalism and of the physiocrats pervaded the thinking of one influential cleric, Bishop José Joaquín de Cunha de Azeredo Coutinho, who had specific recommendations for stimulating the Brazilian sugar industry, and who was committed to social change through a new educational curricula. His influence in bringing the ideas of the Enlightenment to Brazil and on the heritage of peaceful change in the political economy is described in Selection 18.

There can be no doubt that by the eighteenth century the Church in Latin America had ceased to be a missionary agency and that the Bourbon reformers, by reducing the power and jurisdiction of the mendicants, had given lower priority to missions than to diocesan activity. Yet the founding of new chains of missions in the borderlands of North America and the revivified efforts of the Jesuits among the Abipón of South America show that Jesuit and Franciscan friars continued a proud tradition of converting and teaching the Indians. Selection 19 deals with the Argentine missions, and Selection 20 surveys the problems of missiology and the conflict between the Bishop of Durango and the Franciscans of New Mexico, where the transfer of authority to the secular clergy had never been effected.

---

[4] Haring, *op. cit.*, p. 205.

In colonial times the Church was a house of intellect as well as a house of worship. Surely those in the clerical establishment were the best-educated group in the Spanish and Portuguese Empires. These men and women brought culture as well as religion to the areas in which they served. Many colonial scholars were to be found within the ranks of the clergy, and many more were products of Church education. Culture was transmitted to both the humble masses and to the literate classes through religious art and architecture. Cathedrals, religious paintings and statuary, and liturgical music conveyed the grandeur of Iberian civilization. Throughout the Americas, indigenous art and craftsmanship blended with the new Catholicism to produce beautiful hybrid, or mestizo, styles, and Indian variations on Spanish forms produced lasting tributes to the Christian faith. Selection 21 surveys the building and ornamentation of New World cathedrals, and Selection 22 shows the rich florescence of Ecuadorian art, which developed from mestizo origins. Erudition and technical competence in linguistics among the missionary clergy were necessary complements to the techniques of converting and teaching the natives. Only through a relatively sophisticated knowledge of Indian languages, ethnohistory, and archaeology could the friar hope to secure and to retain his converts. The final article, Selection 23, assesses the learning and competence of the Franciscan missionary scholars in colonial Central America.

Professor Charles Gibson has stated:

> Ecclesiastical history remains one of the most difficult branches of colonial Spanish America's past to evaluate accurately. Much depends upon one's conception of the proper role of religion in any society, a matter on which historians, no less than others, disagree.[5]

No one can deny the herculean achievement of the Church in converting Spanish America and Brazil to Roman

---

[5] Gibson, *op. cit.*, p. 89.

Catholicism and in implanting Iberian culture there. The Church was a surprisingly viable, many-faceted institution, never monolithic in administrative character, that cast an aura of influence over the entire range of colonial life and society. This brief essay and the readings included in the volume are designed to help the student assess the extent of that influence.

~§ I §~

# The Church in the Sixteenth Century

# ❦ 1 ❧

## France V. Scholes

————◆❖◆————

# An Overview of the
# Colonial Church

*Born in 1897, France V. Scholes has devoted fifty
years to the study of the ecclesiastical history of New
Spain and the Hispanic southwest. As an investigator
for the Carnegie Institution in Washington, D.C.,
and as a researcher in the principal archives of Spain
and Mexico, he uncovered large numbers of valuable
documents on Church history. For many years professor, graduate dean, and academic vice-president of the
University of New Mexico, Professor Scholes contin-
ues to teach at Tulane University, where he trains
young scholars in paleography and archival techniques. This selection stresses both political and religious dimensions of the colonial Church.*

The guiding principles of Spanish governmental policy
from the age of Ferdinand and Isabella to the nineteenth
century were orthodoxy and absolutism. By the conquest
of Granada, the establishment of the Inquisition as a separate tribunal for the extirpation of heresy, the expulsion of
the Jews, and the initiation of that policy of whittling
down the charter of liberties of the Moors which culminated

From France V. Scholes, "Church and State in New Mexico
1610–1650," *New Mexico Historical Review,* Vol. 11 (1936), pp.
9–19 *passim.* Reprinted by permission of the *New Mexico Historical Review* and the author.

in the expulsion of the Moriscos in 1609–1614, the Catholic Kings completed the territorial reconquest of Spain and assured the triumph of Roman Catholic orthodoxy within their dominions. No less important were their victories over the feudal nobility, the Cortes, and the municipalities by which they laid the foundations for the absolutism of the Hapsburgs and Bourbons. Centralization of political power in the Crown matched the imposition of orthodoxy in matters of conscience, and henceforth the two despotisms, political and spiritual, were identified with Spanish tradition.

But neither the Catholic Kings nor their successors believed that the maintenance of orthodoxy required them to guarantee to the Church all of the privileges it had acquired during the long centuries of the Reconquest. Although ready to recognize the Church as a separate corporation with its own system of organization, law, and courts, with special privileges under the ecclesiastical *fuero* and with rich endowments, the Spanish monarchs were firm in their purpose to assert the preponderance, "or at least the liberty of action," of the State in dealings with the Church, and to limit those ecclesiastical privileges which threatened the sovereignty of the State in temporal affairs. Politico-ecclesiastical relations were characterized by an increasing regalism which culminated in the Bourbon absolution of the eighteenth century.

The discovery of America created new responsibilities, as well as unlimited opportunities, for the business of governing a vast colonial empire raised problems of the first magnitude. It was inevitable that the principles of absolutism and orthodoxy which the Catholic Kings were making effective in the Old World should be applied in the New. The Indies were regarded as separate realms united with the Crown of Castile in the person of the king, and political organization was based on the Castilian model. Royal control was imposed by means of a separate Council of the Indies, appointed by and responsible to the Crown, which acted as the supreme administrative organism for the colonies, and by local administrative officers and tribunals responsible to King and Council. Even the municipalities which in the beginning represented a certain amount of local self government rapidly lost their democratic character. The manner in which the Crown tried to impose its will in colonial affairs is best illustrated by the mass of legislation on details of government and administration. On the ecclesiastical side, the supremacy of Roman Catholic orthodoxy was secured by the imposition of restrictions on the emigration to America of foreigners, Jews, New Christians, and persons who had been punished by the Inquisition, and by the ultimate establishment of the Holy Office in America with very wide powers of independent jurisdiction. The conversion of the aboriginal population was declared to be the most important aim of colonial enterprise, and the Crown expended large sums on the support of missions, the building of churches, and the endowment of ecclesiastical foundations.

The Spanish monarchs were just as eager, however, to assert a preponderance over the Church in the New World as in the Old. In certain respects it was possible to begin with a clean slate in the New World, especially with regard to ecclesiastical appointments, the erection of dioceses, and the establishment of ecclesiastical foundations, and the kings took full advantage of the opportunity. Yielding to pressure from the Catholic Kings who urged their services to the faith as arguments for the concessions they desired, the popes issued a series of important bulls which gave the Crown comprehensive powers over the Church in the colonies.

The bulls of Alexander VI, May 4, 1493, gave the Spanish monarchy (1) title over the Indies, with the conditional obligation of carrying on the conversion of the aboriginal population, and (2) all the concessions, privileges, rights, etc., that former popes had conceded to the kings of Portugal in lands discovered beyond the seas, of which the most important was the right of presenting to ecclesiastical office. Eight years later, November 16, 1501, the same pope granted to the Crown the right to collect the tithes in the

American colonies, with the condition that the Crown should provide revenues for the establishment of churches and missions. On July 28, 1508, Pope Julius II conceded to the Crown universal patronage over the Church in the Indies.

On the basis of these concessions, which were clarified by later papal decrees, the Crown established an unparalleled control over ecclesiastical organization in America. The tithes were collected by the officials of the royal treasury and expended by them according to instructions from the Crown. The consent of civil authority was required for the establishment of every cathedral, parish church, monastic house, hospital, and pious foundation in the Indies. Appointment to all sees and benefices was reserved to the king or his representatives. The establishment and delimitation of dioceses were made by royal authority. The emigration of clergy to the New World was controlled by royal license, and the movements of those who went to the Indies were supervised by the civil officers in the several provinces. The meetings of provincial and diocesan councils and the publication of their decrees were subjected to supervision by the State. Papal bulls and letters directed to the Church in America were examined and certified by the Council of the Indies. It is not surprising, therefore, that these powers were jealously guarded, that the viceroys and lesser colonial officials were instructed to resist any encroachment on the patronage, or that bishops were required to take an oath not to violate the rights of the Crown under the patronage.

In actual practice the Crown exercised direct power of appointment in the case of archbishops, bishops, and cathedral chapters. The nominations of archbishops and bishops were sent to the Pope who formally installed the appointees in office. Appointment to lesser benefices was made by the viceroys and provincial governors, acting as vice-patrons, from a list of nominations made by the local prelates. The person chosen was then presented to the bishop who installed him in office. The Crown permitted private individuals to endow local ecclesiastical foundations, such as chaplaincies, and to exercise patronage over them, but this form of private patronage was under the strict control of civil authority. Rigid supervision was exercised over the monastic orders, and all prelates, visitors, and guardians elected by the orders were obliged to present their patents of office to the appropriate civil officers. Although the tithes were collected by the officials of the *real hacienda,* the sums collected were expended according to a general scheme ordered by the Crown. It was the usual custom to divide the tithes into four equal parts, of which one was paid to the bishop and one to the cathedral chapter. The remainder was divided into nine parts or *novenos,* of which the Crown retained two and the remaining seven were distributed among the lesser clergy, hospitals, and the general fund of the Church. The *dos novenos,* or king's share, were frequently used for pious purposes. Finally jurisdiction in suits relating to the patronage and the tithes was reserved to the civil tribunals.

But this extraordinary measure of control exercised by the Crown was no guarantee of peaceful relations between Church and State. In fact, problems of the patronage and tithes often complicated these relations instead of simplifying them. The viceroys and other local officials had constantly to be on guard against the creation of any rights which, in the course of time, the Church might claim to be prescriptive, although royal legislation specifically stated that prescription could in no way alter the character of the patronage. Evasion of the patronage took various forms, such as assumption of the appointing power by bishops and other prelates, or the building of churches and convents without license. Solórzano cites the case of the bishops of Cuba who disregarded royal cédulas forbidding them to appoint the collector-general of the cathedral church. Occasionally ecclesiastical buildings were actually torn down by royal command as the result of violation of the patronage. The appointment to benefices, the enjoyment of the revenues derived therefrom, and the removal for cause of regularly installed appointees by their prelates were a constant source of controversy involving both the patronage and the canon law. One of the most fruitful sources of embarrassment for the State was the constant need for settling disputes between the secular and regular clergy, especially with regard to the examination of religious appointed to benefices, the supervision of *doctrinas* served by the monastic orders, and the secularization of missions. Suits over secularized missions often dragged on for years and justified the proverb, *si te quieras hazer inmortal, hazte pleito eclesiastico.* The rapid accumulation of property by the Church, by means of private endowment and investments, and the administration of revenues from the same, especially the disposition of *espolios* and the revenues of sees *sede vacante,* created another group of complex and controversial questions. The collection and administration of the tithes raised many issues. What articles of production were subject to the tithes? Were the military and monastic orders exempt from payment? Numerous controversies of a personal character, frequently caused by disagreement concerning precedence at ceremonial functions, engendered bitterness and unduly disturbed the relations of Church and State.

Besides these problems that were created by or directly related to the power of the Crown under the patronage, there were many other conflicts of interest between the two jurisdictions, civil and ecclesiastical. For the sake of convenience, these may be divided into two classes: (1) those which related to the position of the Church as a privileged, corporate institution under the canon law; and (2) those which grew out of disagreement concerning the place of the Indian in the general colonial scheme. It is apparent, of course, that the missionary activities of the Church frequently caused a merging of strict canon law questions with problems related to the administration of the aborigines. Moreover, problems within each class were often complicated by the theory and practice of the patronage.

It was a recognized principle of both Spanish and Indian legislation that the clergy and ecclesiastical property enjoyed certain privileges and immunities. Cases of ecclesiastical discipline and offenses committed by the clergy were normally outside the jurisdiction of lay authority. Ecclesiastical property enjoyed special privileges, such as protection against desecration and immunity from the ordinary jurisdiction of civil officers. The right of asylum was generally recognized. Finally, all lay members of the Church were subject to its jurisdiction in cases ecclesiastical in character. Jurisdiction in ecclesiastical cases belonged to courts presided over by ecclesiastical judges ordinary, such as bishops or their vicars and the prelates of the monastic orders. The intervention of civil authority, except in cases related to the royal patronage, or in cases of open and violent denial of royal authority, was usually unwarranted. On the other hand, for the arrest of laymen and for the execution of sentence on them, the ecclesiastical judges ordinary and their officials were obliged to call in the aid of the secular arm, i.e., of civil authority. Thus there existed two sets of law, canon and civil, and two sets of courts, ecclesiastical and secular. This dual system of jurisprudence had always been a source of conflict between Church and State, for it had never been administered or applied with full satisfaction to either.

The Crown recognized the privileges, immunities, and jurisdictional powers of the Church in the New World, and tried to maintain a just balance between Church and State in matters of this kind. Civil officers were instructed to aid and protect the clergy, to respect the privileges of ecclesiastical persons and things, to refrain from interfering in the exercise of jurisdiction by ecclesiastical judges, and to lend the aid of the secular arm under the customary conditions. Prelates were charged not to usurp or obstruct the exercise of civil justice. But the execution of these instructions presented many difficult problems. The maintenance of order and the suppression of public scandal were functions of civil authority, but how should the civil officers deal with cases involving persons enjoying the immunities of the ecclesiastical *fuero?* Mere investigation of the conduct of clergy by laymen might be regarded as a violation of ecclesiastical immunity. The normal method of procedure was to call a given case to the attention of the appropriate prelate who would make the necessary investigation and impose discipline. If the prelate who had immediate jurisdiction failed to act, then the case was brought to the attention of a superior prelate. Finally, if such measures were ineffective, the Crown might be informed, or, if the offender was incorrigible, the civil authority could, by proper legal formulae, assume jurisdiction. Expulsion of clergy from the Indies was decreed for certain offences, such as abandonment of the habit of a monastic order, chronic and notorious disturbances in the elections of prelates of the regular clergy, and scandalous, public attacks on civil authority. Discipline of this sort was to be arranged, if possible, by joint action of the two jurisdictions, but the civil officers could act alone if necessary.

The right of the Church to protest against injustice and to interpose its influence to obtain a remedy for abuse of authority by civil officers was recognized, but the prelates were instructed to admonish the clergy not to use "scandalous words touching the public and universal government" in the pulpit, and not to preach against the "ministers and officials of our justice." If the civil officers were remiss in their performance of duty, the clergy might admonish them privately. The imposition of censures and excommunications on civil officers for ecclesiastical offenses was subject to appeal, and if appeal was denied, the royal aid could be invoked. Copies of all the papers pertaining to the case would then be sent to the audiencia possessing jurisdiction, and pending the decision of the audiencia all censures would be raised. It was also ordered that absolution of civil officers should be granted in a simple and quiet manner without show or elaborate ceremony.

Two special ecclesiastical tribunals exercised a wide range of independent jurisdiction and exerted great influence in colonial affairs. These were the tribunals of the Santa

Cruzada and the Holy Office of the Inquisition. The sale
of bulls of the Santa Cruzada, or indulgences, was introduced into the colonies at an early date, and in the course
of time the revenues therefrom became an important
source of income for the Crown. The business of the Cruzada was finally put on a permanent administrative basis
by the appointment of a Commissary General Subdelegate
for the capital of each audiencia district who was subject
to the authority of the Commissary General of the Cruzada
in Spain. Each Commissary General Subdelegate was assisted by the senior oidor of the district, a fiscal of the
audiencia and an accountant. Together they formed the
supreme tribunal for the district. Local business of the
Cruzada was in the hands of subdelegates, who had charge
of preaching the bulls, and lay treasurers, who received the
money resulting from the sale of the indulgences. The net
revenues were sent to Spain at convenient intervals. The
district tribunals and the subdelegates possessed jurisdiction
over all business of the Cruzada; appeals from the district
tribunals went to the Commissary General and Consejo de
Cruzada in Spain. The civil courts and the ecclesiastical
courts ordinary were forbidden to interfere in such matters.

The activities of the district tribunals, the subdelegates,
and the local treasurers caused numerous conflicts of jurisdiction. The sale of the bulls and other business operations
of the Cruzada provided opportunities for the abuse of
privilege. Treasurers who were tempted to use their authority for personal profit claimed exemption from all civil jurisdiction. Ecclesiastical members of the organization were
wont to claim freedom from the authority of their prelates.
Although colonial legislation denied these claims for general immunity, the laws were not easily enforced. Moreover,
the Cruzada, like all other tribunals with power of independent jurisdiction, sought to extend its influence whenever possible. It tried, for example, to assert control over
unclaimed property, especially livestock, and to obtain the
management of, or a share in, the goods of persons who
died intestate. By special concessions the Cruzada in Spain

possessed jurisdiction of this kind, but in the Indies no such concessions were made.

The Holy Office of the Inquisition was the most important ecclesiastical court in the New World. Bishops and prelates of the monastic orders exercised jurisdiction in matters of the faith during the early years of the conquest, but in 1569 the Crown ordered the establishment of tribunals of the Holy Office in Mexico City and Lima. In 1611 a third was set up in Cartagena. These tribunals consisted of a board of inquisitors, attorneys, consultants on theology and canon law, receivers of confiscated property, jailers, and numerous lesser officials, and servants. In provincial capitals and important towns local commissioners were appointed to investigate cases of the faith and arrest offenders when so ordered by the inquisitors. These local agents had no authority to try cases; the accused parties were sent to the central tribunals for trial.

The jurisdiction of the Inquisition was wide and elastic. Heresy, apostasy, blasphemy, bigamy, the practice of superstition, sorcery and demonology, propositions subversive of the faith, denial of ecclesiastical authority, lack of respect for ecclesiastical persons, institutions, and censures, solicitation in the confessional, evil sounding words—these were some of the causes for prosecution by the tribunal. No member of the non-aboriginal community was exempt. Spaniards, creoles, Negroes, mestizos, mulattos, clergy and laymen, officials and private citizens—all were subject to its authority. The Indians alone were exempt. In addition to its spiritual jurisdiction in matters of the faith, the Holy Office exercised wide authority of a temporal character. It owned and administered property and exercised temporal jurisdiction over all persons, even lay familiars, who were connected with it in an official capacity. The civil courts were forbidden to interfere in the business of the Inquisition, and appeals from the American tribunals were taken to the Council of the Inquisition (the Suprema) in Spain.

Such a broad range of independent jurisdiction made the Inquisition the most powerful and most feared ecclesiastical tribunal in the New World. It could defy the power of the viceroy, and even the orders of the Crown were frequently disregarded with impunity. In Peru, and to a lesser degree in Mexico, the members of the Holy Office exercised a freedom of action that was not infrequently the cause of public scandal. For the Church the Inquisition was a weapon of great importance in dealing with civil authority, because the broad definition of heresy and related spiritual offenses made it easy to bring charges against officials who resisted the policies of the clergy. Moreover, criticism of the actions of the Holy Office or resistance to its demands could be made cause for action on the ground that the offender was guilty of lack of respect for and opposition to the tribunal as an instrument of orthodoxy. It should not be forgotten, on the other hand, that sometimes the State found the Inquisition a convenient means for dealing with leaders of rebellion and for the suppression of doctrines contrary to accepted theories of government.

# Richard E. Greenleaf

# Religion in the Mexican Renaissance Colony

*Religion in the Renaissance colony is a matter of scholarly controversy. Studies that stress the presence of a vast Christian humanist movement in early sixteenth-century Mexico continue to appear, whereas others claim that the prevailing intellectual attitudes belonged to the Middle Ages or to the Counter Reformation. The application of Christian humanist beliefs and Renaissance utopian thought to techniques of colonization is the theme of this selection. Richard E. Greenleaf, formerly professor of history, dean of the Graduate School of Inter-American Studies, and academic vice-president of the University of the Americas in Mexico, D.F., is currently professor of history at Tulane University.*

The discovery and colonization of America coincided with the period of the high Renaissance in Europe. Christian humanists and other reform-minded individuals were excited with the idea of a "new world" in which they could apply their theories and construct a perfect Christian so-

From Richard E. Greenleaf, *Zumárraga and the Mexican Inquisition 1536–1543* (Washington, D.C.: Academy of American Franciscan History, 1962), pp. 26–32 *passim*. Reprinted by permission of the publisher.

ciety free from the apparent defects of fifteenth and sixteenth-century European society.

These theorists had a relatively simple formula: a return
to the basic precepts of Christianity in its pure form, as it
existed in the golden apostolic age of the Church. The
noble American savage, "blessed by nature, and free from
the taint of fraud and hypocrisy," was to furnish the raw
material for the new order, a society which would be built
upon the indigenous agrarian collectivism. The upshot of
such thinking was the so-called Renaissance Utopia and
its attempted application in America. The thought of
Campanella, More, and Bacon dominated this movement.
The utopian ideas of the northern humanists found an ally
in a reform movement going on within the Spanish Catholic Church whose intellectual mentor in the early years of
the sixteenth century was the Dutch humanist Desiderius
Erasmus. Erasmus' philosophy of Christ fitted in very well
with the plan to adopt utopian rule in regulating the lives
of the natives. Lewis Hanke's thesis of the nature of the
conquest of America adequately sums up this thinking: that
it was

> far more than a remarkable military and political ex-
> ploit; that it was also one of the greatest attempts the
> world has seen, to make Christian precepts prevail in
> the relations between peoples.[1]

The difficulty in implementing the Utopia in Mexico
centered on the fact that the conquistador was not imbued
with the idealism of the Christian humanist and that
furthermore he brought to the American mainland the
very culture which the humanist hoped to exclude from
the colonization. The conflict between Christian humanism
on the one hand and Spanish materialism and greed on the
other created grave problems in the framing of colonial
policy and generated an amazing amount of intellectual

---

[1] Lewis Hanke, "The Contribution of Bishop Zumárraga to
Mexican Culture," *The Americas,* V (1948), 275.

speculation on the nature of the Indian and how he should be treated. Hanke has indicated that the Christian humanist position

> became basically a spirited defense of the rights of the Indians, which rested upon two of the most fundamental assumptions a Christian can make: namely, that all men are equal before God; and that a Christian has a responsibility for the welfare of his brothers, no matter how alien or lowly they may be.[2]

Those who would exploit the natives, both conqueror and clergy, denied in fact that the Indian was a human being. Instead he was some kind of animal being, perhaps a dirty dog, and as such fitted into the Aristotelian hierarchy on the lower level. The royal chronicler Oviedo y Valdes gives us the prototype of this argument. He characterized the Indians as

> naturally lazy and vicious, melancholic, cowardly, and in general a lying shiftless people. Their marriages are not a sacrament but a sacrilege. They are idolatrous, libidinous, and commit sodomy. Their chief desire is to eat, drink, worship heathen idols, and commit bestial obscenities. What could one expect from a people whose skulls are so thick and hard that the Spaniards had to take care in fighting not to strike on the head lest their swords be blunted?[3]

The Dominican Bartolomé de las Casas, as the conscience of the crown and extreme defender of the Indian as the

---

[2] Hanke, "The Contribution of Bishop Zumárraga to Mexican Culture," *loc. cit.*

[3] Cited by Hanke, *ibid.*, pp. 276–277, from Oviedo, *Historia general y natural de las Indias* (Sevilla, 1535), primera parte, Lib. 2, cap. 6; Lib. 4, cap. 2; Lib. 5, prohemio, caps. 2–3; Lib. 6, cap. 9.

noble savage, employed Aristotle to prove that Indians were human beings:

> God created these simple people without evil and without guile. They are most obedient and faithful to their natural lords and to the Christians whom they serve. They are most submissive, peaceful, virtuous. Nor are they quarrelsome, rancorous, querulous or vengeful. Moreover, they are more delicate than princes and die easily from work or illness. They neither possess or desire to possess worldly wealth. Surely these people would be the most blessed in the world if only they worshipped the true God.[4]

The controversy over the rationality of the Indian and his capacity to become civilized and accept and understand the Christian religion consumed the first half of the sixteenth century. In the final analysis the struggle led to a victory of the security of empire and religion over humanism. However, the experiments with utopian ideas and the intellectual speculation behind these ventures provided the philosophical background of the early sixteenth-century Mexican society. In general the Order clergy were divided on the question of rationality, and this issue became inextricably bound up with the question of the ordination of a native Christian priesthood. In general the Franciscans felt that the Indians possessed enough rationality to be converted but lacked the aptitudes necessary for ordination. The eminent ethnologists and antiquarians of the Order, Mendieta and Sahagún, were convinced that the Indians were to be ordered, not to order, and that they were unfit for the priesthood. Many other Franciscans, including Bishop Zumárraga, felt that the Indian was capable of the full cup of salvation, many feeling that the Mexican

---

[4] Bartolomé de las Casas, *Colección de tratados, 1552–1553* (Buenos Aires, 1924), pp. 7–8, translated by Hanke, *op. cit.*, p. 276.

Church was not adequately constituted because there were no Indian priests.

     .     .     .

The rationality controversy seemed to be terminated when Pope Paul III in June of 1537 issued two bulls on the subject: *Veritas ipsa* condemned Indian slavery while *Sublimis deus* proclaimed the aptitude of the Indians for Christianity. The bulls were largely nullified in Mexico when the crown revoked them as interference with the *patronato real*. The controversy continued to rage in Mexico and Spain. Finally, in 1550, a council was convoked at Valladolid to deal with rationality and the treatment of the Indians. Las Casas defended the Indian while Juan Ginés de Sepúlveda upheld the traditional Aristotelian views. The outcome of the Council of Valladolid was indecisive but it generally adopted the Aristotelian view and humanism lost out to Spanish imperial security.

While the rationality controversy was in progress and the Aristotelians were winning out in the decades prior to the Council of Valladolid, another famous Dominican, Francisco de Vitoria, a professor at the University of Salamanca, was attacking the problem of the Indians from a different point of view. He contended that not only Spain's Indian policy but also its fundamental right to dominion in the New World were based upon untenable premises. Vitoria debunked the right of discovery (*res nullius*) as a just title because the Indians were already the lords of the New World when the Spaniard came. Similarly, the *mare clausum* theory instituted by the bull *Inter caetera* of Alexander VI in 1493 was denied by Vitoria as a basis for Spanish rule because he contended that the pope had no temporal power over Indians as non-Catholics. Consequently, the refusal of the Indians to accept papal dominion could hardly be considered a basis for just war against them or the confiscation of their properties or goods.

Vitoria did concede, however, that the Spaniards had

certain rights and responsibilities in America, and were they hindered in the exercise of either, they might wage a just war. In all there were six possible titles to Spanish dominion in the New World. Each was predicated upon a right or a responsibility which, if abridged by the natives, could lead to just war or the assumption of territorial dominium. The first title was derived from the Spaniard's right to travel and to take up residence in America if he did not harm the Indian in doing so. Should the Indian deter him, a just war could be waged. Secondly, the Spaniard had the right to preach and declare the gospel in barbarian lands and if warfare was necessary to do this, it had to be moderate and directed toward the welfare rather than the destruction of the native.

The last four possible titles to dominion were of a more nebulous character. They included the right to intervene and assume power to prevent cannibalism or sacrifice, to deter Indian princes from forcing converted Indians to return to paganism, to establish dominium when the natives truly and voluntarily submitted, and finally, to establish mandates in the natives' interests. The use to which unscrupulous conquistadores put Vitoria's theories need not detain us. The significance of his work lies in the humanist movement of which he was a part and which dominated the thinking of a large segment of the spiritual conquerors of New Spain.

.     .     .

Lewis Hanke has summarized the four large questions which confronted the early Mexican humanist in translating his ideas into reality. They were crucial questions, as we shall see: (1) Could the Indians learn to live like Christian Spaniards? (2) Could Spain colonize by peaceful farmers and integrate the Indian into such an agrarian society? (3) Could the faith be preached by peaceful means alone? and finally, (4) Could the encomienda system be abolished?

The attempts to answer these questions became the first social experiments in America. Obviously, the opponents of Las Casas in the rationality controversy were also foes of these experiments. They were carried on before the conquest of the mainland in the Indies, and afterwards in the Venezuelan, Guatemalan, and Mexican areas. Las Casas himself took the lead in the first mainland experiments. He was able to show only moderate success in the Vera Paz venture in Guatemala (1537–1550), and he failed completely earlier at Cumaná on the Venezuelan coast (1521). Despite failure in practical experimentation, Las Casas remained the inveterate foe of the encomienda system, and it was largely due to his efforts that it was eventually tamed.

The only measure of success of the early Christian humanists came in Mexico. While Bishop Zumárraga certainly had some hand in stimulating the utopian experiments in New Spain, it was the first bishop of Michoacán, Don Vasco de Quiroga, who must be credited with adopting utopian rule in regulating the lives of the Indians.

## ❧ 3 ❧

## F. Benedict Warren

—◆◆◆—

# The Idea of the Pueblos
# of Santa Fe

*Vasco de Quiroga came to New Spain in 1530 as a judge on the second Audiencia. During the next years he developed an abiding interest in Indian policy and techniques of colonization. When the Audiencia made Quiroga responsible for Michoacán affairs during the 1530s, he became attracted to the Tarascan area, and he became intimately acquainted with its problems. Quiroga later decided to enter the diocesan clergy in Mexico. When the Bishopric of Michoacán was established in 1536, he became the obvious man to occupy the see. From 1536 to 1565 Quiroga applied many Christian humanist and Renaissance ideas, especially those from More's* Utopia, *to Michoacán missionary activity. The pueblos of Santa Fe provided models for missionary techniques throughout the Spanish Empire, and especially in the Spanish borderlands in North America. F. Benedict Warren, formerly editor of* The Americas *and currently a professor of history at the University of Maryland, has devoted years of study to Quiroga's activities in New Spain.*

From F. Benedict Warren, *Vasco de Quiroga and His Pueblo Hospitals of Sante Fe* (Washington, D.C.: Academy of American Franciscan History, 1963), pp. 26–42 *passim*. Reprinted by permission of the publisher.

Quiroga found much to admire in the Indians. He was
attracted by their natural, simple virtues—their humility,
obedience, poverty, contempt of the world, and lack of
interest in clothing. To his mind they were like the
Apostles, going about barefooted, with long hair, and without any covering for the head. In fine, they were like a
*tabula rasa* and like very soft wax that was ready to receive
any impression. Quiroga maintained that through congregation into pueblos the Indians could be shaped into
a new and strong type of Christians, like those of the primitive Church. . . . We do not know when Quiroga first
came into contact with More's *Utopia,* although it appears
to have been after he came to the New World.

.   .   .

By the time Quiroga came to write the Ordinances for
the pueblo-hospitals of Santa Fe the influence of More
had been tempered to some extent by experience, by the
introduction of many specifically Christian elements, and
by the fact that his towns had never grown to a size which
justified the complicated governing body of his *parecer*.
Yet, the influence of the *Utopia* is still strongly present, as
is very evident to anyone who compares the two works
carefully.

.   .   .

The Ordinances were completed before January 24, 1565,
since Quiroga mentioned them in his will of that date.
Undoubtedly a set of ordinances for the pueblos existed
before 1554 and the set that we have now represents
Quiroga's final revision. The order and arrangement within
the work is poor, with related materials in entirely separate
places. It gives the appearance of growth by accretion over
the course of time. In presenting the summary which
follows, an attempt has been made to draw together those
ordinances that are related. . . .

## Political Structure

The basic political unit of the society is to be the *familia*
which is to be composed of members of one lineage in
the masculine line, up to ten or twelve couples in each
*familia*. Each *familia* is subject to its *padre de familia*. The
pueblo is to be governed by a body composed of a principal,
regidores, and jurados. One principal, or two if necessary,
is to be elected by the padres de familia. After attending
the Mass of the Holy Spirit, they are to elect him from
among four who were chosen from among themselves by the
poor of the pueblo, either divided into four groups or acting as a unit. His term of office is to be for three or six
years, but he can be re-elected for a longer time. He can
be removed and another put in his place with the permission of the rector. The principal is to be a good
Christian and a man of exemplary life, meek and not too
severe, attracting the love and honor of all but not allow-
ing himself to be despised. His duty is to notify the rector
of what goes on and what is necessary in the pueblo.

The regidores, three or four in number, are to be chosen
annually by the padres de familia. The office is to be
given in turn to all the able married men.

Two padres de familia, chosen by the principal and
regidores, are to assist at the meetings of the principal and
regidores to protect the interests of the poor of the pueblo,
and not the same ones every day but by turns. Above this
council and vested with the ultimate authority in the
pueblo, is the rector. From Quiroga's will we know that
this official was to be a priest devoted to the aims of the
hospital with an adequate knowledge of the Indian languages of the area, appointed every three years by Quiroga
himself or, after his death, by the rector of the College of
San Nicolás in Michoacán with the approval of the dean
and cabildo of the cathedral of Michoacán.

The meetings of the governing body of the pueblo are
to be held every third day, or more often if necessary, in

the familia of the principal. They are to discuss matters pertaining to the hospital, estancias, boundaries, and common works in conformity with the Ordinances and in agreement with the rector. Unless a decision is pressing, it is not to be made at the first meeting at which it is discussed but is to be reconsidered at one or two other meetings before being put to a vote. After reaching a decision on anything of importance they are to give a report on it to the rector. The object of delaying the vote was to give time for deliberation and to make sure that no one would become more determined in defending his vote than in looking for the good of the hospital.

Other duties of the governing body are to visit the boundaries of the pueblo once a year and renew the markers if necessary according to the document of the boundaries. They are also to have a chest in which the documents of the pueblo are kept. Complaints of Indians against one another are to be settled amicably before the rector and regidores without recourse to the courts so as to save expenses, avoid imprisonment, and preserve mutual charity.

Another official of the pueblo is the *veedor general,* or overseer, of the farms. His office puts him in charge of all the farms and ranches. It is his duty to visit the farms regularly and to report on them to the rector, principal, and regidores. He is allowed to live in his own familia in the hospital, going out during the day to make his rounds of the farms and ranches.

## Social Life

The familia was also the unit upon which the social life of the pueblo was built. Parents are to see to the marriages of their sons with the daughters of other familias of the hospital, or, if they are lacking, with daughters of poor people of the neighborhood. Boys are considered marriageable at fourteen, girls at twelve. They are to be married publicly according to the order of Holy Mother Church and with the consent of their parents and familia. The wives must go to live in the familia of their husbands. Each familia is to have eight, ten, or twelve couples. When a familia becomes overcrowded they are to form a new one.

All the members of a familia are to obey the oldest grandfather of the familia; wives their husbands; children their parents, grandparents, and great-grandparents. This will take away the need for servants, who disturb social tranquility. The padres and madres de familia are to report to the rector and regidores the excesses and disorders of the children as well as their own responsibility or negligence in such matters. If such things happen through the inability or negligence of the padres de familia, others are to be elected with the advice of the rector and regidores.

When the members of a familia go to work in the fields, they are to go with the padre de familia, who is to oversee the work and report negligences. The padres themselves are exempted from work but are encouraged to lend a hand for the sake of example, especially at the beginning.

For the sake of recreation one or more of the poor people of the hospital may, with the permission of the rector, principal, and regidores, go to the farms or ranches for a while, where they shall help out if they are in good health and shall be fed as long as their permission lasts.

In regard to vesture they are to maintain uniformity in so far as possible. The clothing is to be of cotton or wool in their natural color, white, clean and modest, without decoration and other costly and curious work, and it shall be made in the familias. It is to be such as to protect from both cold and heat. The people may have two suits of clothing, one for dress and the other for work. In the winter they are to wear hose and woolen jackets or vests stuffed with cotton or wool. Married women are to wear unadorned white cotton veils (*tocas*) over their other garments, which shall cover their heads and the rest of their bodies; single girls are not obliged to wear them.

As for instruction, the children are to be taught their

ABC's. They are also to be trained in farming, as will be explained further on. But of primary importance is the instruction in Christian and moral doctrine and good customs according to the form of Quiroga's printed *Doctrina Christiana*. This doctrina is to form them not only in faith but also in general principles of civilized life and is to be considered as supplementary to the Ordinances in ruling their life. Quiroga's aim is to give them *policía* and prudence, destroying what is evil in their native customs but preserving what was good. Those who have been taught in the hospital are to take with them when they leave the hospital "sound and Catholic Christian doctrine and policía, and crafts" which they will teach to their neighbors.

Those who are not legitimately impeded are to attend Mass on days when it is celebrated. Quiroga gives a list of special feasts, apparently made up primarily for Santa Fe de México. They are to celebrate the feast of the Exaltation of the Holy Cross, the day on which the first tall crosses were raised in both hospitals, although in different years. Bishop Zumárraga had granted indulgences for this day for Santa Fe de México. The feast of San Salvador is to be celebrated in the hermitage of that name in the valley near the pueblo, the feast of the Assumption in the principal church which was under that patronage, and the feast of St. Michael and the other angels in the church of St. Michael to be built above the valley in a place set aside for it. On the principal feasts all the members of the pueblo are to gather for common meals in a large hall built for this purpose. This meal shall be at the expense of the commune. Each familia shall take its turn in preparing one of these meals, which shall not be of strange or skimpy foods but shall be abundant and cheerful.

Quiroga adds some admonitions as to personal habits. The people of the pueblos are to strive for cleanliness of both soul and body, so that the cleanliness of the soul appears outwardly in the body. They are not to paint their faces or bodies except for necessary or useful medicine. They are also exhorted not to make fun of anyone because of poverty, natural defects, or other causes.

## The Work of the Pueblo

The work of the pueblo is to be done willingly and without complaint, for the benefit of the hospital and its hospitality. It is to be regarded as a means of learning *policia* and *prudencia*. Six hours each day are to be employed in works for the common good, the fruits of which are to be distributed equitably according to need. The surplus, after the needy of the hospital are cared for, is to be employed in pious works and for the benefit of other needy people.

There are two main types of work: mechanical and agricultural. Mechanical work includes such occupations as weaving, stonecutting, carpentry, masonry, and blacksmithing. The artisans who are trained in these crafts are to make all necessary repairs on the buildings during the six hours of common labor. The buildings are to be repaired as soon as they show signs of damage before the harm becomes serious. Girls are to be taught womanly arts at home, such as the working of wool, linen, silk, and cotton.

Agriculture is to be the principal occupation of the pueblo and the common work of all the members. Six hours a day are to be devoted to work in the common fields but at times it may be considered better to work from sunrise to sunset two or three days a week according to the demands of the season. Children are to be taught farming with their ABC's. Twice weekly after the time of classes they are to be taken into a field near the school and instructed in agriculture for an hour or two after the fashion of a game or a pastime. What they raise is to be distributed among them according to the quality of their work.

Individuals can have the usufruct of orchards and pieces of land for recreation and subsidiary income, but only for as long as they live in the pueblo. In case of death or long absence from the pueblo without permission, the usufruct passes on to the children or grandchildren or to the most deserving members of the pueblo who do not have land. The immovable goods of the hospital are inalienable.

The farms and ranches are to be staffed from the urban familias, with four to six married couples in each, chosen by the principal and regidores. They are to be changed every two years but if anyone wishes to stay longer he may do so, provided he has the express permission of the rector and regidores. The oldest in each group is to be in charge and the others are to obey him. When the farm familias are changed, the most capable or the oldest is to remain as principal to oversee the work of the new arrivals and the whole familia is to obey him. Slack seasons in farm work are to be filled in by supplementary work, such as cutting and shaping of stone and timber and collecting of wild products.

They are to raise a full list of farm products—fowl, both Spanish and native; sheep, goats, cows, pigs, and draught animals, with preference for oxen; produce of orchards and gardens, and field crops. They are to plant twice as much as is considered necessary for the pueblo, or at least one-third more than necessary. The surplus is not to be disposed of until they are certain that there will be no shortage for the coming year. Then it can be replaced by the new crop. There shall be adequate places for the storage of the produce and from there it shall be distributed to each and all according to need. In each familia there is also to be some place to store what has been distributed.

The income from the sale of produce and from other sources is to be placed in a large chest with three keys which are to be kept by the rector, the principal, and the oldest of the regidores. In this box are also to be kept the account books, which are to be given annually to the rector, regidores, patron, and protectors of the hospital, and to Quiroga until his death.

## The Infirmary

An infirmary is to be built on the plan of a large familia, square, twice as large as the others and a little separate from them. On one side there is to be a large hall for those sick with contagious diseases and opposite it another hall for those with non-contagious ailments. The other two halls at the front and back of the familia shall be for the *mayordomo* and *dispensero* of the sick and for the necessary offices. In the middle of the patio there is to be a covered chapel with open sides where Mass can be said and the sick can attend.

The mayordomo and dispensero are to give of the best and first things of the hospital to the sick when they make a request, and what they do not have they shall buy. A druggist, physician, and surgeon shall be hired to visit and care for the sick. The healthy shall visit the sick, guarding themselves against contagion, but consoling the sick and showing them the greatest possible charity and interest.

## Expulsion from the Pueblo

A member may be expelled from the hospital for any of the following causes: doing a hideous thing or causing bad example, unruliness, living scandalously, being a bad Christian, drunkenness, excessive laziness, consistent violation of the ordinances, acting against the common good of the hospital. Such a person is to be expelled and is to restore whatever profit he has made from his stay. This ordinance shall be executed by the principal and regidores, having consulted the rector.

# Lewis U. Hanke

———◆———

# The Great Debate at
# Valladolid, 1550-1551

*One of the foremost students of Bartolomé de las
Casas and of the Spanish struggle for justice in the
conquest of America, Professor Lewis U. Hanke published in 1959 a perceptive analysis of the issues of
the great debate at Valladolid, which sought to establish for the Spanish crown the guidelines for
proper treatment of Indian populations in the New
World. Differing interpretations of the nature of the
Indian and his capacity to live like a Christian Spaniard led to a lively debate in which Christian humanist views clashed with traditional Aristotelian doctrines. Both major disputants, Bartolomé de las Casas
and Juan Ginés de Sepúlveda, used Aristotle to support particular views. This selection of Hanke's work
is designed to show Ginés de Sepúlveda's position in
opposition to those of Las Casas and the Christian
humanists Zumárraga and Quiroga, which were presented in Selections 2 and 3. After a distinguished
career in the Hispanic Foundation of the Library of
Congress, at the University of Texas, at Columbia
University, and at the University of California at*

From Lewis U. Hanke, *Aristotle and the American Indians: A
Study of Race Prejudice in the Modern World* (London: Hollis
and Carter Ltd., 1959), pp. 38–42 *passim*. Reprinted by permission of the publisher.

*Irvine, Professor Hanke, in July 1969, became the
first Haring Professor of Latin American History at
the University of Massachusetts at Amherst.*

The sessions began in mid-August, 1550, and continued
for about a month before the "Council of the Fourteen,"
summoned by Charles V to sit in Valladolid. Among the
judges were such outstanding theologians as Domingo de
Soto, Melchor Cano, and Bernardino de Arévalo, as well
as veteran members of the Council of Castile and of the
Council of the Indies, and such experienced officials as
Gregorio López, the glossator of the well-known edition of
the Spanish law code known as the *Siete Partidas*. Unfortunately, the great Dominican Francisco de Vitoria, considered by many the most able theologian of the century,
had died in 1546. Had he lived, the Emperor might well
have named him a member of the group and another
classic work from his pen might have resulted. We might
also know whether Las Casas or Sepúlveda more faithfully
followed Vitoria's doctrine, a point upon which much
argument has been expended in recent years.

The disputants were to direct themselves to the specific
issue: is it lawful for the king of Spain to wage war on
the Indians before preaching the faith to them in order
to subject them to his rule, so that afterwards they may be
more easily instructed in the faith? Sepúlveda of course
had come to sustain the view that this was "both lawful
and expedient" and an indispensable preliminary to preaching the faith, while Las Casas declared that it was neither
expedient nor lawful but "iniquitous, and contrary to our
Christian religion."

On the first day Sepúlveda spoke for three hours, giving
a résumé of his treatise. On the second day Las Casas appeared, armed with his own monumental *Apologia* which,
as he himself stated, he proceeded to read word for word.
This verbal onslaught continued for five days until the

reading was completed, or until the members of the junta could bear no more, as Sepúlveda suggested. The two opponents did not appear together before the council, but the judges seem to have discussed the issues with them separately as they stated their positions. The judges also carried on discussions among themselves.

It is no wonder that the bewildered judges requested one of their members, Domingo de Soto, an able theologian and jurist, to boil down the arguments and present to them an objective and succinct summary for their more perfect comprehension of the theories involved. This he did in a masterly statement which was then submitted to Sepúlveda, who replied to each of the twelve objections Las Casas had raised. The members thereupon scattered to their homes, taking with them copies of the summary. Before departing, the judges agreed to reconvene on January 20, 1551, for a final vote.

Most of the information available on this second session, which actually took place in Valladolid from about the middle of April to the middle of May, 1551, comes from the pen of Sepúlveda, who discovered, much to his disgust, that Las Casas had availed himself of the vacation period to prepare a rebuttal to Sepúlveda's reply to him. To this last blast Sepúlveda made no rejoinder "because he saw no necessity; indeed, the members of the junta had apparently never read any of the replies," but he appeared again before the junta and expounded his views on the meaning of the bulls of Alexander VI. It was probably at this time that Sepúlveda composed his paper entitled "Against those who depreciate or contradict the bull and decree of Pope Alexander VI which gives the Catholic kings and their successors authority to conquer the Indies and subject those barbarians, and by this means convert them to the Christian religion and submit them to their empire and jurisdiction." Sepúlveda stated that much of the discussion at this session revolved around the interpretation of the papal bulls of donation, that the Franciscan judge Bernardino de

Arévalo strongly supported his case, but that when he wished to appear again the judges declined to discuss the issue further.

Unfortunately whatever records of the proceedings of the Council were kept have been lost, or at least have not yet come to light. The arguments presented by the two opponents are therefore our only present source. Sepúlveda set forth his position from notes, drawing up no formal brief, but following closely the arguments previously developed in his *Demócrates* in dialogue form, which had circulated widely in Spain in the years preceding the disputation. Leopoldo, "a German considerably tainted with Lutheran errors," takes the part of the man who believes the conquest unjust, while Sepúlveda, speaking through Demócrates, kindly but firmly opposes Leopoldo's ideas and convinces him in the end of the complete justice of wars against the Indians and the obligation of the king to wage them.

The fundamental idea put forward by Sepúlveda was a simple one and not original with him. Thomas Aquinas had laid it down, centuries before, that wars may be waged justly when their cause is just and when the authority carrying on the war is legitimate and conducts the war in the right spirit and the correct manner. Sepúlveda, applying this doctrine to the New World, declared it lawful and necessary to wage war against the natives there for four reasons:

1. For the gravity of the sins which the Indians had committed, especially their idolatries and their sins against nature.
2. On account of the rudeness of their natures, which obliged them to serve persons having a more refined nature, such as the Spaniards.
3. In order to spread the faith, which would be more easily accomplished by the prior subjugation of the natives.
4. To protect the weak among the natives themselves.

It is not necessary to reproduce here the multitude of authorities marshalled by the disputants on Sepúlveda's four propositions. Both men devoted most of their time to the point on which the king sought advice: "How can conquests, discoveries, and settlements be made to accord with justice and reason?" The Valladolid dispute, therefore, must be considered the last great controversy held in Spain to determine the regulations for conquistadores and the proper way to preach the faith. We may note that these old problems, raised in 1513 shortly after the Laws of Burgos were promulgated, and responsible for the adoption of the famous Requirement—of which Las Casas once said that he did not know whether to laugh or weep on reading it— were still unresolved in 1550.

The arguments of Las Casas require little detailed examination. He made a few simple points over and over, with numerous examples and references from the copious literature he had studied, and there is no real question on what he actually meant to say.

The judges at Valladolid appear to have shared the view of the Scottish philosopher who declared "Blessed are they that hunger and thirst after justice, but it is easier to hunger and thirst after it than to define precisely what it means." For they enquired of Las Casas exactly how, in his opinion, the conquest ought to proceed. He replied that, when no danger threatened, preachers alone should be sent. In particularly dangerous parts of the Indies, fortresses should be built on the borders and little by little the people would be won over to Christianity by peace, love, and good example. Here it is clear that Las Casas never forgot and never abandoned his plans for peaceful colonization and persuasion. This proposal has much in common with the idea, put forward by the Catalan mystic Ramón Lull two centuries before, that Spain should Christianize the Moslem world peacefully by establishing a chain of missionary groups at strategic points from Andalusia through north Africa to the Bosphorus. It is clear, too, from the way Las Casas and his Dominican brothers had proceeded in their peaceful persuasion work in Guatemala, that the result Las Casas wanted was a tight control of the Indians by ecclesiastics in paternal but supreme command, like the later achievement by the Jesuits in their famous Paraguayan missions. The plan proposed by Las Casas also bears some similarity to the mission system which Spain actually used in later years to Christianize the provinces north of Mexico including California, New Mexico, and Texas.

# ❧ 5 ❧

## Antonine Tibesar, O.F.M.

◆━◆❯◆━◆

# The Early Peruvian
# Missionary Effort

*Probably the ideas of the Renaissance Church had less effect in Peru than in New Spain. Father Antonine Tibesar describes the difficult beginnings of Franciscan labor among the Indians from 1533 to 1600 in the Peruvian viceroyalty and development of the friar's role as priest of a* doctrina, *or parish. He shows how the stage was set for jurisdictional struggle between the hierarchy and the regular clergy in the sixteenth century as well as the conflict between Spanish and creole friars within the various orders in succeeding years (see Selection 10). Father Tibesar, long director of the Academy of American Franciscan History, now devotes his efforts to the study of the Franciscan Order in Peru and of general ecclesiastical administration in colonial Latin America.*

The religious who came to Peru with Pizarro not only were to act as missionaries, but they were also to be agents in the conquest of the country. At least such was the mind of the Spanish Crown. While Pizarro was to conquer and secure the land militarily, the religious and, to a lesser

From Antonine Tibesar, O.F.M., *Franciscan Beginnings in Colonial Peru* (Washington, D.C.: Academy of American Franciscan History, 1953), pp. 35–50 *passim*. Reprinted by permission of the publisher.

extent, the diocesan clergy were to conquer the hearts and the minds of the natives and to introduce among them the religion and the culture of Spain. In this task they were to receive the aid of the governor, and they were to co-operate with him in furthering the political organization and pacification of the country. The civil and the religious rulers were, therefore, co-ordinate instruments of the Spanish Crown for the conquest of Peru. Pizarro enjoyed pre-dominance in so far as the affairs of the Spanish conquistadors were concerned; the religious or clergy, in regard to questions of Indian policy.

According to the instructions of the Crown, the religious were to investigate the conquered Indians and decide with the governor whether these Indians were to be divided among the Spanish encomenderos and on what terms. In the beginning each religious was appointed a protector of the Indians against the conquistador and the royal official. The religious also were to live among the Indians on the encomiendas, a practice generally forbidden to Spaniards and after 1555 even to the encomendero. Thus the religious were frequently the sole direct representatives of the royal authority among the Indians, at least until the institution of the Corregidores de los Indios by Licenciado Castro in 1565.

During the first years (1533–1548) the Franciscans had few, if any, residences in the Indian pueblos, and their mission activity was carried on by a few friars who went from province to province instructing the Indians. When in need of rest, the missionaries returned to the residences in the Spanish cities. The second period of Franciscan activity (1548–1570) is characterized by the establishment of converts among the Indians. The friars used these convents as centers to which they could retire for prayer and rest at the end of their missionary travels, although the friars usually now concentrated their efforts on the Indians who resided within the confines of the province in which the convent was erected, even though exact limits had not yet been determined by the authorities. This period also marks the acceptance by the Franciscans in Peru for the first time of certain Indian parishes, or *doctrinas,* an event of 1557. The last period (1570–1600) is distinguished by a further development of the movement begun in the preceding period. While the convents erected in the Indian country were not abandoned, the Franciscans who were to labor henceforth among the Indians were entrusted each with definite Indian parishes, or *doctrinas,* with definite limits and each with a definite term of office. It now became customary for such friars to be approved beforehand by the viceroy, i.e., *la presentación real.* This form of mission organization persisted substantially until 1752, when the Franciscans in Peru were separated from their *doctrinas* by the Bourbons in an effort to weaken the influence of the friars among the people.

In part the three periods reflect the progress of Peru towards a stable political system, and in part they show the fact that the Franciscans who first came to Peru from Europe were unfitted for their work. For centuries the Franciscans in Europe had been excluded from the administration of parishes by papal decrees issued in the latter half of the thirteenth century; as a result, when the conquest of Peru began, the Franciscans did not know how to fulfill many pastoral obligations. These decrees had been intended to delimit the spheres of activity between the then recently founded Mendicant Orders (Augustinian, Dominican, Franciscan and Mercedarian) and the parochial, or diocesan, clergy. Friar and parish priest were henceforth to work side by side in the service of the Church, but the activities of the two were distinct. The parish priest, usually born and trained within the immediate vicinity of his parish, and hence intimately acquainted with the problems of the locality, restricted himself to the work of administering his parish and of tending to the daily needs of his people. The friar, on the other hand, often an outsider by birth and training, ministered to the people through sermons in the public squares, schools, and especially through special religious and social groups. Moreover, the friar was not bound by a parish; he worked wherever the opportunity presented itself or his superiors commanded.

This centuries-old division had grown so venerable by the time of the conquest of Peru that it had become a law almost without an exception that no friar should administer a parish. It should, therefore, not be surprising that the Franciscans did not organize parishes immediately after their arrival in Peru. Not only were they too few in numbers to undertake such a task, but also by training they did not know how, and their mentality would certainly have proved a bar even to their learning. To the Franciscan friar of the sixteenth century, parish work was not a friar's work. In short, the friars who came to the Americas as missionaries in the earlier part of the sixteenth century were untrained for the work in the *doctrinas,* for the friars in Europe had no similar institution. Some friars, indeed, never adapted themselves to the change. We suspect that this was true of many of the Franciscans who came to Peru within the first decades of the conquest of that country. How else may we explain the fact that it was only in 1557, after friars had come from Mexico, that the Franciscans in Peru began to accept parishes of Indians? Later, of course, when creoles and mestizos, who as youths had seen the Franciscans serving as parish priests, joined the Order in Peru, they accepted the role of *doctrinero* without question. Yet until such youths began to form the major part of the Franciscan personnel, the old-world tradition would continue to constitute a serious handicap to the full employment of the friars in the Indian parishes. Even later, this prejudice would remain in the minds of Spanish friars sent to Peru to serve as commissaries general or provincials; they would tend to look upon a *fraile doctrinero* as a friar on the road to ruin.

.      .      .

An idea of the situation during these first years is given by Guamán Poma de Ayala. In some provinces there was only one priest. When he was not available, pious laymen would instruct the Indians in the rudiments of the faith in Spanish, but it is doubtful that many Indians understood what they were saying. When a priest visited the Indians, he would say the usual prayers for the Indians in Latin. He would then try to preach in the native tongue, using signs generously to make himself understood. Neither these priests nor the laymen took money from the Indians, but they received food. They did not beat the natives or punish them but tried with all love and kindness to persuade them to submit to the king and to the pope. The actual work accomplished among the Indians by the missionaries during these first years must have been very little. It was a period of contact and of beginnings, and almost certainly not one of deep penetration into the soul of the native. The four thousand converts who Lorente states were in Cuzco at the time of the death of Pizarro in 1541 could hardly have been deeply convinced Christians.

After Pizarro's assassination the religious policies were continued by Vaca de Castro, the royal governor. Castro erected four monasteries in as many provinces—Chincha, Guailas, Jauja and Huamanga, possibly all Dominican foundations—as centers of religious instruction and Indian settlement. Castro also evidenced the same interest as the earlier Spaniards in the conversion of the caciques, whose prestige could be useful both to the religious and the civil leaders. He is evidently proud to inform the king that the cacique of Guailas had been converted with all his relatives. When he returned to Spain, there were, he said, more than four hundred thousand Christian Indians in Peru. Granted, of course, that this figure may be padded, it still indicates that the missionaries had met with a favorable response from the Indians despite unfavorable circumstances of many kinds.

That these Indian neophytes were not too firm in their faith is seen in the account of Bishop Solano of Cuzco, written in Lima in 1545. The bishop had landed earlier at Paita in the extreme north and journeyed overland to the City of the Kings. In his letter he describes the conditions which he observed on this journey. He found that the Indians had almost completely abandoned the Christian churches after the promulgation of the New Laws by the Viceroy, Blasco Núñez Vela. The Indians understood the New Laws to signify that they were free from Spanish control, and thus they abandoned not only their Spanish encomenderos but their Spanish priests as well. The caciques also had their own interpretation of the laws and saw in them an opportunity to reconstitute their own power. Some of the Christianized Indians who returned to their own pueblos were killed by their caciques, either because they had served the Spaniards or because they were considered traitors to their pagan gods, to whom they were now offered in atonement. All this boded ill for the progress of Christianity among the Indians, and this foreboding was not relieved in any way by the ensuing rebellion of Gonzalo Pizarro, which was to keep the entire country in turmoil for four years.

It is surprising though to discover that even Gonzalo Pizarro in the midst of this grave struggle still had time, according to Gómara, to insist that the encomenderos, under penalty of forfeiture of their grants, see to it that their Indians were instructed in the Christian faith. On the other hand, under the circumstances, there is little cause for wonder if the work of conversion slackened during these wars, as the same author notes. The important point to remember is that despite the disturbances of the Spanish civil war and of Indian insurrection, despite the many distractions of conquering and of organizing a new country, the rulers of Peru, even the illegal claimants, cooperated with the clergy in a sustained effort, of unequal intensity certainly, to convert the Indian to the Christian faith. At the very least, the contact made during the period, 1533–1548, would render the work of later missionaries much easier when peace would be restored to the coun-

try. Certainly also during the same period some solid work
had been done, and some of the fundamental policies upon
which the conversion was to be carried through were laid.
In particular, the emphasis on the conversion of the
caciques and the gathering of the Indians into pueblos,
together with the practice of educating the sons of the
caciques and of other principal Indians, was to survive
and to be enlarged in succeeding decades of the sixteenth
century.

·      ·      ·

While the establishment of residences in the Indian
country was a move in the right direction, it did not
signify immediately that the Franciscans would be able to
give much more attention than formerly to the individual
native. For some time to come these friars were still to be
wandering missionaries, though instead of wandering from
province to province they would now wander within one
province. In 1548 there were not enough friars to permit
them to concentrate attention on small groups of natives.
Thus in Cajamarca in 1548, there were more than five
hundred Indian villages and only a handful of friars. This
meant that the missionary could spend only a short time
in each pueblo. Much the same condition existed in the
valleys south of Lima where a friar might remain a week
in a village once in about every two months. But after
1548, as the number of friars slowly increased, the periods
of visitation were lengthened, though for many years the
uninterrupted instruction of the same group by one friar
was still impossible.

Such instruction could be offered only in regular parishes
manned by permanent groups of friars. In other words, uninterrupted instruction could be given if the Indians were
organized in parishes and if the friars were retained on a
permanent basis. But this was a slow development. It was
not until May 10, 1557, that the Marqués de Cañete at the
request of the Franciscan superiors granted the *pase real*

to the papal privileges which permitted the Franciscans to assume the permanent care of Indian parishes or *doctrinas*. While the friars may have administered such parishes before this time, it was probably only now that such a responsibility became a permanent part of the Franciscan policy of mission activity in Peru. After receiving the *pase real,* the friars, in August of that same year, accepted the *doctrina* at Magdalena, and in December that of Surco, both near Lima. Thus began a new phase in the Franciscan missionary effort in Peru. If Christianity was to be implanted firmly among the natives, this type of spiritual care was clearly imperative.

The slowness of the development was due largely to two causes: the hesitancy of the Franciscan superiors to accept parishes as a permanent obligation, and the reluctance of the bishops, who were mindful, perhaps, of the unhappy experiences in Mexico, to entrust these parishes to the religious. The religious orders in Peru were exempt from the jurisdiction of the bishops and were governed directly by their own superiors or provincials, who in the Spanish Empire occupied the same administrative level as the bishops. Thus to the bishops of Peru, each *doctrina* given to the Franciscans and to the other Orders signified a curtailment of the episcopal power and frequently also loss of revenue as well. In 1562 Archbishop Loaysa complained that the Indians in the *doctrinas* knew the friars and not their bishops. Hence, although Loaysa, who controlled all of central and northern Peru, had a high regard for the Franciscan *doctrinero,* he was not anxious to entrust *doctrinas* to them or to any other religious, even though he did not then have enough diocesan clergy to staff these Indian parishes. Yet, the blame must also be shared by the Franciscan superiors who were anxious, perhaps overanxious, to withdraw from the work among the scattered Indian pueblos and to gather their friars back into the convents where strict conventual life could be followed with its determined times for silence, prayer and labor.

The Franciscan superiors, for example, withdrew their men in 1569 from the *doctrinas* of Cajamarca entirely on their own initiative. In 1584 the same thing was attempted by Fray Jerónimo de Villacarrillo without any pressure from the bishops and surely contrary to the wishes of the Indians. Villacarrillo would have given up even more, if he had not met with determined opposition from many quarters. A strong hand was required to overcome the hesitancy and reluctance; Viceroy Toledo supplied it.

When Francisco de Toledo arrived in Peru as viceroy in 1569, he found all the residences of religious in Lima well populated, and with his customary energy he set about remedying the reluctance of both the bishops and the religious superiors. When he had landed at Paita, the Indians from Cajamarca had met him and requested that he should send back the Franciscans to care for them. One day, shortly after his arrival in Lima, Toledo entered the Franciscan convent at mealtime. At his request he was conducted to the refectory. Calmly the viceroy counted the number of friars at table and summarily ordered the superiors to send friars to reoccupy the *doctrinas* of Cajamarca. The other Orders, as also the reluctant bishops, were treated with just as little ceremony. As Toledo traveled about the country on his visits, he used his power as royal representative not only to delimit parishes but also to entrust these parishes to the friars. To the Franciscans, apparently without bothering to consult the interested bishop, he assigned those parishes which they were administering at the time of his visit. This, together with his policy of uniting the scattered small settlements of Indians into pueblos of such size that each could support a priest— about four hundred tribute-paying Indians to each reduction—finally rendered truly effective work possible. This is not to say that before 1570 the missionaries had accomplished nothing; for it does seem that by that date the Christian faith was firmly established in Peru. We would like to emphasize, however, that because of Toledo's reorganization, the missionaries were permitted to operate under conditions more favorable than formerly; they were now able to concentrate their efforts and thus would have more reason to hope that Christianity would take a firmer root in the soul of the native.

# ❧ 6 ❧

## Arthur Ennis, O.S.A.

————◆❖◆————

# The Conflict Between the Regular and Secular Clergy

*One of the most difficult chapters of Latin-American colonial Church history deals with the struggle between the hierarchy and the missionary orders during the sixteenth century. The contest for the allegiance of the native populations and the more technical disputes over faculties, jurisdiction, and finance led to intemperate language and unnecessary hard feelings. Even after King Philip II decided to uphold the authority of bishops over the order clergy in 1574, the struggle continued well into the next century and in some areas of the Empire until the eighteenth century. The Augustinian Arthur Ennis, in a brilliant biography of Fray Alonso de la Vera Cruz, leader of the Augustinians in Mexico, gives a sophisticated treatment of the conflict.*

The story of the conflict that developed between the missionary friars of the Augustinian, Franciscan and Dominican Orders on the one hand, and the secular clergy, especially the bishops, on the other, is one of the sad chapters of the history of sixteenth century Mexico. . . .

———————————————————————————

From Arthur Ennis, O.S.A., *Fray Alonso de la Vera Cruz, O.S.A. (1507–1584)* (Louvain: Imprimerie E. Warny, 1957), pp. 100–107, 123–125, 136–137 *passim*. Reprinted by permission of "Augustiniana."

While a truly enormous amount of paper and ink was consumed in the numberless letters and reports written by both sides, the quantity of documentation in itself means nothing. Many of the reports were extremely long-winded and contained very little substance. Both sides were anxious to maintain their own position, neither hesitated to exaggerate freely and bring in extraneous matters with little or no connection to the immediate problems. Consequently, it is a mistake to take this conflict too seriously, or to put full credence in everything that was written. The following opinion of Mariano Cuevas is a reasonable one, though somewhat too lenient.

> The violent language employed in these disputes, their inexplicable prolongation over so many years, and even certain insults and discourtesies orginating therefrom, never reached the point of serious defects, nor do they signify anything more than affairs engaged in by hot-blooded Spaniards.[1]

.    .    .

The conflict has its origin in the very nature of the Spanish missions in the New World. At the inception of these missions at the end of the fifteenth century the Popes granted extensive powers to the Catholic Kings of Spain, Ferdinand and Isabel, as Patrons of the missionlands. The members of the religious orders, especially the Franciscans, became the special emissaries of the Crown and the favored missionaries within the realm of the Royal Patronage. In order to make their work possible in an area where the Church had never been established, the Holy See gave the religious very extensive faculties for the administration of the Sacraments, faculties that normally rest in the hands of the bishops. These powers were transferred to the missionaries by the very fact of being designated to the missions by

---

[1]Cuevas, *Historia de la Iglesia,* II, 176.

their superiors and the King. Hence, within a short space of time, with the very rapid expansion of the missions, what was really an extraordinary setup became the ordinary functioning of the Church in the New World; the religious became strongly entrenched in their favored position. The trouble began when the time came to establish dioceses in the missionlands; the first Bishop in Mexico, Juan de Zumárraga, was appointed in 1528. The bishops found themselves in a disadvantageous position. They were, practically speaking, without authority, because the secular clergy were very few, and the religious operated totally independent of episcopal jurisdiction. The friars were the pastors of the churches, but they did not regard their territories as parishes, but rather as *doctrinas,* unique organizations with no dependence upon the normal diocesan establishment. Obviously, such an arrangement could not go on indefinitely and conflicts of jurisdiction soon arose. It became a question of which side was going to make concessions, and how much.

The religious, as we shall see, were very reluctant to make any concessions, and sometimes even tended to extend their authority beyond previous limits. They constantly fell back upon their privileges and regarded their own rights and those of the Crown, both granted by the Holy See, as one. Their attitude is summed up in a statement by Grijalva where he mentions the rights of the Spanish king in ecclesiastical affairs. This statement was occasioned by an attempt on the part of the bishops, in 1555, to demand that the friars get permission before building a church or monastery within the diocesan territory. The King came to the defense of the religious, and Grijalva says that the King had the right and duty to defend the friars on three counts. First, the bishops were subject to the Crown because they owed their appointment to the King. Second, in this specific instance, the Crown was not interfering in ecclesiastical matters because the King was merely settling a question of temporal justice on the basis of the privileges enjoyed by the religious. Third, and more fundamental, the King possessed delegated authority from the Pope to govern all matters within his realm with regard to the good of souls, granted to him especially by Pope Alexander VI.

Upon examining these three points we shall see that the first two are correct, but the third one demands closer scrutiny. As to the appointment of bishops, it is true that the Spanish king enjoyed the right of appointment to all benefices. Not only was he empowered to nominate bishops, but he could also set the boundaries of the diocese, determine the collection and distribution of rents and tithes, and appoint all beneficiaries within the diocese.

With regard to the second point, it is easy to see that the religious felt quite free to build monasteries at their discretion. Before the establishment of dioceses they were free to operate in that respect, needing only the approval of the royal government upon whom rested the responsibility of sponsoring the missions and defraying the expenses of building and maintenance. With the coming of the bishops, the religious saw no need to change their position. The privileges and exemption of the friars were based upon Bulls granted by the Popes, especially the *Alias felices* of Leo X, given April 25, 1521, and the *Exponi nobis fecisti* of Adrian VI, given May 9, 1522. The Bull of Leo X confirmed all previous faculties granted for the administration of all the Sacraments, including ordination to minor orders, with the sole restriction that those faculties which normally pertain to the episcopal office be not exercised in any place where there is a bishop. The Bull of Adrian VI was known as the *Omnimoda* because it contained a very extensive phrase, granting to the religious superiors *"omnimodam auctoritatem nostram in utroque foro,"* in all places where there was no bishop or where, at least, the friars were a distance of *dos dietas* (about 40 miles) from an episcopal seat. The word *omnimoda,* because of its elasticity, was to become the shibboleth of the religious in all their disputes with the Hierarchy. Both these Bulls were granted in favor of the Franciscans, but all their privileges were extended equally to the Augustinians by Clement VII, successor to Adrian VI. Hence, the friars possessed their faculties from the Holy

See through their own superiors; they had no need of either permission or approval from the bishops. As for the specific point about which we were speaking, that is, the right to found monasteries and churches, although this right is not mentioned in the Bulls of the sixteenth century, the friars reasoned that such foundations were obviously essential to the mission given to them by the Popes, so that no further permission was needed from the Hierarchy.

One of the effects of this unusual type of ecclesiastical organization was a deep attachment between the Indians and the particular friars who served their villages. The Indians paid loyalty and respect to the missionaries who had come to live among them, but they knew nothing of the bishops. Consequently, the bishops were sometimes chagrined to see the high regard paid to the friars, while their own office went unrecognized. The lofty position and independent jurisdiction which the missionaries enjoyed sometimes prompted them to assume authority in questions where even the bishop would hesitate to act. The Augustinian Juan de Medina Rincón, after he became Bishop of Michoacán, is quoted as saying: "When I was a religious, the simple prior of a monastery, I had more courage and audacity to make decisions than I do now as a Bishop." [2] An example of this kind of conduct is found in the method adopted by Agustín de Coruña, also an Augustinian, in handling a case of idolatry amongst some Christian Indians. He called the people together in the village of Olinalá and pronounced himself inquisitor by authority of the Bull *Omnimoda,* even though the Inquisition did not exist in Mexico at that time. He then threatened to declare the villagers relapsed and impenitent, if they did not reveal the place of the idol. The Franciscans also were accustomed to employ this method of procedure. But the *Omnimoda,* elastic though it was, could not justify such audacious claims.

Another aspect of the conflict between religious and

---

[2] Ricard, *La "conquête spirituelle,"* p. 293.

Hierarchy arose when the bishops tried to replace the friars with diocesan clergy in some of the churches. This should have been a natural development in the ecclesiastical organization, but the religious were understandably reluctant to relinquish the churches which they had established and built by much sweat and toil. Furthermore, relinquishing the services of the church to the secular clergy also meant leaving their monastery which was attached to the church. It was not simply a question of handing over the office of pastor of souls; it meant also a great loss of property and income. The reply of the friars to the demands of the bishops was that the secular clergy were not fit; they did not know the Indians and could not speak their languages, they were poorly educated and lacking in zeal and self-sacrifice. In general, these charges were true, especially in the early years, because there were no seminaries for diocesan clergy in the New World, and sometimes the clergy who came from Spain were seeking opportunity more than priestly labor. There were, however, some worthy and capable priests among them, but the friars made no distinction; they were opposed to all efforts of replacement.

Of all the points of conflict the most hotly contested was the question of tithes[3] . . . Grijalva . . . had said that the King possessed delegated authority from the Pope to govern all matters that pertain to the good of souls. This rather all-inclusive statement identifies something which later came to be called the "Royal Vicariate of the Indies." It is true that the king enjoyed very extensive ecclesiastical authority granted to him by the Holy See. In virtue of various Bulls given at the end of the fifteenth century and beginning of the sixteenth, he was declared the Patron of all the lands in the Spanish Empire with the right and the duty of sending missionaries to evangelize the heathen peoples; he was

---

[3] The order clergy denied the validity of collecting tithes from the Indians in the New World, since there was no need for the diocesan clergy, normally supported by the tithe. See Ennis, *op. cit.*, pp. 148–149, 153–162 [ed.].

granted the right of receiving ecclesiastical tithes with the consequent obligation of supporting the future churches in the new territories, the right of appointment to all benefices, of setting the boundaries of dioceses and of dividing dioceses under certain circumstances. All these privileges together constituted the Royal Patronage, by means of which the Spanish king enjoyed exclusive control over the newly-discovered lands. In return, he was pledged to sponsor, aid and support the Church in all her affairs. These privileges, along with those granted to the religious in the *Omnimoda,* welded into one the aims and the efforts of the Holy See, the Spanish Crown and the mendicant Orders. As a result, the King, through his Council of the Indies, exercised complete supervision and control over the Church in the Spanish Empire.

Hence it was that in the conflicts with the Hierarchy the friars always appealed to the king and the Council of the Indies, who, in turn, usually defended the religious, although that was not always the case. In favoring the religious there was an element of economy. . . . In the course of time, through the many appeals to the Crown in every kind of ecclesiastical affair, it came to be intimated that the king actually enjoyed papal delegation, vicarious spiritual powers above and beyond the rights of Royal Patronage; that is the idea behind the term "Royal Vicariate." This idea had its beginnings in the writings of some of the religious, principally Juan Focher, a Franciscan, and Alonso de la Vera Cruz. Unique though it was, the idea was taken up by the royalist ministers of the Crown, particularly in the next century, and especially in opposing the move by the Holy See to send Vicars Apostolic to the Spanish mission lands. In order to avoid direct interference by the Holy See within the empire, appeal was made to the apostolic delegation enjoyed by the king. Egaña, in his exhaustive study of the "Royal Vicariate," concludes that there is no evidence to show that the Popes actually willed to concede vicarious powers to the kings of Spain, and therefore, the theory of the "Royal Vicariate" must be regarded as false. But that is not to deny that the Popes did concede the office of universal patronage, and even a kind of super-patronage, embracing the wide range of powers that have already been mentioned. These powers were so extensive that it was sometimes difficult to determine the limits; it was by exceeding those limits that the theory of the "Royal Vicariate" had its origin.

.    .    .

We find that the year 1555 was especially significant in the conflict between the Hierarchy and the religious orders. In that year the first provincial synod of the archbishopric of Mexico City was called by Archbishop Montúfar. In this meeting the bishops surveyed their situation and issued some new legislation, much of which was opposed to the privileges of the friars. The religious, of course, took immediate steps in opposition to the move made by the bishops. In the years following, a great flow of correspondence crossed and re-crossed the Atlantic as each party presented its case to the royal government. The bishops were eventually upheld when in 1564 Pope Pius IV issued the Bull *In Principis Apostolorum Sede,* revoking the privileges enjoyed by the religious in the New World which were not in conformity with the decrees of the Council of Trent. The friars, however, viewing this as the destruction of their missions, worked hard to convince the King and the Holy See of their point of view. Their efforts were rewarded when Pius V issued the *Exponi nobis nuper* in 1567, restoring the previous privileges. . . .

. . . There were several points of conflict created by the synod of 1555. The bishops declared that all matrimonial cases were reserved to themselves and therefore the religious had no power to judge such cases, that permission of the Ordinary was necessary for the building of a monastery, and that the religious could be dispossessed and replaced by secular priests in those foundations where said permission had not been obtained. . . . In regard to the matrimonial cases, the opposition of the religious was equally determined.

They maintained that the position taken by the bishops was not only contrary to the papal privileges, but it was also impractical. The bishops and their staffs could not possibly handle the numerous cases arising among the new Christians, especially because of the custom of polygamy. Furthermore, it was frequently impossible, because of the distance separating some of the missions from the episcopal seat, to refer all the cases to the bishop. There was in addition a question of extra burden on the Indians, if they had to pay the fees entailed in conducting formal tribunals. . . .

. . . the friars felt that the efforts of the bishops would make their mission work impossible. Because of the still primitive condition of the Church in Mexico, it was necessary for the religious to maintain their privileges, and they contended that it was up to the Holy See to decide when and how the missionaries' privileges were to be curtailed. They were defended by a royal order sent to the bishops in 1557, commanding the bishops not to upset the previous method of procedure, especially in regard to the matrimonial cases. Such royal orders, however, never permanently settled these disputes. With each new order new appeals followed, and each party did its best to win the King over to its opinion.

.    .    .

Summing up this whole question of the disputes between the Hierarchy and the religious orders, it is difficult to see just how a peaceful solution might have been arrived at. Looking back over the various factors mentioned in this chapter, one sees that the problem had very many complications. García Icazbalceta has pointed out that there were two basic failures which aggravated the situation. One was the esprit de corps of each camp, a thing good in itself, but often giving rise to prejudice and excess; the other was the failure to recognize the fact that circumstances change and no institution should exist after it has ceased to serve the purpose for which it was created. The first of these two factors obviously played an important part in the problem.

But the second one was more than just a failure, it was the very heart of the problem. How was it possible to decide when the extraordinary system of privileges enjoyed by the religious had ceased to serve its purpose? In the centers of population the regular diocesan organization was easily established, but in many of the outlying districts the Church still existed in a primitive mission situation. As long as the whole problem of ecclesiastical organization was looked upon as being one piece, there could be no solution. It was necessary to find some line of demarcation between the two extremities, but neither side was willing to limit its sphere of authority. Of the two, Hierarchy and religious orders, probably the greater blame is due to the religious, because they should have recognized that they must give way to the episcopal authority, and the sooner they had been willing to work out an understanding, the better it would have been for all concerned.

## Jerome V. Jacobsen, S.J.

◆◀◆▶◆

# The Jesuits in Brazil

*Perhaps the greatest figure in the history of sixteenth-century Brazil was the Jesuit missionary Manuel da Nóbrega. Born in 1517 and educated at the University of Coimbra, Father Nóbrega arrived in 1549 in Brazil as part of the entourage of Governor General Thomé de Sousa. Until his death in 1570, Nóbrega was the guiding force in Jesuit mission-building in Brazil. On the firm foundations built by Nóbrega in the sixteenth century, the integration of the Indian into Portuguese society continued, and Nóbrega's efforts provided the background for the momentous efforts of his Jesuit compatriot António Vieira in the seventeenth century. The distinguished Jesuit scholar and editor of* Mid-America: An Historical Review, *Father Jerome V. Jacobsen, has done the primary analysis of Nóbrega in Brazil.*

Toward the end of 1548 . . . the king completed arrangements for making something out of the scattered, badly managed settlements, or captaincies, of Brazil. He appointed Thomé de Sousa governor general in full charge of building a capital and bringing the individual colonies under one central headship. The Jesuits were asked to

---

From Jerome V. Jacobsen, "Nóbrega of Brazil," *Mid-America: An Historical Review,* 24 (1942), 151–187 *passim.* Reprinted by permission of the publisher.

carry out the religious and cultural phase of the unification. Simon Rodrigues, superior of all the Jesuits in Portugal, to the satisfaction of John III and Thomé de Sousa, named Nóbrega superior of a chosen band of six.

.    .    .

The fleet was the largest ever to go to Brazil to that time—three ships, two caravels, a brigantine, and two other boats. All told there were over a thousand men, including functionaries, soldiers, colonists, and four hundred *degredados;* the latter, a group of exiles made up of various human derelicts and offenders not wanted in Portugal, who might, it was thought, make a new start in America. The voyage was completed without incident, no storms, no seasickness; in fact, the Jesuits were in better health after their trip. They followed a strict religious order each day, and by sermons and talks ultimately got everyone to go to confession. In exactly eight weeks, on March 29, they reached the Bay of All Saints.

The disembarkation from the armada was made with both display and caution. The soldiers landed in battle array fully prepared to meet any resistance. The fathers followed chanting a hymn, one (Nóbrega?) holding aloft a crucifix. "But," said Nóbrega, "we found the land at peace and forty or fifty dwellers in the settlement already there. They received us with joy. We found a sort of church, close to which we soon lodged the fathers and brothers in some houses [made] like it." [1] These were thatched mud huts made by the fathers. Nóbrega said the first Mass on the following Sunday, March 31, and preached where the new city of Salvador was to rise, while Father Navarro preached half a league away to the people of the old city settled by Francisco Pereira Coutinho.

.    .    .

The difficulties of constructing the city were minor com-

---

[1] Nóbrega to Simon Rodrigues, from Bahia, 1549, in Afránio Peixoto, *Cartas Jesuiticas,* 3 vols. (Rio de Janeiro, 1931–1933), Vol. I, p. 71.

pared to those encountered in constructing a new social, moral, and intellectual order. Nóbrega was a realist. He soon saw what confronted him in the way of a spiritual task. Rather than being discouraged after one horrified look at the prospect, he took the moral measure of all of the people and then launched a two-fisted, twenty-year campaign against the evils of the land.

The Indians were in general one rung above the brute stage on the ladder of civilization. First of all they had the bad habit of eating one another. Living in groups in the jungle or along rivers they preyed upon their neighbors like animals, carrying off males and females to be bartered into slavery or fattened for a feast. The constant tribal warfare was motivated by hate and vengeance rather than by desire for power; the satisfaction of these passions was complete at one of the cannibalistic orgies only when all were glutted and intoxicated. They remained in one place for a short period, moving elsewhere when their mud hovels fell apart or became too filled with filth for free movement. They frequently killed children to get them out of the way. They knew nothing of God, of moral laws, of monogamy; led by medicine men they feared the devil and worshiped various idols; they grubbed, hunted, fished, and warred for food; they did nothing about clothing. Were it not for the few more civilized natives around Bahia, Nóbrega might well have despaired of elevating the Indians of Brazil.

Equally bad were the conditions among the whites and half-breeds. "The people of the land live in mortal sin," Nóbrega wrote.[2] This was a blanket charge covering all classes who knew right from wrong. The *donatarios,* the planters, poor whites, and riff-raff were all living with many wives, "Negresses" as the native slave women were termed. They had children by them and by the free women. None went to confession. The half-breed children, *mamelucos,*

---

[2] *Ibid.,* p. 72.

were neither known nor a responsibility to parents as they grew up. Many went into the *sertão* living naked and as promiscuously as the Indians. Since the procedure had been going on nearly twenty years, nobody could tell whether brothers were cohabiting with sisters, fathers with daughters, mothers with sons.

Most of the clergymen were as evil as anybody else. There were several unnamed priests at Bahia, several at Pernambuco, and a handful down south at São Vicente. How and why they got to Brazil cannot be stated. They had become victims of their surroundings, attached to an estate and dependent upon the owner for support. They could do nothing but condone slavery and concubinage, or even apostatize, as at Pernambuco. They had neither bishop nor vicar to check their idleness and waywardness. The remedy for this was promptly suggested by Nóbrega. In letters to the king he begged that a bishop be sent.

Definitely, the ax had to be laid to the roots of paganism. To correct the widespread social evils Nóbrega planned an aggressive, detailed campaign, consulting frequently with the governor and officials regarding procedures. Father Leonardo Nunes and Brother Jácome were sent south to Ilhéus to care for the people there. He and the others set themselves to learning the native tongue. With customary enthusiasm he worked on a translation of prayers and sermons into the native language but apparently ran into insurmountable obstacles. The natives not only could not read but they were "so brutish that they have no vocables" to express ideas. The Jesuit leader determined to have the fathers live in the villages, there to acquaint themselves with native habits and means of communicating ideas. The chieftains of two main villages, falling in line with the plan of Christianization, made houses for Navarro, who lived alternately in each and visited other places near Bahia.

Attention was centered upon small boys and girls with happy results. Brother Rodrigues caught their fancy and soon had a small school of reading and writing. One of the chieftains accepting the challenge to learning mastered the ABC's in two days. Another, already baptized, made up for his lack of such promising scholarship by his truly Christian fervor and friendship; he paternally cuffed his village into order. The children went with Nóbrega through the streets in solemn processions, drawing the people by their chants. The Indians assembled to hear the father inveigh against war, homicide, polygamy, idolatry, and the crime of "eating one another." In time, one after another of the "thou shalt nots" came to be known and respected in the old and new city of Bahia. Within five months about one hundred had been baptized, and "600 or 700 were catechumens," according to Nóbrega (who had the peculiar habit exhibited here of speaking in round terms such as "ten or twelve," "forty or fifty").[3] Still, instructing the children brought up the further problem of keeping them secure in the faith amid adverse conditions, for any convert was in constant danger of death.

Efforts to organize the adults into respectable communities called for the greatest amount of patience. Coaxing them to build homes and villages more permanently, leading them to clear and till a specific area, to make a home for one man, one wife and family, instructing them to be responsible for infants and children, became the slow, painstaking task of Nóbrega and his men. They taught the peoples of the poverty-stricken land what to eat and how to grow food. Nóbrega soon asked for clothing for the women to wear, at least when they came to church. Caring for the sick, baptizing dying infants, visiting the slaves on the estates were in the day's work.

Part of the daily toil consisted of steps taken to discredit the superstitions of the medicine men, the *feiticeiros,* who were the backbone of the opposition to Christianity. These went about bestirring all with the doctrine of hatred of fellow men, calling Indians to their ancient idolatry, devil

---

[3] Nóbrega to Dr. Navarro, August 10, 1549, in Peixoto, *op. cit.,* p. 93.

worship, wars, and pagan rituals. Through such firebrands the backwoods tribes were aroused to fury against the padres' condemnations of the vice of cannibalism. When they led raids on the new settlement the strong military arm of the governor was bared. Laws were promulgated. By legislation, punitive campaigns, and paternal instruction the idea of justice was brought home to the people. Abused Indians found a court of appeal, bad Indians felt the force of the law, that is, if they did not scamper into the jungles.

The *feiticeiros* were accustomed to come as angels of light to the villages, where they were welcomed with a great fanfare of songs and dancing. They promised to heal any sickness, especially that contracted from the "poisoned water" poured during the Christian baptisms. Nóbrega, who considered them the devil's emissaries, sought ever to counteract their work. On one occasion he came upon one in the market place haranguing a throng. Nóbrega strode through the Indians and asked him if he received his power to heal from God in heaven, or on earth, or from the devil in hell. The conjurer's astounding reply was that he had this power himself since he was the son of God, and the others mentioned his relatives; he was even in communication with deities that Nóbrega had never heard of, in the clouds and storms. The padre immediately emitted a wild cry against the blasphemy; he summoned the whole village to the scene; he called upon the people to witness his denunciation. Without any arguments he literally shouted and gesticulated the fellow into confusion. As a result, the *feiticeiro* admitted his falsehoods, begged God's pardon, and asked to become a Christian with some of his followers. Once such religious leaders were discredited or were brought into the fold the fathers became in the eyes of the indigenes the great religious guides. Instances of this type later were multiplied all over Brazil.

. . .

The dire economic needs were a constant problem to

the Jesuit leader. Simply stated these consisted of supporting ten Jesuits, the seven orphans, two Indian seminaries, and constructing houses, a church, and a college on the total sum of one dollar and thirty cents a day. Legalities and religious regulations complicated the situation.

From Porto Seguro Nóbrega had written to his Portuguese provincial for a clarification of his authority. What permission had he to build, to accept funds, to acquire lands and properties including slaves, to establish a college? Since these orphans were sent he assumed that he had somehow to provide them with shelter, food, clothes, and education. But his religious vows and the Jesuit regulations against individual or corporate ownership were in conflict with practical needs. He presented his reasoning as follows: living quarters were necessary, and therefore must be obtained; food could not be begged from people so poor as those in the colony, therefore a farm and herd of cattle were essential; but the farm could not be worked by fathers already building houses and doing missionary work, and hence labor had to be obtained; the hire of native or white labor for farming and herd-tending was expensive, and there was no money at hand; slaves, the alternative, were also expensive.

Thomé de Sousa was approached with a statement of the facts. During the year and a half that had elapsed since their arrival, the missionaries had received, besides the plot of ground in the city and the king's subsidy, twelve cubits of dark cloth, twelve pairs of shoes, two sombreros, and fourteen yards of cloth for shirts, the whole valued at 7,080 réis, or $54. The other needs were mentioned, the most urgent of which pertained to Nóbrega's adopted poor boys. Thomé cooperated with alacrity. The two leaders formed the Colégio dos Meninos de Jesus, that is, "incorporated" the boys as a unit, housed them in a hall, and formulated regulations for the "college." A farm site was allotted for its support. Nóbrega acquired three slaves from among those sent by the crown from Guinea, promising payment to the crown in two years. Some cows were purchased on similar terms. Within a year the cotton fields, gardens, and farm were in operation, though one of their slaves died of fever. These acquisitions later gave rise to religious scruples on the part of some of the fathers and brought about a stout defense from Nóbrega.

This college of orphans began to flourish. The boys were very useful for instructing natives. They received education, starting Latin in 1553, and the brighter ones were sent back to Portugal for higher studies. The king granted 5,600 réis a year for clothing. As a youth movement this Bahia foundation was important. When these and others of the type later sent grew up we find Nóbrega still watching over their welfare, even to the extent of asking that orphan girls be sent who might become wives for those who did not have a religious vocation, and with the boys build new homes in the colony.

Meantime, the children of the land were not neglected. In the two nearby villages, Navarro had organized the Indian and mestizo lads into two seminaries, housing the groups in adobe huts built by the fathers. These were taught reading, writing, grammar, composition, and singing. Navarro could easily have two hundred in each place if they could be fed and lodged. Children's processions became common sights in places only shortly removed from barbarism. Many boys came to the door in tears begging admission to the select groups.

. . .

The time came for Thomé de Sousa's inspection tour of the coastal cities. With him sailed Nóbrega, Francisco Pires, and four orphan boys, at the end of 1552. The first stop on the 1,000 mile voyage was at Ilhéus. At Porto Seguro they met Navarro. They found Father Braz and a brother making good progress at Espírito Santo. The seminary for Indian boys with its grammar school was flourishing, while natives, slaves, and whites were under instruction. Proceeding to the bay of Rio de Janeiro they did not land because the tribes were warring. Near the captaincy of

São Vicente a big storm struck the ships, but all came safely to the island village of São Vicente in the Bay of Santos. There the fathers were warmly welcomed in January 1553 at the Jesuit house by Leonardo Nunes and eighty boys and Jesuits living there.

Nunes had made remarkable progress in the vice-ridden land of João Ramalho, the wealthy renegade, whose many *mameluco* sons lived wild and naked with the free Indians. The father had fourteen youths in training as Jesuit novices. In his school reading, writing, singing, the flute, and some Latin were taught. He had built the best church on the coast and had a large house. Nearby, the "father of São Paulo metallurgy," Brother Noguiera, operated a shop in which boys were trained to be smiths, carpenters, and weavers, while in the gardens and orchards others learned agriculture and horticulture. The two fathers were maintained by the king's small subsidy; alms were begged for the others; two benefactors gave some farms. In view of the development Nóbrega officially made this group of buildings the Colégio de Meninos on February 2, 1553, preaching a special sermon on the occasion. Thus the coastal center was well established for its purposes.

There was, however, a great desire on the part of the fathers to missionize the *sertão,* the backwoods, beyond the estates immediately surrounding the bay. The nearby area was a moral eyesore, due chiefly to the ancient Ramalho who lived three leagues inland. From over the mountains came invitations to the fertile plains and valleys where natives were neither fickle nor cannibalistic. This *sertão,* even to the villages of the gentle Guaraní, was to *mame lucos* ideal for vicious slave raids, but to the fathers "a mine of souls." Nóbrega soon paid a visit to the nearer tribes.

In view of the reports he determined in June 1553 to establish a great city for Indians one hundred leagues west, and another in the plain twelve leagues from São Vicente. The former plan was fulfilled in the Paraguay Reductions, the latter in the great city of São Paulo. The birth date of São Paulo de Piratininga falls in the very last week of August 1553. Then, on this site Nóbrega brought together converts and neophytes from three villages for better instruction. Here, isolated from contacts with whites, they could establish their own economy, enjoy village life, and be tutored in grammar, crafts, agriculture, and grazing. Father Manuel de Paiva was placed in charge with some brothers. Father Nunes was sent by boat to Bahia to conduct south some missionaries who had arrived there on July 13. He returned to São Vicente on December 24 with two fathers and two brothers, one of whom was José de Anchieta, as yet not ordained nor famed. Moreover, he brought word of the departure of Thomé de Sousa and of the arrival of the new governor, Duarte da Costa. And to the joy of all except the superior he handed over letters patent from Ignatius Loyola designating Nóbrega provincial of Brazil. In this capacity Nóbrega held the official opening ceremonies of the Colégio de São Paulo de Piratininga on January 25, 1554. How the city of São Paulo grew around this institution whose first houses were built by Jesuit hands, has been frequently told.

Elevation to the provincialate did not change much the nature of Nóbrega's worries. Apparently, all legalities were satisfied only by May 1555, when he pronounced the vows of the professed. One special concern was getting men; another was keeping them in the field. Thomé de Sousa on his arrival before King John III, giving high praise to the work done under Nóbrega's leadership, urged that more men be sent. He carried his plea to the Jesuits of Lisbon and Coimbra, cajoling and prodding them to go to Brazil. Nóbrega, after repeatedly begging help, sent Father Nunes to Portugal to procure it, but on the way the ship was wrecked, June 30, 1554; survivors saw the valiant missionary go down, cross in hand, exhorting all to constancy in the faith. He was the fifth of the Jesuits to die, for a father and brother were overtaken suddenly by death at Bahia in 1553, and on June 8, 1554, two brothers were slain by Carijós. By 1554 seventeen Jesuits had come from Portugal and twelve had been received in Brazil. Nóbrega obtained no more from Portugal to the end of his provincialate in 1559, when seven arrived (of whom two survived), but during this time he admitted nineteen more in Brazil.

From January 1554 until May 3, 1556, Nóbrega lived at the Colégio de Meninos of São Vicente and the Colégio de São Paulo, though he made trips to villages of the *sertão*. He had many administrative duties: giving instructions in moral theology, settling cases of conscience, settling points of canon law, obtaining faculties even from Rome for absolution and tangled marriage problems, writing to Portugal and to Ignatius for interpretations of the Jesuit constitutions and for instructions as to procedures, distributing his men. With the new governor at Bahia he had practically no communication owing to the infrequency of boats between north and south Brazil. He was aware that a quarrel had arisen between the governor's son and the bishop, which was instrumental in causing the bishop to resign.

Practically, Nóbrega did much to consolidate his province and the people. Jesuits were sent to study at Piratininga, where from 1554 secondary education was in progress. This led to the official establishment of the college there in 1556. At São Vicente the "college" for boys flourished. To tie the natives of the *sertão* down into organized social units, five *aldeias,* villages of reduced Indians, were established at Maniçoba, Mairahaia, Geribatiba, Ibirapuera, and Santo Amaro, each with its church and primary school. The provincial's leadership in this concerted drive to form and elevate Indian society was notable, but requires a book to fill in the details. He had of necessity to make trips into the backwoods. On one such he went by canoe and on foot some one hundred twenty miles, passing through villages with four lads who attracted the people by chanting litanies. In one place they came upon tribesmen in the act of butchering a number of slaves. Nóbrega wished to baptize the unfortunates, but the crazed cannibals refused him. Nevertheless, he secretly and with great danger to his life performed the rite by squeezing holy water from his hand-kerchief. In this year of 1554 the fathers brought a local war to a halt and nipped a budding revolt in the interior.

The village of Maniçoba was significant. Ninety miles from São Vicente it was established by Nóbrega as a step toward Paraguay where he yearned to go. The peoples of this land originally lured him south, and now that his centers were established, his eyes ever turned westward. Paraguay, however, was the land of the Spanish Emperor, and King John III early gave orders to Thomé that no Portuguese were to go beyond the Line of Demarcation into Spanish-owned lands. Because of his great desire to be off to the west, Nóbrega hoped soon to be relieved of the provincial's duties. Probably illness would have prevented his going, for he says he was very near death from an infirmity which no one escaped in this land—a tumor or swelling of the stomach. At least, from his writings, Portugal, Spain, and Rome knew there was a promising missionary field in Paraguay thirty years before the *reductions* were begun.

## II

# The Seventeenth-Century Church

## ⋅⋖ 8 ⋗⋅

## Irving A. Leonard

◆━◆━◆

# A Baroque Archbishop
# Viceroy

*Little has been written about the Church as a political
institution or the hierarchy as civil administrators.
In this selection by Professor Irving A. Leonard, who
was the Domingo Faustino Sarmiento Professor of
Spanish-American History and Literature at the University of Michigan until his recent retirement, we
have a personal glimpse of an archbishop who assumed the office of viceroy of New Spain. The pag-
eantry and the Baroque culture of the seventeenth-
century colony are dealt with in a masterful way by
Professor Leonard, who writes history in the literary
tradition.*

For the sixty-two vessels that had sailed from Cádiz on
June 12, 1608, it had been a good crossing, notably free
of the customary threats of storms and pirates.

⋅    ⋅    ⋅

   Surrounded by a numerous retinue and mountainous lug-
gage, an imposing figure, in the panoply of high ecclesiastical office, stood on the foredeck of one of the ships

From Irving A. Leonard, *Baroque Times in Old Mexico* (Ann
Arbor: University of Michigan Press, 1959), pp. 1–16 *passim*.
Reprinted by permission of the University of Michigan Press.

slowly picking its way toward [the port of Vera Cruz]. Among the swarm of expectant inhabitants lining the shore word had quickly passed that the conspicuous personage was no less than a great Prince of the Church, the Archbishop newly appointed to the See of Mexico, Fray García Guerra by name and renowned for his vast learning and stirring eloquence. Increasingly visible to these eager onlookers, as the vessel hove to, was the commotion on deck caused by the obsequious crew and personal servants who scurried about to initiate the formidable task of lightering ashore the distinguished dignitary and his multitudinous effects.

.     .     .

The Vera Cruz, at which the travelers were disembarking, had an aspect of raw newness for, indeed, it was not yet a decade old. An earlier site of the port farther south was abandoned at the close of the sixteenth century because the fortified rock of San Juan de Ulloa offered better protection from the heavy gales which descended from the north and from the fierce pirates who might descend from anywhere. Otherwise, there was little to commend the location for human habitation and, important as the settlement was as a trading center and entrance to an opulent viceroyalty, its population barely exceeded two thousand. Situated in a dreary stretch of sand broken by tiny, sluggish streams, swampy bogs, and shallow pools of stagnant water, the moist heat, swarms of mosquitoes, gnats, and other noxious insects made the vicinity singularly unhealthy. The frequent, heavy downpours during the long rainy season, now approaching its end when the fleet put in, left a humid, dank atmosphere that was almost suffocating, and in it every sort of pest and repulsive creature seemed to proliferate.

On that August day of 1608, however, the dismal town strove to offer a more alluring appearance. The coming of the annual fleet was a great event of the year, and on this occasion it was anticipated with more than normal excitement. Preparations, as elaborate as the meager resources of the community permitted, had been arranged, and the whole motley population was on the waterfront to welcome the great prelate. The *cabildo,* or council, of the Cathedral in Mexico City had already sent down two of its eldest and most distinguished canons to greet this illustrious personage, though advanced age compelled one of them to remain in the more salubrious vicinity of Jalapa. The hardier clergyman was already in Vera Cruz, to which he had brought an ample supply of tasty foods and fruits along with forty servants, saddlehorses, mules, and other animals to convey the Archbishop's retinue and the enormous quantity of baggage to the highland capital. For the ease and comfort of this ecclesiastical Prince, the Cathedral council had also provided a spacious carriage drawn by well-trained mules.

The prosperous merchants and the clergy of the port town had no wish to be outdone in the homage paid to this powerful minister of God whose esteem they craved, and they spared no effort to insure the comfort and pleasure of the temporary guest. The priests and canons of the local cathedral in their vestments, and the religious orders in their dusty gray, black, and brown habits, had formed a procession, each with an upraised Cross at the head of its column. Chanting a *Te Deum Laudamus,* they picked their way through the muddy streets where scrawny fowls pecked about the refuse, mud-caked pigs rooted in the offal, and spectral *zapilotes,* or vultures, fed on carrion. This solemn parade moved slowly toward the beach, passing raucously braying donkeys protesting under heavy burdens of faggots which almost concealed them, and lumbering, ox-drawn carts, called *chirriones,* whose tortured axles filled the air with shrill squeaks and strident squeals.

.     .     .

Small, naked children, and slightly more clothed adults, mulattoes and Negroes for the most part, ran along the line of friars, or brought up the rear. The ebony skin of these inhabitants glistened with sweat in the humid sunlight, while the marching members of the religious orders perspired profusely beneath their heavy vesture. The dank air seemed oppressive, and its steamy vapor was redolent of the mingled odors of decaying fruit, carrion, excrement, and the sweaty bodies of man and beast.

Now safely on the waterfront Fray García Guerra, in resplendent vestments, stood under an ornate palium to receive the obeisance of clergy and laymen, while cannon shots resounded sharply from the anchored ships and from the island fortress. Looking slightly harried by the intensity of the obsequious throng, the Archbishop and his servitors who surreptitiously mopped their brows, were slowly conducted through the miry streets amidst further chanting and responses to the rude church and convent of the Dominicans, of which order the honored guest was a member. In due course the friars of other congregations returned to their cloisters while their superiors entertained the prelate in a more private manner.

Fray García Guerra hardly wished to linger in these unhealthy surroundings and, as everything was in readiness for his journey to Mexico City, he began the slow advance inland accompanied by a long caravan of horses, pack mules, coaches, litters, creaking carts, and pedestrians. It was a triumphal march and the progress of his carriage was deliberately slow to permit all his flock along the way to behold the majesty of a Prince of the Church and to pay homage to this intermediary of God. Well over a month elapsed before he made his ceremonious entry into the viceregal capital.

.    .    .

The arrangements for the crowning event went forward —the magnificent spectacle of the entry into the Cathedral under the episcopal palium. The liveried magistrates, who had met Fray García on the outskirts of the city, now took positions as a guard of honor. Each held an ornate staff supporting the purple and gold palium with brocade trimmings which sheltered the Archbishop robed in glittering vestments. So massive was this canopy that it required twenty-two of the uniformed *regidores* to hold it aloft in this fashion. This dazzling tableau moved slowly through the streets lined with the awed populace. From the walls, windows, and balconies of the buildings on either side hung rich tapestries and bright-hued bunting. At length the procession halted in front of the Cathedral, still far from completion. Before the ponderous portal stood a gigantic arch with a Baroque profusion of sculptural details, of complex symbols, of ornamental figures, and of erudite quotations.

Leaving the palium on the Cathedral steps the Archbishop, with attendant priests and acolytes, moved majestically into the gloomy splendor of the interior and advanced toward the gleaming effulgence of the candlelit altar while the great nave resounded with the swelling paeans of the *Te Deum Laudamus,* sung by an augmented choir. To the edification of all assembled this mighty Prince of the Church prostrated himself before the Cross with ostentatious humility. After an appropriate pause in this position Fray García Guerra slowly arose to his feet and the profound solemnity of the moment yielded to an almost gay burst of melodious song, secular and festive in character. This sudden transition heightened the emotional effect and drama of the scene, filling the audience with a kind of rapture. The Archbishop, a dazzling figure in the magnificence of his episcopal robes, then seated himself near the high altar to witness a brief, allegorical play ingeniously staged in the chancel. Elaborately costumed performers, in witty dialogues of prettily worded phrases, explained and interpreted the fanciful designs and symbols embellishing the enormous arch at the Cathedral door. At the conclusion of this sprightly interlude the Dean, prebendaries, and other ecclesiastical dignitaries approached the prelate in single file to offer their obeisance with impressive humility. The object of this adulation was now more than ever the cynosure of admiring and reverent eyes.

For Fray García it was a supreme moment. His fortunate

career had brought him to a pinnacle of glory in the neo-medieval world that Spain was expending its blood and treasure to maintain and that it passionately believed was the fulfillment of God's will on earth. But like the civilization that he personified, he was already an anachronism and his own fate epitomized the destiny of that age. Unforeseen by all that throng was the certainty that, in a few brief years, his dissected and decomposing body would lie interred in the very place where he now sat amid so much pomp and circumstance. Long after in the same century a distinguished citizen of Mexico City, moved by other portents, would exclaim: "O sacred and most just God, how removed from human reason are Thy incomprehensible and venerable judgments! And how true are the Scriptures when they state that laughter is mingled with tears and that sorrow follows upon the greatest joys!"

The newly inaugurated Archbishop did not fail to display the piety, benevolence, and oratorical gifts that so clearly justified his designation to the richest See of the New World. To his flock he seemed the perfect embodiment of an exemplary minister of the Gospel and a saintly administrator of the Church of God. In those first months of his office he appeared to strive for justice for all with an impartiality, a lack of precipitation, and a compassionate rectitude. His varied duties he performed with punctuality, and so zealous was he in distributing alms personally from his vast income that his meals were often delayed. Faithfully he visited all parts of his broad diocese, and in the churches he preached with that moving eloquence and great learning that unmistakably marked him as one set apart to do God's work.

All who came into the presence of this ecclesiastical Prince acquired a conviction that Fray García was, indeed, an inspired person happy in fulfilling a great destiny. Yet a close observer might have perceived that, with all the homage daily bestowed upon him, with all the Croesus-like wealth at his disposal, and with all the assurance of an eternal reward at the end of his earthly existence, a disquieting urge vaguely stirred deep within his consciousness. Omnipotent as he was in the social and economic as well as the spiritual lives of his flock, an unspoken longing, which was growing in intensity, possessed him to dominate the political affairs of the realm as well.

.     .     .

Like most at the summit of human institutions, the prelate's existence was essentially a lonely one. As the accepted instrument of God he was the recipient of obsequious demonstrations of awe, veneration, and fear wherever he went. Nowhere did his basically gregarious nature find the intimate companionship and confidence that it craved. With all his appearance of piety and of a dedicated servant of the Lord, and with all his ascetic ostentation, he longed for the milder sensual delights of his flock. He loved the sweet melody of instrumental music, the singing of ballads and folk songs, the gustatory pleasures of the table, and the strong tonic of spectacles of the bull ring. To satisfy the first of these tastes Fray García had fallen into the habit of dropping into the Royal Convent of Jesus and Mary in the afternoon to visit Sister Mariana de la Encarnación and Sister Inés de la Cruz, whose company he found especially congenial. Both nuns were skilled instrumentalists and singers who infallibly charmed the Archbishop by lively renditions of popular airs. With perfect mastery they played liturgical music on the convent organ, and with effortless ease they shifted to the guitarlike *laúdes* and *rabeles,* strumming accompaniments to worldly songs that told of sentimental longings, of blighted loves, and of forsaken hopes. This musical potpourri they interlarded with sprightly chatter most relaxing to a prelate surfeited by the ceremonious formality of his daily life. The culinary arts of these talented ladies, manifested in sweetmeats and dainty dishes, added delight to these restful occasions, and rarely did Fray García miss these agreeable afternoon visits.

This was a common practice of clergymen noted a few years after this time by Thomas Gage, the "English American" who reported: "It is ordinary for the Fryers to visit their devoted Nuns, and to spend whole days with them hearing their musick, feeding on their sweet-meats. And for this purpose they have many chambers, which they call Loquitorios, to talk in, with wooden bars between the Nuns and them, and in these chambers are tables for Fryers to dine at; and while they dine, the Nuns recreate them with their voices. Gentlemen and citizens gave their daughters to be brought up in these Nunneries, where they are taught to make all sorts of conserves and preserves, all sorts of musick, which is so exquisite in that City, that I dare be bold to say, that the people are drawn to their churches more for the delight of their musick, than for any delight in the service of God." [1]

Even this gentle and harmless association did not exempt Fray García entirely from the solicitation and importunity that often beset the powerful and influential, for the hospitable nuns were not wholly without guile. They, too, had dreams and ambitions. Long cherished was their hope of founding a new convent under the rule of the reformed Carmelites, and already a wealthy patron had willed a sufficient sum for a building and given part of the endowment. This benefactor had named the Archbishop an executor, and only the approval and a supplementary grant of funds by Fray García were needed to convert a dream into reality. Hence the devout ladies exerted themselves to charm their opulent guest who remained curiously immune to their overtures. This intimate communion with the nuns, however, had brought forth a confession of his own aspirations of becoming the viceroy of Mexico, and whenever pressed for action on the beloved project of his hostesses he invariably put them off by exclaiming: "Ah, my dear sisters, if God is pleased to bestow upon me the office of viceroy, I shall surely help you to start the convent that

---

[1] Cf. A. P. Newton (ed.), *Thomas Gage, The English American. A New Survey of the West Indies, 1648* (London, Guatemala City, 1946), p. 90.

you so rightly desire! And what a splendid one I shall make it!"

"Must we wait until then, Sire?" the anxious nuns pleaded.

"Yes, my dears," was his constant answer. "It can only be when I become the viceroy."

Fray García's afternoon visits continued regularly and with equal regularity, as they plied him with appetizing tidbits, melody, and conversation, the nuns repeated their pleas. Invariably the obdurate Archbishop vouchsafed the same reply: "When I am the viceroy . . ." Even when Sister Inés de la Cruz professed to have had a vision in which the viceregal office was bestowed upon the ambitious prelate, Fray García remained unmoved. Until the prophecy was fulfilled he would make no commitment, and the impatient nuns could only pray more fervently for divine intercession.[2]

.    .    .

The spring of that year brought the long-expected summons to Don Luis de Velasco to vacate his viceregal office and return to Spain to serve as president of the Royal Council of the Indies. The same decree formally designated Fray García Guerra as his successor in Mexico. The prayerful and seemingly modest acquiescence of the Archbishop did not wholly conceal his inner delight, and his ostentatious humility hardly veiled his keen pleasure in supervising the elaborate plans for a second triumphal entry into the capital, this time with the full panoply of the viceregal office. He gave his closest personal attention to the details of erecting an ornate arch, of selecting the sonorous verses and Latin inscriptions to adorn it, of preparing the magnificent display of fireworks and the illuminations of the façades of public buildings by night, of rehearsing the *Te Deum Laudamus* and the lighter music

---

[2] Cf. Artemio de Valle-Arizpe, *El Palacio Nacional de México* (Mexico City, 1936), chap. iii, *passim*.

that so delighted him, and of the construction of the grandstands along the line of march. Absorbed in these pleasurable activities all thought of his promises to the hospitable nuns at the Convent of Jesus and Mary fled from his mind. Indeed, the financial assistance pledged for the new Carmelite establishment was diverted to a pastime close to Fray García's heart—bullfights. To celebrate his elevation to the supreme rank of Archbishop-Viceroy he decreed that these taurine spectacles should take place every Friday for an entire year. And presently he prevailed upon a reluctant city council to construct a private bull ring within the Palace since it hardly seemed fitting for one of his ecclesiastical eminence to attend such functions in public places.

· · ·

Before assuming his new office Fray García had retired to an outlying village to await formal notification of the departure of his predecessor from Vera Cruz and to make a ceremonial entry into Mexico City as viceroy. When the welcome word arrived that Don Luis de Velasco had sailed the Archbishop's first act was to abase himself publicly before the shrine of the Virgin of Guadalupe. This rite performed, he permitted his attendants to address him by the coveted secular title "Your Excellency."

The inaugural march into the capital on June 19, 1611, duplicated the pomp and splendor of his earlier entry as Archbishop with, however, features of a more secular character. This time he rode a beautiful mare of the most pure blooded stock of the realm, the gift of the city council. Beneath the episcopal palium supported by the *regidores* on foot, who were dressed in velvet uniforms of brilliant crimson, the Archbishop-Viceroy presented a gallant figure. Next in order came the judges of the Royal Audiencia, the magistrates of other tribunals, and the flower of the vice-regal aristocracy, each group vying with the other in theatrical splendor.

· · ·

The glittering procession resumed its course toward the triumphal arch which simulated a huge fortress gate decorated by an intricate pattern of symbolic figures painted on its façade. Here the Corregidor administered a ceremonious oath to the new viceroy and handed him a large golden key. The ponderous doors of the imitation stronghold then swung open and the bright column, with Fray García in the lead, wended its way to the Cathedral where the thunderous *Te Deum Laudamus* reverberated through the nave. Presently the Archbishop-Viceroy, accompanied by the city's principal magistrates, departed by another door and entered the viceregal Palace on the east side of the central square. There his accompaniment of judges of the Royal Audiencia and other officials obsequiously took their leave and Fray García retired into the chambers of his secular predecessors to relish the first moments of his ascent to the supreme authority of the State as well as of the Church in the fairest of Spanish realms. Outside, in the plaza, deafening explosions of bombs and artillery-pieces saluted the new viceroy. That night the whole city seemed ablaze with lanterns in doorways and windows and roaring bonfires in the streets and squares.

## ·§ 9 §·

## Antonine Tibesar, O.F.M.

# Social Tensions Among
# the Friars

*As the Peruvian viceroyalty entered the seventeenth
century, a preponderance of the order clergy came
from the colonies rather than from Spain. Very often
the various orders tried to reserve the important offices for peninsular Spaniards, since they questioned
the ability of the creole clergy to administer religious
affairs. Hard feelings and conflict within the orders
led to the imposition of the* alternativa, *a forced
alternation in office of the creole clergy and the peninsular churchmen. Friar Antonine Tibesar has examined masses of archival documentation in relation
to the* alternativa *in Peru, and he has shown how the
institution shaped clerical attitudes in the seventeenth-
century colony.*

Within recent years there has been increasing interest in
those aspects of Spanish American history which represent
a growing political consciousness among the inhabitants of
those lands especially during the seventeenth and eighteenth centuries.

From Antonine Tibesar, O.F.M., "The *Alternativa:* A Study in
Spanish-Creole Relations in Seventeenth-Century Peru," *The
Americas: A Quarterly Review of Inter-American Cultural His-
tory,* 11 (1955), 229–283 *passim.* Reprinted by permission of the
Academy of American Franciscan History.

Perhaps nowhere can the growth of this sentiment be studied with greater ease than in the religious orders. By their development, the religious orders, the Augustinians, Dominicans, Franciscans, Jesuits, and Mercedarians, came to consist almost exclusively of *criollos* (descendants of Europeans born in America) and *Chapetones* (friars born in Europe, in particular in Spain): the two groups which were to be the leaders of the two contending parties in the wars of independence. The ultimate estrangement of these two groups developed during the colonial period in the course of which the rising creole desire to manage their own affairs encountered increasing opposition from the Spanish Crown. The encounters were not always peaceful. The participants, on both sides, in good faith held to their principles with a deep conviction of which the incidental vehemence is perhaps the clearest proof. Neither side yielded readily. This is true also of the friars.

By their constitutions, most religious orders held elections every three or four years in which the friar-delegates freely elected their provincials and his council. Of course, these elections afforded the creoles, and the Spaniards too, a perfect opportunity to voice their sentiments regarding the type of candidate which they preferred with comparative freedom and immunity. Thus the chapters of the religious orders may in a certain sense be regarded as the first forum in which the creole was able to state for the first time his preference in regard to his ruler. There was perhaps little political significance, at least in the beginning, in the decisions of these chapters. The friars were not revolutionaries seeking to overthrow Spanish authority, though they may well have wished to restrict the extent of the Spanish monopoly of positions and power. Neither were these chapters wholly without political significance. Many friars in the seventeenth century were members of powerful creole families. Their relatives, who did have political ambitions which were regularly thwarted by the royal policy of preferring *Chapetones* exclusively for the highest offices, regarded these chapters with more than passing interest. In them their unspoken protests found voice. This was realized by the royal officials and in an effort to curb creole aspirations the Crown imposed the *alterna-tiva*: the forced alternation in the higher offices of the respective provinces of Spanish and Peruvian friars.

The first friars who arrived in Peru were, of course, almost exclusively Europeans. The bulk of these were Spaniards, though we do find Portuguese, French, and even Germans in their ranks. The Dominicans and the Mercedarians came with Pizarro in 1531 with the Franciscans following their example after a few months. The Augustinians came in 1551 and the Jesuits in 1568. From the very beginning, the Dominicans do not seem to have received any Indians or those with Indian blood in their ranks, and all available evidence today points to the conclusion that the Dominicans as a rule received only Spanish or creoles. The Mercedarians at an early date, certainly before 1548, had already established the policy of admitting Indian and mestizo boys—a fact which may help to explain the attitude of that order towards the Pizarros and also its loss of social acceptance by the Spaniards which resulted in its royal suppression in 1568. The Franciscans seem to have adopted in the beginning the Dominican attitude, although there are some indications that they may have admitted Indians as lay brothers, though not as priests. In general also the Augustinians accepted the Dominican policy and at a comparatively early date, 1571, forbade the reception of mestizos. The attitude of the first Jesuits towards the mestizos is not clear but after the arrival of Father Joseph de Acosta in 1572, the Jesuits, for a time, became the devoted protectors of the mestizos and admitted a number into their Order, among them the famous Blas de Valera. The experiment, however, did not prove happy and in 1582 the Jesuits also excluded them. From that time, until possibly the middle of the eighteenth century, the religious orders in Peru with the exception of the Jesuits were to be made up almost exclusively of creoles and

*Chapetones.* After their sad experiences with the mestizos, the Jesuits proceeded to limit also the numbers of creoles who might join their company. This limitation was not removed until late in the eighteenth century.

The other Orders had placed no limit on the reception of creoles and accordingly as the century advanced an ever greater proportion of the total number came to be drawn from this class. The desire to manage their own affairs grew apace with their numbers and importance and before the end of the sixteenth century encountered considerable opposition from the Spanish friars who had founded the provinces in Peru and had enjoyed a monopoly in their government for a number of decades. In particular was this true of the Dominicans who had been the first religious to organize a province in that country and apparently also the first to receive candidates. It is understandable therefore that this problem would become acute first of all among them. As early as 1565, Castro informed the Crown of the existence of factions among them. Castro did not specify the cause of the division, but in 1588 Viceroy Villar reported that the desire of the creole Dominicans to govern themselves was the cause of internal difficulties. At the same time, the viceroy added that the Spanish Dominicans were few in number. By 1592, the creoles were so firmly entrenched among them that they were able to pass a law which prohibited the entrance of any Spaniard into the Dominican Lima province. The situation must have been very similar in the other Orders, for by 1593 the majority of the friars in all Orders in Peru were creoles, though none of the others is known actually to have forbidden the reception of Spaniards.

.  .  .

For in 1619, we see that the Spanish-born Franciscans of Mexico, who numbered only fifty out of the 630 friars of the Province of the Holy Gospel, unhappy with the *alternativa,* were appealing for the establishment of a *ternativa*: the forced sharing of the offices of the provinces in succession among these three groups: the creoles, the Spaniards who had entered the Order in Mexico, and finally the Spanish friars who had come from Spain. This last group asked for the *ternativa* and they got it too on April 5, 1627.

Once the *alternativa* was established in Mexico, it was not long before it was begun in Peru also, though the *ternativa* seems to have remained the unique glory of Mexico. The Augustinians of Lima received it through a decree of March 11, 1629, and they may well have been the first in Peru to have it, although there is good reason to believe that the Dominicans of Quito had it by November 4, 1625. The Dominicans of Lima certainly had it by 1654, though at this time it is not known when it was begun. The Mercedarians of Lima did not even enjoy the privilege of the *alternativa* but were commonly governed by Spanish friars. Thus, at the middle of the seventeenth century, only two Orders in Peru, the Franciscans and the Jesuits, still remained exempt from the *alternativa*.

.     .     .

At any rate, there were some vague stirrings of the creole Franciscans of Peru during the first decades of the seventeenth century. At the same time the numerical position of the creoles was improving. These two trends seem to have united about 1650. Up to that year, of the thirty-one provincials of Lima only nine had been creoles. From 1650 to 1678 there were eight provincials in Lima; six of these were creoles. In Cuzco the situation was just about the same. From 1607 to 1650 (this province had suffered two short interruptions) there had been ten provincials, nine of these had been Spaniards. From 1650 to 1678, there had been eight provincials, only one of whom had been a Spaniard. In Cuzco, therefore, after 1650 one-eighth of the provincials had been Spaniards, while in Lima in the same period two-eighths had been. These proportions were comparatively close to the total numerical strength of the Spaniards in the provinces at large. In 1675, there were 291 creole priests and clerics in the Lima province and

61 Spaniards. In Cuzco, there were 247 creoles and 44 Spaniards. In other words, in Lima the Spaniards formed a little more than one-sixth of the total priests and clerics, while in Cuzco they formed just a little less than one-sixth. On the basis of numbers, therefore, the Spanish friars were receiving a fair representation in the election of the provincial—the highest office in the province filled by direct and free election of the members of the province. However, the disturbing element in the picture was the constant trend against the Spaniards, and these had little hope for improvement in the ratio. This disquieted the Europeans and rumbles of their dissatisfaction with the turn of events are discernible in their letters to the Crown beginning already in the 1640's. The ready-made equalizer was the *alternativa*. For some years this device was not invoked.

The peninsulars took advantage of a general chapter to be held in Rome in 1664 to begin the campaign to regain what they considered to be their rights. In the Franciscan Order a general chapter is a sort of convention held at periodical intervals, generally every six years, in which delegates from each province meet to elect a new general superior called the Minister General or simply the General. At this time each province had the right to send two delegates to the chapter. These delegates were selected through a special election held in each province. This special election was held in Lima and Cuzco in 1662. Lima sent as its delegates Father Ignacio de Irraraga, a peninsular, and Father Francisco de Andrade, a Peruvian. Similarly, Cuzco elected two delegates, one of whom was also a Spaniard, Father Francisco Pérez de Ybieta, and a second, who was presumably a Peruvian, whose name is not recorded.

Unfortunately, the Peruvian Andrade was taken ill shortly after his arrival in Rome and was forced to keep to his quarters. Thus he was not able to learn what was taking place at the chapter. Irraraga took advantage of his absence on May 18, 1664, to present a petition to the chapter in the name of the seven Franciscan provinces of South

America asking for the imposition of the *alternativa* in all seven provinces "for the sake of harmony and so that all may share equally in the offices." [1] This petition was signed by one delegate from each of the provinces—all of them Spaniards. This important fact, however, was not mentioned. Neither did the petition mention another fact of perhaps even greater importance. None of these delegates had been instructed by their provinces to ask for the *alternativa,* although the petition read as if the provinces themselves were anxious to have it. Thus misled, the chapter granted the petition on June 5, 1664, with these words: "the *alternativa* is granted presupposing the request of the provinces." On the following day, June 6, this decree was submitted to the Congregation of Bishops and Regulars for their ratification and approval. It was evidently considered a routine matter by the cardinals of this congregation for the requested approval was granted on that same day. Next the decree was submitted to the Pope for his final approval and for the decree which would make it law. There had been no opposition to the *alternativa* and so on June 20, 1664, Pope Alexander VII issued the decree approving the decision of the cardinals. In a final clause, the Pope expressly safeguarded the jurisdiction of the cardinals in the matter in case of appeal. Apparently this final clause was added as a result of Andrade's activity. This Peruvian friar during his illness had not been informed of the activity of his colleagues and he did not learn of the petition to impose the *alternativa* until the decree had already been approved by the cardinals and had been submitted to the Pope. Andrade immediately appealed to the committee of cardinals against the *alternativa* with the result that on June 16, 1664—four days before the day when the pontifical confirmatory decree was being issued—the cardinals issued a decree suspending the *alternativa* until both sides could be heard. Andrade now tried

---

[1] *Informatio. Facti et Juris in Causa Peruana Alternativae* (Rome, 1683), fol. 17.

to contact Irraraga, only to learn that as soon as that friar had received a copy of the decree he had set out post-haste for Spain, aided by the Spanish officials in Rome. Andrade set out in pursuit but in Genoa his health failed again and there he died without ever contacting his fellow delegate and his papers fell into the hands of the Spanish authorities. Irraraga continued on to Madrid where the papal decree imposing the *alternativa* was granted the *paso regio* on September 13, 1664, although the suspensive decree of the cardinals was then seemingly already known in Madrid.

The suspension, however, was ignored and on September 16, 1664, the king sent a decree to the royal authorities in Lima and Cuzco to impose the *alternativa* on the Franciscans in their jurisdictions. No word was said of the intervening suspension. It is evident from all this that the full weight of the prestige and organization of the Spanish monarchy was being thrown into the balance against the creoles. Under the circumstances, it was foolhardy for the creoles to oppose the measure. All the advantage lay with the Spanish friars who were anxious to have the *alternativa*. At this time, however, the creoles apparently thought that the Crown would remain impartial in a dispute in which both sides were fellow vassals—each with equal claims upon the royal consideration. Before the question had been settled, the Peruvians were to find that through every twist and turn of this tortuous question, the prestige and full power of the Crown would be thrown only to one side—that of the Spaniards. The Peruvians had to learn that they were fellow vassals only in legal theory; in practice they were colonials.

.        .        .

The tensions engendered by the *alternativa* affected both State and Church in Peru. Politically, this struggle helped to emphasize the fact that while in law the Peruvians and Spaniards were equal vassals of the same king, in fact the Peruvians were regarded by the Crown as colonials. Hence, there is reason to agree with those who profess to see in the *alternativa* one of the factors which fostered the growth of a Peruvian national consciousness and thereby, at least indirectly, of a desire for independence. Certainly at the time when other factors rendered the decision in favor of national independence feasible, the *alternativa* would have done much to prepare the minds of the Peruvians to concur in and to favor that decision.

More pronounced, perhaps, were the effects, both direct and indirect, upon the Church itself. Directly, to judge from the records of the Franciscans, the clergy suffered a continuing loss of both prestige and numbers. During the decade, 1680–1690, relatively few Peruvians entered the Franciscan Order in Lima, while before that date the annual increase averaged nearly twenty-four. At the same time, the young men after 1690 who did become Franciscans seem definitely to have belonged to a lower social class than had those who had been received before that decade. Also the average of the annual entrants never seems to have reached the volume maintained earlier. Both of these latter trends seem to have continued well into the present.

It is possible that the Church may have suffered also indirectly from the *alternativa*. At that time, there was union of Church and State. In the earlier decades of Peruvian history, the Church had undoubtedly profited from this union. Now the State demanded its payment. At a time when Spanish prestige was declining throughout the world, the Crown needed all the support it could muster. In this effort, it forced the Church, at least in the *alternativa* affair, to identify its interests with those of the State. Perhaps any other position at that time would have been unthinkable. It would seem to be just as unthinkable, although at this time there is little concrete proof for or against this theoretical conclusion, that the later revolutionary political leaders should have cherished the Church while hating the State with which it was identified.

In the long run, therefore, the *alternativa* seems to have

been a mistake for both Church and State. The creole friars tried to persuade the royal officials to adopt this belief. They had failed. Accordingly, on January 6, 1686, the *alternativa* was finally imposed on the Lima Franciscans by explicit royal order.

# ⋘ 10 ⋙

## W. Eugene Shiels, S.J.

◀━◆❙◆━▶

# Seventeenth-Century Legal Crisis in the Missions

*The Jesuit historian W. Eugene Shiels, an expert in-*
*terpreter of the vast supervisory powers exerted by*
*the state over the Church in the Spanish Empire, ex-*
*amines in this selection the aftermath of the crown's*
*decision in 1574 to enforce episcopal jurisdiction over*
*missionary districts. Legal crises in the missions and*
*jurisdictional conflicts engendered by this decision*
*lasted for the better part of the seventeenth century.*
*The shortage of diocesan clergy dictated that the mis-*
*sionaries remain at their posts and thus continue to*
*control the Indian doctrinas. But to whom were they*
*suffragan? To the episcopal see or to their own prel-*
*ates? Who was to dictate policy? During the seven-*
*teenth century, the king and the Council of the In-*
*dies became involved in complicated litigation over*
*these issues.*

The liveliest administrative worry in this period was the
matter of episcopal jurisdiction over missionary districts.
Jesuits had come to America prepared for high enterprise.

From W. Eugene Shiels, "The Legal Crisis in the Jesuit Missions
of Hispanic America," *Mid-America: An Historical Review*, 21
(1939), 253–276 *passim*. Reprinted by permission of the publisher.

Their men were well trained and thoroughly disciplined in close organization. They enjoyed the special favor of the hierarchy, of the viceregal officers, and of the royal government. Officialdom furnished them with a set of exemptions and privileges enabling them to go rapidly to work and to carry on unencumbered by exterior restraint. Their privilege amounted to a policy of unusual freedom and a frank recognition that they, as a religious order, had their own special regimen providing for effective and exemplary conduct on the part of their membership. The crown distributed work to them and expected them to make a success of it. Nor was their success questioned. Together with the Franciscans and Dominicans they made an enviable record with their missions, and during the latter sixteenth and early seventeenth centuries they gained the universal good will of the prelates whose helpers they were.

As years passed and colonial government reached the outlying sections, differences of opinion caused friction with the ordinaries. The original mission idea fixed ten years for the religious to do missionary work in a chosen sector. After that period would come the normal appointment of the secular clergy. Such was the spirit of the New Laws and the famous 1573 *cédula* of Philip II. But the theory was more simple than the practice. Actually few mission *partidos* reached civilian status within the specified time. The diocesan clergy failed to become proficient in the native languages, particularly the Otomi, the most difficult tongue. Native political management did not achieve trustworthy development. Native economy could not stand against European competition. The childish simplicity of the tribesmen made them easy prey for grasping individualists.

Then, too, there was the point of relinquishing thriving institutions which the religious considered parts and units of general fields marked off by tribes, languages, mountains, and rivers. Quite naturally, the privileged independence would come into contact with diocesan expansion. The successfully organized *partidos* would be yielded up to the parochial clergy and the pioneers would go farther in the field. Such a move had been foreseen. In fact the character of the Jesuit order made it a "light cavalry," subject to instant orders, ready to go wherever needed, to relinquish any post for another more in distress. From the broad point of view of the general in Rome, the administration was always prepared to make such changes, but the human nature of missionaries on the spot was prone to repine at quitting a cherished position. The local units saw their labors fruitful among their beloved Indians and they feared that others might not carry on the operations with equal facility.

A more severe trial arose in what the religious considered an improper extension of episcopal power, the effort to force them into diocesan organization. There were two grounds for their privileged status of working independently of viceregal and episcopal control in the missions: the internal organization of the religious order, and the external need for a well-equipped body of compactly organized men to conquer the uncivilized and un-Christianized portions of the colonies. When once these territories were sufficiently settled for the ordinary clerical forces to operate, the religious knew that their day of independent action was on the wane. The external need in that sector would pass, and with it the missionaries must go. The point, however, was to determine just when mission territory became diocesan. And the judge in this point was the man who held high control over religious regulations, El Rey, in his capacity of chief patron of all churches in Spain and in the Indies.

In several cases it appears that one or other bishop tried to hurry that day. Such a situation seemed chronic to the diocese of Guadiana, the present Durango. That diocese comprised most of the northern and northwestern missions where the best Jesuit work was done. Another focal point was Puebla de los Angeles. The effects of these efforts were serious. Generally speaking, the prelates put such pressure on the missionaries that there was earnest discussion in provincial meetings on abandoning all mission work.

Now why should all this have happened? The prelates appreciated the value of the work done, and the religious respected the position of the prelates. Perhaps the tithes were a motive, for the endowments supporting mission work were exempt from these payments. Possibly the best answer is that history was moving onward, that the locale of unrestricted opportunity was receding into the far north, that territory closer to the capital was organized in normal functioning wherein the episcopate were the directors of ecclesiastical work. As their field widened, so might they expect to embrace all the operations within their effective rule. And yet this need not have changed the character of the religious regimen. The religious had to keep their manner of life, but they did not have to keep their stations here and there in the organized bishoprics. It was no small matter to work out this compromise, for, aside from the native difficulty of the arrangement, various human factors contributed irritations and emotional displacements.

To begin, the colonies of Spain in the early days were forcing-beds for lawsuits. The hierarchy of jurisdiction, with its final court in the Council of the Indies, made for interminable appeals. Almost everybody of importance in New Spain was involved in cases concerning property rights and the limits of power in civic offices, and the Jesuits were no exception. Lest they waste time in these cases and alienate good will, the general was at pains to remind them to stay out of legal involvements. The colonial era was one of continuous readjustments. The constant shifts of rights resulting from new *entradas* of conquest or economic or missionary penetration, explorations, the creation of new political divisions and bishoprics, all revised the original simple system into a complex fabric of life. The juxtaposition of natives and Europeans, of creoles and Peninsulars, of the secular priesthood with a multitude of orders and their particular privileges—necessary for the work but irritating to officialdom—and the pronounced penchant for litigation in the colonies of Spain, made for decades of legal action to establish and re-establish the rights of persons and corporations.

Individuals might be quarrelsome. The struggle of missionary life did not make for placidity and the calm of leisure. The change in title of productive *haciendas* could not go unfelt in a milieu where there was much fear of insolvency. The wonder is not that there was difficulty but that so much was done. From the suits and cases there resulted a smoother administrative machinery. One only element of basic risk remained, the *Patronato Real,* with its power to remove, to suppress, to withdraw support and the right to exist. This, however, is not the place to show how that power was used to destroy the missions after 1750. . . .

The extension of episcopal power is the nub of the story. In many places the bishops sought to bring the religious under a control proper to the secular clergy but scarcely consistent with the independence requisite for carrying on a religious order. This independence enables an order to achieve close control of its members, to supervise virtuous living and correct ministry, and to beget the special obedience to religious superiors who must necessarily have the freedom to remove men for causes that might not permit of external consultation. The conflict is often called the *doctrina* controversy because it involved what were known in Spanish law as the *doctrinas.*

A *doctrina* was, roughly speaking, a mission district. The word is also used for the systematic catechism of Christian doctrine as it was taught to the Indians. The head of a *doctrina* was a *doctrinero*. If he were a secular priest, he would be called a *cura,* a name signifying his charge and at the same time his dependence on his bishop who could both appoint and remove him, who as an agent of the crown could give him the usufruct of the *doctrina* revenues, and who had the right of regular inspection called visitation. If the *doctrinero* were a religious such as a Jesuit, he could claim no salary, and, as he was not sent by the bishop, he was not in charge of a *cura*. The *doctrina* is sometimes referred to as a *partido* or division of the mission field or of the tribe being evangelized.

From the first days these *doctrinas* were maintained in

territories where the heathen predominated in numbers. With no stable residence they formed only the nucleus of a settlement which had to be Christianized little by little. Spiritual jurisdiction among them did not belong to any diocese but was derived directly from the Holy See. Religious were destined to convert them according to the will of the king, to whom the pope had committed the charge of sending men fit for the preaching of the Gospel. These men penetrated into the unorganized territory with authority emanating immediately from the Holy Father to whom they were directly subject. They exercised all their necessary ministries without dependence on any diocesan ordinary but only on their religious superior, who was the channel, through his major superior, from the Holy See.

As time brought civilization and Christianity to the natives, the missionaries should ordinarily have come under the control of the bishop in the newly formed diocese. In America, however, there was a scarcity of secular clergy, and to place the regulars directly under the episcopacy would bring a double jurisdiction and tend to hamper the work of the orders and to contravene their regular character.

With this problem in mind, Philip II asked the Holy See for a dispensation from the ordinary discipline as set down by the Council of Trent and published through the Spanish dominions by the same Philip II in 1564. He wished the religious to continue the administration of the *doctrinas* and of the sacraments as though they were parish priests, yet depending only on their superiors and not on the bishops. This petition was granted by Pius V in his brief *Exponi Nobis* on March 24, 1567.

Opposition to this arrangement broke out in time and the attack was so serious that it threatened to end the corporate work of the Jesuits in their missions. Other orders were not so worried. The Franciscans and Dominicans were on the scene earlier when there was no diocesan clergy, and from this fact it followed that members of these orders were appointed prelates. The effect was a fusion, and a confusion, of jurisdiction, to some extent, though at certain periods these two orders suffered similar missionary ordeals in company with their later co-workers.

By a queer coincidence, the first troubles of the Jesuits had their origins in the urging of viceroys and bishops that the religious take away from them some of their own prerogatives. The first occurrence is in Peru, where the renowned viceroy Francisco de Toledo demanded that the Jesuits accept two diocesan parishes or *curas* with all their rights and possessions and manage them independently of episcopal provision.

A concrete example of this whole subject is the story of the *doctrina* of Tepotzotlán which appears in many letters of the *Colección de cartas inéditas de los Padres Generales*. Tepotzotlán was the center of a small group of Indians about twenty-five miles north by northwest of Mexico City. In 1581 the Archbishop of Mexico, Pedro Moya de Contreras, asked the Jesuits to send some men there. The previous curates had not known the native languages, Otomi, Masaguan, and Mexican, said to be the most difficult tongues in the viceroyalty. Due to the death of the incumbent, the *doctrina* was unprovided with its *cura*.

The Jesuits were just beginning to attack the missionary problem, and their Father Visitor, Juan de la Plaza, requested the archbishop to find them a place where they could both aid the natives and learn their speech. His petition coincided with that of Moya and early in 1581 the Jesuits arrived. Quickly the scattered natives were "reduced" into one pueblo. Alegre tells us that their coming voluntarily and without the use of force was an altogether new thing in New Spain. The conversion of a very "bad" Indian caused it all. Families of other linguistic stock joined the *población*. Instructed and baptized, they soon became exemplary Christians. The archbishop had offered to turn over the regular stipend proper to a *cura*, but the fathers refused to take title to the ordinary revenues and they distributed the surplus of several rich *haciendas* to the natives for the construction of a civilized community.

In the very next year the provincial tried to recall his men from Tepotzotlán because the general, Claude Aquaviva, refused to allow them to become *curas* in the canonical sense. Accepting "presentation" from the archbishop would make the Jesuits subject to the will and appointment of the prelates in the future. Aquaviva felt that such a concession would cut into the religious regimen; it would give his men two superiors with equal authority; it would hamper the provincial power to make readjustments; it would dissipate the "light cavalry" character of the order, both in settling men in fixed positions and in dividing the command.

The Indians heard of this intention and sent delegates to see the archbishop. Alegre copies out their petition. They asked for a compromise arrangement. The upshot was the appointment of a secular *beneficiado* as the canonical pastor with all his perquisites and responsibilities. To the Jesuits were given the residence and garden which they had been occupying there. They were to live in Tepotzotlán and assist the *beneficiado*. This appointee was a man who got along well with the fathers and the combination worked in harmony for many years. In 1584 the Jesuits opened the Seminario de San Martin as a school for native boys. Two years later the novitiate was moved to Tepotzotlán, and in 1604 a college was founded there. In this institution the Indians came to such remarkable intellectual development that some of their number later on, as priests and religious, became professors of their language and even of so difficult a science as canon law.

In those days men were bold, striking out daringly to build new patterns of life. A later age would point out the folly of expecting consistent unity between the *beneficiado* and his helpers. The fact is that for twenty-two years there was peace between them, until in 1608 we find the *cura* going to Mexico with a set of complaints and a request for an appointment elsewhere. The fathers also had their story of the differences. It finally appeared that a new arrangement was imperative. The *curas* had not learned to speak in Otomi and the seminary and college had won the affection of the natives. The archbishop accordingly asked the viceroy to realign the situation.

The viceroy, Luis de Velasco II, wrote to His Majesty in 1610. The long letter is given in full in Alegre. He said that His Majesty had asked for a report on the *doctrina* of Tepotzotlán. It seemed that, for the discharge of the royal conscience and the good of the Indians in that *partido,* it would be better to give the *doctrina* entirely to the Jesuits. They had done well there as helpers of the secular clergy. However, they did not wish to accept the post as a *cura.* Never had they accepted *doctrinas* in the Indies except the two which Viceroy Francisco forced them to take in Peru, those in Lima and Juli. Disturbance had arisen in Tepotzotlán from the overt acts of the clerics there, who, it was thought, should not be sent back. The Jesuits, on the other hand, had a seminary there for boys, a novitiate, and a college. Velasco's thirty-five years' acquaintance with them in the Indies convinced him that they did not want *doctrinas* for any selfish aims. Everywhere they acted as helpful associates of the diocesan clergy. The Indians there were very devoted to the fathers. The father general had lately granted, with much difficulty, permission for his men to try out the plan of acting as *doctrineros* in this one pueblo. It would be a great benefit to the natives there. His Majesty should concede this grace to the fathers and give them that *doctrina.*

In 1618 all hearings on the case were finished, and Philip III sent a *cédula* to the viceroy, now the Marqués de Guadalcazar. The incumbent *cura* was to be promoted to the cathedral of Mexico, and the king proceeded:

> You know well, from our law and the apostolic bulls, as well as from my right as King of Castile and Leon, that to me pertains the presentation of all the dignities, canonries, appointments and ecclesiastical benefices, both here in Spain and in the Indies, and in the islands and lands of the Ocean Sea. It is likewise mine to provide for the *doctrinas* of those realms, to unite

or divide benefices for those of my vassals who have
learning, conscience and a good life. And now as I
watch over that right and patronage, I give order
that . . . you hand over the said benefice to the said
Company of Jesus. Done in Madrid, June 5, 1618.

The King.

Aquaviva had given his consent in 1609. In reply to a
petition addressed to him by the Seventh Provincial Congregation of the Province of New Spain, he wrote:

PETITION: That you grant that our men be allowed
to act as parish priests wherever they live, both in the
Tepotzotlán College and in the others.

RESPONSE: By no means does it seem proper to concede this faculty, for it is opposed to our Constitutions, and experience has taught us that the thing
does not work out. Meanwhile let trial be made of it
in that one college. Time will show what final decision we ought to take in this matter.

Indeed time would show. At the moment the provincial
made a summary note at the end of the document, thus
showing his interpretation of the response. He wrote: "Our
men are not to take the office of *curas* in other colleges but
only in Tepotzotlán." From the context this concession for
Tepotzotlán appears to have been made before the larger
petition was sent to Rome, very likely in the same year.

Year by year brought an increasing number of royal
*cédulas* with further regulations and restrictions. That of
1637 was particularly disturbing. All religious who now exercised the office of *cura* in a *doctrina,* or would do so in
future, must submit to an examination in doctrine and
language. Likewise they must conform to episcopal provision, collation, canonical institution, visitation, correction,
and removal at the will of the ordinary.

The ruling viceroy sent back to Madrid such a eulogy of
the Jesuit work at Tepotzotlán that the authorities suspended action on the *cédula* and left them in peaceful
possession of the *doctrina*. Not till 1652 did the question

come up again. In that year a definitive *cédula* required all religious to conform to the fullest royal regulation under the *Patronato*. The *doctrina* was given up in the following year. The decision is part of the larger story on which we must now embark.

The history of the Tepotzotlán *doctrina,* its opening in 1581, the agreement of 1618, and the document of 1653, exemplify the general trend of the adjustment in religious jurisdiction throughout Hispanic America. A document of 1640 will show a larger part of the picture. It is headed: Reply of our Father General Mutius Vitelleschi to a memorial which Father Pedro de Velasco, Procurator of the Province of Mexico, presented to him on the subject of *doctrinas,* on April 6, 1640. The memorial follows, and below it is the reply:

PETITION: The religious of the Company of Jesus in the Province of New Spain, subjects of Your Paternity, in obedience to the laws of their institute and their duties to their lords the Catholic Kings of Spain, have been and are employed in the conversion and instruction of the barbarian Indians of this province, especially the missions of Nueva Vizcaya. There, eleven of our Company have shed their blood at the hands of the barbarians for Christ. They have entered into the Province of Cinaloa, once all pagan, and they have gained more than 200,000 souls. They have brought more than 130 leagues of that country under the obedience of the Church and of the Catholic King. They have founded pueblos and churches which they now administer, and they visit other more remote provinces of gentiles. There are no other clerics or religious of any other order in their district.

The Company is excused from accepting *doctrinas* of Indians in the now pacified districts which are administered by clerics and other religious. They hold only one of this kind, the *doctrina* in the pueblo of Tepotzotlán in the archbishopric of Mexico. This *doc-*

*trina* those of the Company have cared for during the past thirty years, for just and reasonable causes, since the King Our Lord Philip III entrusted it to them, and another rather small one in San Luis de la Paz, of the bishopric of Michoacán. This one the Viceroy entrusted to them in order to further the pacification of the Chichimecos Indians, a project which had involved grave damage and very high expenditure of the royal funds. Once these Indians had come willingly into the *doctrina,* these burdens of government were lifted.

It is well known that the religious of the Company have attended with all diligence and good example to the teaching and instructing of these natives and to the conversion of the gentiles, with many happy results and the discharge of the duty of the royal conscience,—a charge that belongs to the King as he is Patron of this conversion and the *doctrinas* of these natives.

Now we have received intimation of a *cédula* of His Majesty, sent in common to all the religious who administer *doctrinas* in New Spain. He desires complete obedience to the ordinances of His Majesty, basing his claim on the debt owed him by our whole Society and especially by this province, and most of all on the great harm that would follow if we abandoned these *doctrinas* where we are actually supported by the royal funds and liberality.

Under our care is a great number of souls. Their disposition is inconstant. Politically speaking, the peace of this barbarous and militant race is highly desirable, while their disturbance would cause serious and perhaps irreparable consequences. The pacification of the Tepeguan nation alone, who form but a tenth part of the Indians under our charge, has cost 900,000 pesos to the royal treasury.

Wherefore, seeing that this Province of New Spain cannot on its own decision subject itself to the de-

mands of the new *cédula,* disagreeing as it does with
our institute and manner of life—and noting that before this *cédula* came we hindered no one but our
help was acknowledged gratefully, and we served God
Our Lord and His Holy Church, and His Catholic
Majesty and the good of souls in these realms—therefore, as the institute which our order professes places
the decision in this matter with Your Paternity as
our general and head, we ask Your Paternity to give
instructions for our conduct in this situation.

RESPONSE: I praise and congratulate your province for
its affection and devotedness in obeying with all punctuality the orders of His Majesty and the Royal Council of the Indies, as far as our institute can allow.
You know I have charged you to do this, for the important obligations which our Company recognizes.
In particular your province has done well in sending
its petition dutifully to me, in good form, and leaving
for me the resolution of the present case in which
your province is unable to decide, for such determina-
tions depend on the general.

Now I know the singular zeal of His Majesty and
the Royal Council. I am sure, too, that they admire
the training, doctrine and exhortation of the Indians,
and the sufficiency and good example of those who
are their teachers and pastors. Trusting in this piety
and Christian spirit of His Majesty I know he will
listen kindly when he is informed of all these matters
(as I order the Father Procurator to inform him, in
the name of the Company and of myself). He will find
that his policies will obtain greater advantage and
blessing if he keeps the Company in the regime in
which it has exercised its ministry for so many years
to the glory and service of the Divine and Human
Majesties and the increasing profit of so innumerable
a conversion of gentiles.

As to our style of government, particularly instituted and distinct from that which others employ, I

shall ask His Majesty to deign with His Royal Clemency to retain his esteem for the manner of our past work among the Indians. I shall represent with proper submission that in whatever does not contravene our institute, as in our men being examined in doctrine and language facility by whatever persons are named, he will see us agreeing to his wishes with all promptness and joy. I shall ask that he prevent only what subverts our constitution.

I feel certain that when His Majesty and the Royal Council are informed on this point, the Company will receive new favor and encouragement in its manner of life, its rules and governance. He will recall that in our enterprises among the Indian missions we find no utility nor any human interest save the service of Our Lord and of His Majesty. This is a grand reward, even though it cost us much suffering, labor, hardship, and not a few lives—either taken by the hands of the infidel or hurried to their term by the labor and hard environment. There will be no lack of devotion and obedience to His Majesty, which may the Divine Grace guard. Rome, April 6, 1640. Mutius Vitelleschi.

Therein the reader may see that a critical point has been reached. The very length and diffuseness of the letter testify to the worry felt by the order in Mexico. The authorities wished to force the Jesuits to accept *doctrinas* in the pacified districts and thus to place themselves directly under the bishops. Should the order find it impossible to accept this arrangement, great harm loomed for the Indian system. King, Council, viceroy, and episcopate would feel that their previous liberality was now ungenerously forgotten in the readiness to abandon the missions on account of the regulatory acts which the authorities deemed imperative. On the other hand, the general could not see how to give in completely without dissolving the constitutional principles of his order.

## 11

## C. R. Boxer

# Brazil in Crisis

*Much is known about the missionary activities and
the framing of Indian policy by the Jesuit António
Vieira during Brazil's crisis-ridden seventeenth century. Professor C. R. Boxer, the foremost historian of
colonial Brazil, who was the Camoens Professor of
Portuguese in King's College, University of London,
until 1969, has examined other dimensions of Vieira's
career—his work as an economist and entrepreneur
and his liberal and humane attitude toward the
Jews. In this selection, Boxer shows how Father Vieira
launched the Brazil Company in 1649, and how he
sought to use the funds of Portuguese Jewish investors to help shore up the political economy of Brazil,
as Portugal struggled to counteract the Dutch invader.*

Three hundred years ago, the national existence of Portugal and Brazil was at stake. This may not readily be realized today, when Brazil is the greatest nation in more
than mere size on the South American continent, whilst
Portugal possesses the third largest colonial empire in the
world. But those who have more than a passing acquaintance with the history of the seventeenth century may remember that for fourteen critical years (1640–1654), Portu-

From C. R. Boxer, "Padre António Vieira, S.J., and the Institution of the Brazil Company in 1649," *Hispanic American Historical Review,* 29 (1949), 474–479, 482–486 *passim.* Reprinted
by permission of Duke University Press and the author.

gal's chances of survival as an independent nation seemed slim indeed, whilst there was a distinct possibility of Brazil becoming a Dutch possession, either in whole or in part.

The fall of the one would, in all probability, have involved the collapse of the other. Portugal could not carry on her twenty-eight years' war of independence against Spain (to say nothing of fighting Holland for most and Cromwellian England for part of this time) without the economic resources provided by her Brazilian "milch-cow" —as King John IV aptly if crudely characterized his most profitable colony. Conversely, Brazil could not indefinitely sustain her struggle against the stubborn Hollanders ensconced at Pernambuco, unless means were found to break the Dutch mastery of the South Atlantic Ocean (even if only temporarily), so that men and munitions from Portugal and slaves from Angola might provide her with the sinews of war and of agriculture.

.    .    .

Padre António Vieira, . . . was not only fully alive to the desperate nature of the situation, but had a concrete remedy to propose for it. On reading the numerous references to maritime affairs in the letters of this remarkable man— perhaps the greatest that Portugal has ever produced after Afonso d'Albuquerque and Luis de Camões—one is inclined to believe that the Portuguese navy lost a potentially outstanding admiral when the young Vieira took a Jesuit's *roupeta* at Bahia in 1623. Throughout his long life, Vieira evinced a remarkable grasp of the importance of sea-power, and he took an intelligent interest in the Anglo-Dutch wars which revolutionized naval tactics. He obviously knew a good deal about shipbuilding, for his observations on the relative qualities of Dutch, French, and Dunkirk frigates in 1647–48 reveal sound sense and acute observation. Had his plans for the building and purchase of a fine fleet of frigates been followed, Portugal might well have recovered more of her colonies than Angola and Pernambuco.

Vieira was at one time the protagonist of a scheme for

the purchase of Dutch Brazil for an indemnity of three million *cruzados*, and an annual tribute of sugar for a decade
or so. Apropos of this suggestion (which naturally encountered great opposition in Portugal) he wrote in August,
1648, that the Hollanders had taken more sugar in six
months than the ten thousand chests which would have
been paid to them in a decade according to his plan. It is
arguable whether the Dutch would in fact have been con-
tented with an average of a thousand chests a year, when
there were so many more to be had for privateers' pickings.
Privateering in the United Provinces was almost a national
sport, as witness the popular Zeeland proverb, *Schijt in den
Handel alseer Buyt te halen is*. But Vieira, ever fertile of
ideas, had another and as it proved more practical suggestion.

This was the formation of a powerful chartered company,
something on the lines of the Dutch West India Company
which had proved so effective with ledger and sword—
chiefly with the latter it must be confessed. Vieira's original
plan (in 1641) was for two companies, one for India and
one for Brazil, but the former never progressed beyond the
paper stage. His idea was that the capital for these two
chartered companies should be furnished by the New-
Christian (or crypto-Jewish) financiers of Lisbon, and by
the Portuguese Sephardic Jews who had fled to Northern
Europe in order to avoid the rigors of the Iberian Inquisi-
tions. In order to induce these oppressed classes and exiles
to invest their capital in the projected Portuguese companies (and to leave the Dutch India Companies in which some
of them were interested), it was essential to guarantee all
investors from persecution by the Inquisition. It was on
this point that the scheme first broke down, since that all-
powerful tribunal utterly refused to countenance what it
regarded as an infamous pact with Satan's emissaries.

·     ·     ·

But the critical situation, and the efficacy of Jewish financial
coöperation in preparing the Portuguese armada of 1647,

had finally resolved King John IV's doubts. This monarch now strongly supported Vieira's project for the creation of a chartered Brazil Company, whose financial sinews were to be supplied by Portuguese Jews, crypto- and otherwise, both at home and abroad, in return for the exemption from confiscation of their capital (whether invested in the Brazil Company or elsewhere) by the Inquisition.

.　　.　　.

It will thus be realized that António Vieira stirred up bitter opposition when he formulated his proposal to attract Jewish capital to his projected Brazil Company, by specifically exempting investors therein from the penalty of confiscation of either goods or capital, even if convicted of the crimes of "Heresy, Apostasy, and Judaism." The inquisitors were already deeply suspicious of those New-Christians who had been formally "reconciled" with Holy Mother Church. The reverend gentlemen complained (no doubt correctly) that such reconciliations were mere shams, the victims still continuing to obey the Law of Moses in their hearts whilst outwardly conforming to Catholicism lest worse befall. One inquisitor advocated that not only should all such New-Christians be refused the Eucharist, but added that if the precepts of canonical law were enforced, any *christão-novo* who once relapsed should pay for it with his life, quoting Saint Augustine as saying *Lupus nadit, Lupus reddit.* This was perhaps an extreme view, but there was more general support for the stand of the inquisitor-general (Dom Francisco de Castro) and his council, who declared on the 25th June 1647, that the penalty of confiscation was the one most dreaded by crypto-Jews; for the formal stigma of Judaism meant little to them, whilst they could avoid death by an outward recantation. "And if with such a heavy penalty, Judaism has continued to flourish recently for our sins, what will happen when it sees itself free and immune therefrom?"

Vieira had, however, scored a great point in getting the vacillating King Dom John IV on his side; since if this

monarch, at the Jesuit's prompting, really decided to waive
the enforcement of the confiscatory clause, the Inquisition
had no means of getting hold of the Jews' money, as it
came ostensibly through the channel of the crown fiscal.
The battle was now fairly joined, and this round went to
Vieira and against the "Fortress of the Rocio" (Fortalesa do
Rossio), as the great Jesuit termed the Inquisition after the
name of the Lisbon square where its headquarters were
situated. Devout Catholic as he was, Dom João did not venture to take so drastic a step merely on the promptings of
Vieira, but he submitted the proposal to exempt Jewish and
crypto-Jewish capitalists from the penalty of confiscation
(*izenção do fisco*) to a large number of theologians and ex-
perts in canon law, as well as to the inquisitors. Needless
to say, the latter were wholly hostile to the proposal, and
claimed that the king had neither the right nor the power
to enforce any such measure without the explicit written ap-
probation of the pope. The Jesuit theologians of São Roque
and Santo Antão, on the other hand, unanimously declared
(in August, 1647) that such a measure was not only lawful
but necessary, and that King John could enforce it with a
clear conscience.

The king and Vieira now went ahead with their plans,
but the formal incorporation of the Brazil Company was
delayed for six months, partly because Duarte de Silva and
others of the principal intended directors were busy with
the preparation of António Teles' armada and Salvador
Correia's squadron throughout the autumn, and partly because the theological wrangles with the Inquisition and its
supporters still continued. The arrest of Duarte de Silva,
one of the principal investors in the projected Brazil Company, by the Inquisition in 1648 also delayed things, it is
to be presumed. By 6th February, 1649, all was ready, and
on that day the king sent for the bishop-inquisitor-general
and his council. On their arrival at the palace, he had the
terms of the *alvará,* or decree formally embodying the Brazil
Company, read over to them. These terms expressly included the *izenção do fisco,* whereupon the bishop and his

colleagues respectfully but emphatically protested against
them. The king in his turn equally politely, but still more
emphatically, rejected their protest, telling them that the
danger to Portugal and Brazil was so great that the foundation of this company (which other theologians had assured
him was justified) was the only possible means of saving the
situation. He added that they would be very unwise to make
any outward demonstration of their opposition, which he
would strongly resent. He then dismissed the fuming inquisitors.

The inquisitor-general subsequently suggested that the
matter should be referred to Rome for approval or rejec-
tion, but the king replied (on 29 March) that this was inad-
visable at present, since the Papacy could hardly adjudicate
fairly on the question, being hostile to the Portuguese government, but that he would do so in due course. Meanwhile,
however, the Lisbon inquisitors had appealed on their own
initiative to the pope, who promptly sent them a brief
declaring King John's move null and void. The king was
much annoyed when he heard this news, and sending for
Dom Francisco de Castro and his colleagues once more, he
read them the riot act in no uncertain terms. Portuguese
kings have always been distinguished for their devotion and
often for their bigotry; and seldom can a Lusitanian monarch have taken so strong a line with such puissant representatives of the church. He not only upbraided them for
their disloyalty and warned them against attempting to enforce the papal brief, but reminded them that a few years
previously the inquisitors had availed themselves of his support in refusing to recognize the validity of a papal brief
obtained by the Jesuits against them in a bitter sectarian
dispute with the Evora Inquisition.

But Bishop de Castro and his colleagues evidently knew
their man. Secure in both papal and popular approval of
their stand, they refused to yield, and in the end it was
they who had the best of the struggle. Despite Vieira's per-
suasive eloquence and the subsequent development of
events, the king gradually weakened under the strain of

such intense disapproval in nearly all quarters. Two years later he reluctantly recognized the validity of the papal brief, albeit he did insist that money invested in the Brazil Company (as distinct from Jewish money invested in other enterprises) should remain immune from confiscation, save in very special circumstances and on certain conditions agreed with the company's representatives. Meanwhile Vieira could at least boast of having achieved something which had earned him more than a night's repose; for the Companhia Geral do Estado do Brasil which he created was the means of saving Portuguese America from the Dutch.

## 12

Bernard Moses

# The Colonial University
# of Cordova

*For many decades dean of Latin-American historians
at the University of California at Berkeley, Bernard
Moses was the first North American to write multi-
volume studies on the Spanish Empire in South
America. His interest in intellectual history led him
to investigate colonial universities in the provincial
areas of the viceroyalties of Peru and Río de la Plata.
This selection is primarily an administrative history
of the University of Cordova in the seventeenth century. Founded by the bishop of Tucumán, the University functioned in a medieval ambience in the
Baroque era until it experienced the impact of Enlightenment ideas and the expulsion of the Jesuits.*

The survival of medievalism in the society of the Spanish
colonies is very well illustrated by the history and character
of the University of Cordova. In point of age this University holds the third place in America. It was preceded by
the University of San Marcos in Lima, and by the University of Mexico. It was founded by Friar Fernando de Trejo
i Sanabria, bishop of Tucumán. Bishop Trejo was one of

From Bernard Moses, *South America on the Eve of Emancipa-
tion* (New York: Cooper Square Publishers, 1965), pp. 143–166
*passim*.

the few creoles who, under the Spanish régime, attained to the episcopal dignity. He was born in Asuncion in 1554, sixteen years after the foundation of the city. He studied in Lima, and here became a member of the Franciscan order. He had been provincial of the Franciscan province of the Twelve Apostles of Peru, and was guardian of the principal monastery of Lima, when Philip II appointed him bishop of Tucumán. He was consecrated in Quito by Bishop Luis de Solis, and assumed the duties of his diocese in 1595.

Trejo held the office of bishop of Tucumán for nineteen years, and during this period he made his influence felt as the protector of the generally despised Indians and negroes. He caused them to be organized in brotherhoods in connection with the churches in all the reductions and towns within his jurisdiction. But his supreme claim to the grateful memory of his countrymen rests on his zeal in behalf of the education of youth, at a time when it was difficult to penetrate the dense ignorance that overshadowed them. In the heart of the continent, with long stretches of the wilderness on all sides, with no schools, no books, and no associations except such as made for barbarism, it required more than ordinary hope and courage to undertake the task of educating that depraved generation. In Santiago del Estero, Bishop Trejo established, in 1609, a school under the name of *Colegio de Santa Catalina*; and a few years later he carried out his desire to found a university, in which "Latin, the arts, and theology" would be taught. By a formal document, dated June 19, 1613, he agreed to give within three years to the proposed University forty thousand dollars. In the meantime he would give fifteen hundred dollars a year for the support of the instructors and the building. And as there might be needed more than the two thousand dollars which it was supposed the forty thousand dollars would yield, he agreed to make to the University a donation

pure, perfect, and irrevocable, which the law calls *inter vivos,* of all my property real and personal,

which I have or may have, money, wrought silver,
books, slaves, and inheritances, and in particular that
which I have called Quimillpa, within the jurisdiction of the City of San Miguel, with all the lands,
mills, goats, asses,

and all the other property.

The bishop did not live long after making this gift. Finding his health failing while in Cordova in 1614, he acted
on the advice of his physician and set out to return to Santiago del Estero. The Jesuits, to whom this donation was
made and with whom he was living in Cordova, opposed
his going; but he persisted, and on the second day of the
journey he was obliged to halt. Knowing his end was near,
he sent Padre Vasquez Trujillo on to Santiago to take possession of his property, which he had donated for the establishment of the University. He died on the 24th of December, 1614, and his body, in accordance with his request, was
taken back to Cordova and buried in the church of the
Jesuits. Before his death, however, he issued a second document confirming the gift of 1613.

In February, 1614, the institution founded by Trejo, under the title of *Colegio Maximo,* opened at Cordova with
fifty students, but it was not until eight years later, 1622,
that it was formally authorized by Pope Gregory XV. At
this time it assumed the name and character of a university
as then conceived. Like all other documents issued by the
pope relating to American affairs, this bull of authorization
was submitted to the council of the Indies. After it had
been approved by that body, the king ordered his officers
and subjects in the Indies to comply with its terms and assist in its execution.

The death of Bishop Trejo before his foundation had
been approved left the institution without a certain important force it would have had in case his life had been
prolonged. In fact, the forty thousand dollars which he had
agreed to convey was never actually turned over to the
Jesuits. They, however, inherited at his death all, or the

greater part, of the articles of property which formed his patrimony; yet these did not amount to the sum specified in the instrument of his gift.

By the approval of the pope, confirmed by the king, the Colegio Maximo assumed the rank and dignity of a university in 1622, and in the following year it awarded its first degrees under its new title. In the early period of the University the degrees were conferred by the bishop of the diocese, whose seat was not Cordova but Santiago del Estero. The students who were prepared to receive their degrees were, therefore, obliged either to wait until the bishop might come to Cordova, or to make a journey to the place where he might then be. Both courses involved inconvenience and expense. This system, moreover, provided ample opportunity for fraud. It was sometimes easy for a person wishing a degree, although he had not made the requisite studies at the University, to deceive the bishop. There were serious abuses growing out of the power of the bishop to confer the degrees of the University wherever he might happen to be when the applicant presented himself; and knowledge of these abuses came to the king, as may be seen from the decree issued by Philip IV in 1664. In the introduction to this decree the king affirmed that the bishop had given the degrees "sometimes to those who had not studied at the University, nor attended the examinations." As a remedy he ordered that whenever the bishop was absent from Cordova the *"maestre-escuela"* might give the degrees. Somewhat later other steps were taken to set aside this difficulty. In 1680, the king authorized the rector of the University to confer degrees in the absence of the bishop and the *"maestre-escuela."* Then, in 1700, Cordova became the seat of the bishop.

In the fifty years immediately subsequent to its foundation the University passed through a preliminary stage of imperfect and unstable organization. But in 1664 it adopted a fundamental law that determined its form and usages for about one hundred and fifty years, or until its reorganization in the beginning of the nineteenth century. This law is an important source of information respecting the character of the University during the colonial period. It recognized Ignatius Loyola as the patron saint of the University, and required that his statue or picture should be assigned a conspicuous place, and that the anniversary of the saint's day should be solemnly celebrated, and the celebration be attended by all the doctors and masters.

The University should keep as its archives all papers, such as papal bulls, royal decrees, and other provisions, relating to it, as well as all books of record. It should have a chest in which to keep all of its funds and all funds entrusted to it, such as the *propinas,* or fees to be distributed on behalf of the candidates for degrees. The chest should have two keys, one held by the rector, and the other by the dean or the doctors residing in the city, or by the treasurer; and it should not be opened except in the presence of the holders of both keys and of the secretary.

.    .    .

Like most medieval universities, the University of Cordova was primarily a school of theology. It embraced two faculties, a faculty of arts and a faculty of theology; but the studies of the first—logic, physics, and Aristotelian metaphysics—constituted a preparation for those of the second. A knowledge of Latin was prerequisite for the study of philosophy. Of the study of Latin, here, Dean Funes, later rector of the University, said it was carried on "without that accumulation of trifles which makes the memory groan." It was conducted with great efficiency and profit by excellent instructors. The students acquired familiarity with the best Latin authors, whose writings became their models for compositions both in prose and verse. Having shown their proficiency in this subject by a public examination, they were admitted to the study of philosophy with the faculty of arts. The studies with this faculty were continued for three years. The first year was devoted to the study of logic, the second to physics, and the third to metaphysics. There were two lectures daily of one hour each. The lecturer devoted a quarter of an hour after each lecture to answering questions and solving the difficulties that had arisen in the minds of the students. In the course of time the discipline became more strict, and the attendance of the students was rigidly required. The course of instruction was then concluded with an examination before "five incorruptible judges," and still later, examinations of greater length were held.

After three years of philosophy, the student passed to the study of theology, which was continued at first four years, and later five years and a half. Of this longer period, the student was required to be in residence only three and a half years. At the conclusion of two and a half years of theology, he might receive the degree of master of arts; and at the end of the whole course, the degrees of licentiate and doctor.

Writing of the quality of this instruction, Dr. Funes said that these studies were corrupted with all the vices of their century. Logic suffered notable defects. The ideas of Aristotle obscured by the barbarous comments of the Arabs could not enlighten the reason. Dialectics was a science of vague notions and insignificant terms, better adapted to forming sophisms than to discoursing with effect. Metaphysics presented phantasms which passed for true entities. Physics, full of formalities, quiddities, forms, and secret qualities, explained by these means the most mysterious phenomena of nature.

Theology was in no better state. Like philosophy it was also corrupted. The philosophy of Aristotle applied to theology, formed a mixture of things sacred and profane. Theology had abandoned the study of the Fathers to devote itself to frivolous and irrelevant questions. Purely human reasoning, subtleties, deceptive sophism, this was what had come to form the dominant taste of these schools.[1]

---

[1] Funes, *Ensayo Historico,* i, lib. II, chap. 16.

In each of the faculties there were three degrees. Those of the faculty of arts were bachelor, licentiate, and master. Those of the faculty of theology were bachelor, licentiate, and doctor, the doctorate of theology being the highest degree conferred by the University. In order to attain it, it was necessary, among other things, to pass five "rigorous" examinations. The first of these covered the first part of the *Summa* of Thomas Aquinas, and dealt with the subjects, God, predestination, the trinity, and angels; the second, beatitude, good and evil, laws, sin, and grace; the third, faith, hope, and charity, contracts and restitution; the fourth, incarnation, sacraments, penitence, and the eucharist, the third part of the *Summa;* the fifth was called the *ignaciana,* in recognition of the patron saint, and lasted five hours, divided between the morning and afternoon.

.     .     .

The primary purpose of the University in the mind of the founder, a Franciscan friar, was instruction in theology, to prepare young men for service in the Church. In keeping with this design, the fundamental law of 1664 provided that the taking of holy orders was a prerequisite for receiving the degree of doctor. One hundred years later, in 1764, seven candidates were absolved from this requirement, and were given their degrees, but under certain other restrictions. This was the beginning of a liberal policy with respect to graduates, and it was made more liberal after the Franciscans came into control of the University on the expulsion of the Jesuits. By the end of the eighteenth century all restrictions of this kind with respect to graduation had been swept away. In the meantime, another restriction had come into force. The early law did not raise the question of the legitimacy or illegitimacy of the candidate. When, therefore, in 1710, a person of illegitimate birth applied for a degree, it was conferred upon him, since there was no special prohibition touching the subject. It was, however, later definitely provided by the *claustro* that no degree should be given by the University to any person who was not of legitimate birth and whose legitimacy had not been established.

The expulsion of the Jesuits effected important changes in the affairs of the University. The *Instructions* of March 1, 1767, framed by the Count of Aranda, required that, in the towns which might have houses or seminaries of education, secular priests should be substituted for the Jesuit directors and masters, that the schools and seminaries should be continued by these substitutes, and that the instructors who were not priests should remain and continue their instruction. The provisions of Aranda's instructions were, however, not carried out, and the places of the Jesuits Aires, and afterwards in the viceroy. By virtue of his powers the royal will. After the departure of the Jesuits, the independence which the University had enjoyed under their administration was in a large measure lost. The superior authority in its affairs became vested in the governor of Buenos were filled by Franciscans, apparently in direct violation of as vice-patron, he appointed the rector and the professors and almost immediately the institution began to experience the baneful effects of its political dependence. The first evidence of political scheming was the project to have the University transferred from Cordova to Buenos Aires. Aranda opposed this project, and begged the king to allow the University to remain in Cordova; and when the arguments for and against removal had been considered by the council of the Indies, the conclusion was that it should remain in Cordova, as being there in the most central position. At the same time the king and his council decided that the peculiar doctrines of Jesuits and their books should be excluded from the instruction.

. . .

The first important step out of the depths of medievalism was the introduction of the study of jurisprudence, in 1791. A practical beginning was made by establishing a professorship of the *Institutes*. With this the University ceased to be purely theological; yet it was the last of the universities in Spanish America to depart from its primary plan. Gradually other chairs in law were established and the University acquired the right to confer the degrees of bachelor, licentiate, and doctor of civil law. The first degree of doctor of civil law was conferred in 1797.

A contest between the Franciscans and the secular clergy for the control of the University marked the last forty years of its history under the old régime. As clearly indicated, the *Instructions* of the Count of Aranda, of March 1, 1767, ordered that the Jesuits should be replaced by members of the secular clergy. In spite of this expression of the royal will, Bucareli, the governor of Rio de la Plata, handed over the government of the University and of the affiliated college of Montserrat to the Franciscans. By this the expectations and aspirations of the secular clergy were defeated. They, therefore, began a struggle to acquire the authority which their rivals had usurped. This little war brought into the dull and monotonous life of Cordova a subject that interested everybody; but, in spite of the arguments and appeals to the law, the Franciscans held their position. The governor favored them, and his support was more immediately effective than the will of the king in opposition. In 1800, the subject was finally before the council of the Indies, and that body rendered a decision justifying the claims of the secular clergy. The decree was issued on the first of December of that year. It had the form of a new act of foundation. The sovereign resolved that there should be founded and erected anew in the city of Cordova, in the edifice which belonged to the Colegio Maximo of the Jesuits, "a greater university with the privileges and prerogatives which are enjoyed by institutions of this class in Spain and the Indies with the title of Royal University of San Carlos and of Our Lady of Montserrat."

## 13

## James H. Carmichael

---

# Recurrent Idolatry and Religious Syncretism

*One of the most perplexing problems of the colonial Church was how to enforce orthodoxy among the Indians. Many parish priests, especially in provincial areas, were acutely aware of paganism, which lurked behind the formal Catholicism of many converted natives. They were concerned that the spiritual conquest had resulted in a fusion of paganism and Christianity. Often harsh tactics were used to eradicate native Indian beliefs, but paganism remained an undercurrent in Spanish colonial religion, and many anthropologists attest to its survival today. James H. Carmichael, a student of ancient Oaxaca, became interested in an Oaxacan priest's attempts to re-educate his flock in the seventeenth century. In this selection Curate Gonzalo de Balsalobre explains to his bishop the dimensions of the problem.*

About eighty kilometers south-southwest of the city of Oaxaca lies the Zapotec Indian town of Sola de Vega. During the Spanish colonial era it was known as San Miguel Sola, and from 1634 to 1655 there acted as curate

---

From James H. Carmichael, Jr., "Balsalobre on Idolatry in Oaxaca," *Boletín del Instituto de Estudios Oaxaqueños*, no. 13 (1959), 1–12 *passim*. Reprinted by permission of the editor.

of this village and of the surrounding countryside a priest named Gonzalo de Balsalobre. Around December of 1653, this diligent cleric became aware of a startling fact: the active survival in his parish of certain native religious beliefs and practices which had supposedly died out at the time of the Conquest. Further investigation by Balsalobre revealed that these religious habits virtually dominated the spiritual life of many of his parishioners, although they feigned obedience and submission to the Church.

The priest naturally reported this matter to his superior, the Bishop of Oaxaca, Diego de Hevia y Valdés, who sanctioned further inquiries. During the subsequent years, Balsalobre, aided by another priest, carried out numerous investigations and trials of "idolatry" in his parish; and, incidentally, he recorded a substantial amount of information about this native religion which he obtained through the confessions of repentant parishioners. It was revealed, among other things, that (125 years after the Conquest!) the natives still applied to their own "priests" for advice and guidance; that these priests consulted "books" of native manufacture which prescribed favorable and unfavorable days for certain activities; that the priests frequently ordered the Indians to perform various penances and sacrifices to propitiate the ancient gods, who numbered thirteen; that the Indians still travelled to their ancient shrines to perform religious rites; and that they also used the Christian churches as places for venerating their thirteen deities.

Since it was evident that the native priests were principally responsible for the survival of the ancient religion, Balsalobre took measures against them, even imprisoning an individual known as Diego Luis. Also, he confiscated and apparently destroyed the "magical books."

In 1656 a book by Balsalobre entitled *Relación Auténtica de las Idolatrías, Supersticiones, vanas Observaciones de los Indios del Obispado de Oaxaca* (*An Authentic Account of the Idolatries, Superstitions, and Vain Observances of the Indians of the Bishopric of Oaxaca*) was printed by order of the Bishop and began to circulate throughout other parishes in order to stimulate further inquires by the Church. Besides this book, Balsalobre submitted numerous other written accounts to his superiors. These, since that day, have remained in the National Archives of Mexico, Inquisition Section.

.     .     .

## An Account of the Idolatries, Superstitions and Abuses in General of the Natives of the Bishopric of Oaxaca

Most Illustrious and Reverend Sir:

Moved by the zeal of reverence for God Our Lord, and zealously concerned by the slight satisfaction which the natives of this kingdom give generally in things of the Faith, and to fulfill the obligations of my office, I have for some time had strong doubts regarding my parishioners and many of the natives of this bishopric. Although in public, whether forced by Ministers of the Doctrine, whether from habit, or whether to palliate the disobedience of their repeated and perfidious idolatries and superstitions that have continued from heathen times until now—with loss of many souls that have died and are dying disobedient and impenitent in that detestable crime, into which they are born, for they have inherited it from parents to children to grandchildren, by succession from one to the other (except those that die in the state of innocence preserved in Baptismal grace)—they perform acts suggestive of true faith, and pretend to appear as true Christians.

And by the experience that I have acquired from communication with them during *twenty-two* years as Minister of the Doctrine, desiring with tireless care by all roads to set them upon that of the State of

Blessedness, I have always found them inwardly very far removed from it, although outwardly they show the contrary. And living among them with this sorrow and affliction, motivated by the causes referred to, Our Lord permitted that the falsity of their simulated faith commence to show itself in a case of relapse that I prosecuted on the twenty-third of December of the past year, fifty-three, against Diego Luis, elder and teacher of these same natives, and himself a native of a barrio under the jurisdiction of my afore-mentioned district, whom a little more than nineteen years ago I punished for these same transgressions.

This and other teachers who are there, and who are called in the common language "wise men" and "teachers," have continually taught those same errors that they held during their heathenism, for which purpose they have had books and handwritten note-books of which they avail themselves for this doctrine; and in them [are prescribed]* the customs of and the teaching about thirteen gods, with names of men and women, to whom they attribute various effects, such as the ruling of their year, which consists of two hundred and sixty days; and these are divided into thirteen months, and each month is attributed to one of these gods who governs it according to the condi-tions of the said year, which is also divided into four seasons, or "lightnings"; and each one of these "lightnings" consists of sixty-five days, which alto-gether make up the said year.

From these [books], with sorceries, they take their different magical answers and prognostications; such as for all kinds of hunting, and for any fishing; for the harvest of maize, chile, and cochineal; for any sickness and for the superstitious medicine with which cures must be effected; and in order to ward off hard-

---

* Bracketed interpolations are Carmichael's [ed.].

ship and death, that these will not come to their houses; for success in pregnancy and childbirth among their wives, and that their children prosper; for [the interpretation of] the songs of birds and animals that to them are auguries; for dreams and their explanation, and for the outcome of one thing or another; and in order to counteract the omens which are predicted for them.

Finally, for any thing which they need they apply to one of these wise men or teachers, who, casting lots with thirteen grains of maize in honor of the aforementioned thirteen gods, teaches them to make horrendous idolatries and sacrifices to the Devil, of small dogs, of native hens and cocks, beheading them and sprinkling with their blood thirteen pieces of copal, or native incense, and burning it and offering it in sacrifice to the god of whom they expect the remedy for the affliction which they hope he can set right; for which purpose they make fasts of twenty-four hours, in the manner of the Jews, especially like the fast of Queen Esther, mixing these with many superstitious rites and ceremonies.

And I specify this particularly: on collecting the first ears of green maize from their fields, on the day indicated by the teacher of these rites, they sacrifice a black native hen, sprinkling with its blood thirteen pieces of copal in memory of their thirteen gods, and burning this copal, and with the rest of the blood sprinkling the patio of the house.

This they offer to the god of maize and all food, called in their language *Locucuy*, in thanksgiving for the good harvest that they have had; and on offering it they say certain words in a very low voice as when they pray. And they do the same on cutting the first chile, offering the sacrifice to the god of lightning called *Lociyo*, in the manner described above.

And on planting the nopal cactus, or on gathering the cochineal, they sacrifice a white native hen to the god whom they call *Coqueelaa,* and they say he watches over it [the cochineal]. And for the hunting of deer and other wild animals [they make this sacrifice] to the god of the hunters called *Niyohua,* or in the event of not succeeding in the hunt through the intervention of this god, they make sacrifice a second time with penance for three days and a fast of twenty-four hours.

For the same purpose [they sacrifice] to *Nocana,* [god] of their ancestors. In pregnancies and childbirths [they sacrifice] to the goddess *Nohuichana,* and to this same [goddess] on fishing for trout; to her they burn copal and light wax candles at the edge of the fishing hole at the river, for success in fishing.

And [they sacrifice] to the aforementioned goddess about the alms that they bring to the church. For sicknesses and medicines to cure them [they sacrifice] to the gods of those things, who they say are called *Lera acuece, Lera acueca.* To the god thirteen called *Leta acquichino,* and to the god of the sorcerers whom they call *Lexee,* [they sacrifice] for dreams and auguries and their interpretation. To the god *Nonachi* [they sacrifice] for several different kinds of happenings.

[They sacrifice] to the god of hell, invoked by them with three attributes: namely, *Coqueetaa,* the great and supreme Lord; *Leta ahuila,* the god of hell, and *Coqueehila,* the lord of hell. And to another goddess from that place, who they say is his wife, commonly called *Xonaxihuilia,* they make sacrifices for the dead, and to ward off sicknesses and death, that these will not come to their houses. This is done in the following way:

When a person expires, they wash the body and head with cold water; and if it is a woman they comb her hair and tie it with a white cord of cotton, and they shroud her with the newest clothes that they have; they put on the body two or three pairs of skirts and *huipils,* more or less, depending upon the wealth of each one, and over this they usually put an ordinary shroud, placing inside of it a number of small stones tied in a cloth, in memory of the sacrifices that had been made in order to cure this dead person, or [in memory] of the superstitious remedies that the wise men applied to them, to no avail.

Before or after the burial, they again consult the wise men, or one of them, about this death; and the latter, casting lots with thirteen grains of maize in honor of their thirteen gods, orders them to do that penance which they have to do; and the usual thing is that, for nine days if the dead person is a male, or for eight days if it is a woman, they do not wear clean clothes, nor take anything in their hands, nor give or receive anything by hand, nor sleep with women; and they must bathe at dawn in the river; and at the end of the said penance they must fast for twenty-four hours, one, two or three days, depending upon how the cast lot indicates the fast. And [he orders them] to make ready, in the same way, little dogs, and native hens and cocks, and copal for the sacrifice that they have to make at the end of the last day of the fast, which having arrived, and the twenty-four hours having passed, the wise man comes to the house of the deceased, taking with him one or two persons most closely related to the deceased.

And [with] these hens, or cocks, little dogs, copal and fire, he goes out of the town, and having come to a place which seems to him fitting, he digs one, two or three holes, each about a foot deep, one after the other; and breaking into pieces the aforementioned copal, he throws into each hole thirteen pieces of it in reverence to his thirteen gods; and he orders one of his assistants or ministers to behead the native hen or cock, or the dog, and to sprinkle the copal with its blood, and to pour the rest [of the blood] into the said hole; and likewise in exactly the same way for the other holes, if he has to make this sacrifice more than once; and placing on the outer edge of each hole a piece of copal without blood he orders that this copal be set on fire; and it having burned, he throws into [the hole] the dog or native cock (but if it is a large hen he orders it to be taken to the house of the deceased in order that, cooked, it be eaten in company by those who have fasted); and he makes them cover the hole with dirt, saying these words, or others like them:

"This sacrifice I offer to the devil for this deceased one; namely, to the god of hell, and to the goddess his wife, and to such and such god," if the sacrifices go on from one to two to three to four, depending upon what the cast lot showed him; [this he does] to ward off from the road sicknesses and deaths, that they will not come out of this place nor to the house of the relatives of the aforementioned deceased. And with this, the sacrifice and fast are ended, all of them returning to sup at the house of the deceased.

At other times they make sacrifice for the dead, after the penance and fast, and in the same apartment or room where the death took place, beheading there a native hen and sprinkling this place and thirteen pieces of copal with its blood and burning the said copal; and with the rest of the aforementioned blood, sprinkling the said room and offering it in the manner referred to.

On this occasion they usually have some other ceremonies and superstitious rites; and since all of them end up as sacrifices to the Devil, although at times they vary the mode of making the sacrifice, in substance it is always one and is directed to one end.

They are accustomed likewise in pregnancies, childbirths and other types of confinements to promise that if all goes well they will sacrifice to such and such a god a small dog or native hen, in the manner related above, offering it to the said god; this has been preceded by consulting some wise man of this jurisdiction, and the latter, casting lots, has told them that such and such a god is imposing justice upon the ill or imprisoned, and that in order to placate him they must make him that promise, which the aforesaid and those of his household accept and make; and they fulfill it punctually in thanksgiving for the fortunate outcome.

And the same thing happens with pregnant women and women who have just given birth; and for this they have designated places to which they go to fulfill their vows; such they have on a hill within the jurisdiction of my province, called in the common language of the natives *Quijaxila,* which is about half a league from the Pueblo of San Juan, distant from the seat [San Miguel] by another half-league, on whose summit are seen the ruins of a building which is commonly known to have been a temple of their idols in heathen times; and there they go to carry out their sacrifices.

For offering alms in the church, they have good and bad days; and these are indicated to them by some counselor who judges of that, according to his computation from the book of their doctrine. If the day is good, although it be during the week, all or many of them come together to light candles or to bring other offerings, which, it is evident by their own declarations, they do in reverence of their thirteen gods.

For example: if such a day is good for offering, and the counselor told them to perform it at the altar of the Virgin offering or lighting so many candles, they do it; and they offer them in reverence of the goddess *Nohuichana*; and if at all of the altars they perform this sacrifice, it is done in reverence of all the thirteen gods; and the other offerings are made in the same respect.

They are accustomed to perform many other ceremonies and rites on burying the dead, upon getting married, on copulating with their wives, on building their houses, on sowing, and on gathering their harvests; and finally, all that they do in general is superstitious and so varied that only with difficulty can it be reduced to number and form.

Everything contained in this account is verified by a large number of witnesses, judicial confessions of many of the prisoners, and statements of others. Either induced by fear of punishment or by the repentance which they claim to feel, they have accused themselves, asking for mercy and planning to make amends.

# III

# The Church in the Bourbon Century

### ◦§ 14 §◦

## Karl Schmitt

———◆◗●◖◆———

# The Clergy and the Enlightenment

*As the most articulate group of intelligentsia in the Spanish colonies, many of the clergy were* au courant *with European intellectual change. Many priests and friars read and discussed the new philosophies and literature of the Age of Science and the Age of Reason with voracious curiosity. Often they embraced philosophical eclecticism and tried to apply the new ideas to established forms. Other colonial clergy steadfastly rejected philosophe thought as dangerous to orthodoxy, and they combatted the new ideas from abroad. To generalize about the clergy and the Enlightenment is, however, risky. Professor Karl Schmitt of the University of Texas examines in this selection consensus and conflict among colonial clergy in the intellectual milieu of the second half of the eighteenth century.*

Several currents of "enlightened" doctrine ran swiftly and strongly through Latin America by the end of the eighteenth century. Scholarly work of the past two decades obviates the

From Karl Schmitt, "The Clergy and the Enlightenment in Latin America: An Analysis," *The Americas: A Quarterly Review of Inter-American Cultural History,* 15 (1959), 381–391 *passim.* Reprinted by permission of the Academy of American Franciscan History.

need to prove that the new philosophy, the new science, and the new politics found acceptance in the Spanish world. Forbidden books made their way into Latin America with relative ease, the Inquisition proved ineffective in preventing the spread of new ideas, and the Spanish crown itself not only promoted useful knowledge but encouraged "modern" philosophical studies. Aside from special studies on the Enlightenment, however, the more general histories of Latin America too frequently take the position, implicit if not explicit, that the Catholic clergy, monolithic in their obscurantism, constituted the primary obstacle to the complete victory of "enlightened" ideas. It appears . . . that this point of view is somewhat inaccurate. . . . The clergy were seriously split on practically all aspects of the Enlightenment. Some supported, some opposed, and many were indifferent to or ignorant of "enlightened" notions. The degree of support or opposition varied, and not all who opposed or supported the movement, supported or opposed it *in toto*.

Before launching into my subject, let me set some limitations. . . . First, I shall concentrate my inquiry primarily in three areas of Latin America: Mexico, Colombia, and Argentina. Each of these in the late colonial period constituted the heart of a viceregal administration, but each in a different stage of development. Secondly, I intend to center attention on the period between 1750 and 1820. And thirdly, I shall discuss "enlightened" ideas in their four primary aspects: the philosophical, the scientific, the economic, and the political in that order. One more word of introduction is necessary. Both in Spain and in Latin America the anticlerical and antireligious character of the Enlightenment, prevalent elsewhere, was muted, and political agitation for constitutional government, insignificant until the 1790's. Furthermore, Latin American independence movements failed dismally prior to the overthrow of Ferdinand VII and the assumption of the throne by Joseph Bonaparte in 1808. The Jesuits with their doctrine of "probabilism" and their teaching of Suárez and Mariana on the limitations of authority caused some stir in the early and middle years of the eighteenth century. These teachings were outlawed with the expulsion of the Society in 1767, but were revived, in Argentina at least, after 1808.


# Philosophy

In previous discussions of the new philosophy in Latin America, emphasis has been placed upon the book trade, upon the prevalence of forbidden books in libraries, upon Inquisitorial records which indicate the possession and reading of forbidden literature. That a considerable number of the clergy possessed and read such books need not be labored. Let us rather consider how some of them reacted to the new philosophy.

It appears that the introduction and acceptance of the "modern" philosophers into Latin America resulted not so much from the attractiveness of their philosophy as of their methodology. In their adoption of new philosophical concepts, the Latin Americans tended to be eclectic. Descartes' methodical doubt, and Bacon's and Newton's emphasis upon experimentation both in philosophy and in science, found a ready audience among a number of Latin American scholars surfeited with a sterile and decadent scholasticism. The Jesuit Francisco Clavigero, best known for his *History of Ancient Mexico*, "embraced with youthful fervor modern or experimental philosophy," and among his works is listed the "Dialogue between Filaletes and Paleófilo against the argument of authority in Physics." And a canon of the Cathedral of Mexico persisted in a life-long opposition to scholasticism as a result of the obsolete theories taught him in the physics section of his philosophy course.

By the last quarter of the eighteenth century some Mexican priest-philosophers had begun to adopt some of the new concepts into their own writings. One of the earliest and perhaps the most important of these was Father Juan Gamarra's *Elements of Modern Philosophy*, first published in 1774, and received with general and even glowing approval by its reviewers. These included a professor of mathematics at the university, a professor of Sacred Theology at the College of St. Michael, and a committee composed of the doctors of the university and the priest professors of Sacred Theology in the city of Mexico. In the purely philosophical sections of the work, hardly original, Gamarra does not break fully with the scholastics, although he accepts with some limitations the Cartesian theory of innate ideas. It is in the section on physics, however, that he directly attacks the scholastics for their reliance on authority rather than on experiment. The reviewing committee in an apparent reference to this section noted that Gamarra's teaching could not "be ignored or controverted without dishonor or ignominy." Scholasticism, of course, was not overthrown by this single blast, but it is revealing that of some forty known authors of philosophical treatises in eighteenth-century New Spain, about ten may be considered members of the new school, and of these all were of the second half of the century.

In Buenos Aires and Bogotá the Jesuits played a leading role in introducing the new philosophical concepts, with the Franciscans continuing their work after 1767. Like Gamarra in Mexico, both Jesuits and Franciscans tended to be eclectics in their adaptation of the "moderns" to the scholastics. What they rejected of modern philosophy was what they considered to be in opposition to Catholic doctrine. Major changes in philosophical studies were introduced into New Granada by Viceroy Manuel Guirior in the mid-1770's when he ordered the *Institutes of Moral Philosophy* by Gregorio Mayáns to be used in the courses on Moral Philosophy at the colleges of St. Bartholomew and the Rosary. Mayáns' work, characterized as "secularized moral theology," omits all reference to the scholastics and contains brief, though favorable, references to Bacon and Descartes. Although the bishops appear to have played a small part in the introduction of the new philosophy, their passive assent may be assumed; and in 1786 the Archbishop-Viceroy of Mexico did introduce the *Institutes* of François Jacquier, the modernist French priest, philosopher, and mathematician, into the philosophy course in the pontifical seminary.

## Science

Closely related to the purely philosophical controversies of the age was the dispute over the relative merits of experimentation vs. authority in the natural sciences, then a section of the philosophy course. Both within and without the schools the clergy were foremost in the ranks of the combatants. A running battle was fought throughout much of the eighteenth century, and despite all the evidence, a goodly number of the philosophy professors continued to teach physics on the basis of Aristotle. By the latter part of the century, however, leading proponents of the new approach to science were largely concerned with experimentation and study of nature rather than with controversy.

In both New Granada and New Spain the outstanding scientific investigators were priests: José Celestino Mutis and José Antonio Alzate. The Plata region produced no such luminaries either lay or clerical. Mutis, best known for his organization and leadership of the great botanical expedition in New Granada, was also an astronomer, mathematician, and physician. Though not a university professor, he trained a number of young men in the sciences, and though not a politician, his foremost student, Francisco Caldas, became a hero in the wars of independence. Alzate worked largely through the press, founding several newspapers, some of prime importance, between 1768 and 1794. His interests ranged from his own studies on the migratory habits of swallows to Benjamin Franklin's studies on optics and heat waves which he published in his newspaper.

Nor were these two priests lone clergymen crying in the wilderness. Mutis had the direct encouragement and assistance of his archbishop, and Alzate had at least the tacit approval of his superiors in his scientific work. Furthermore, Mutis' subdirector on the botanical expedition was a priest, and of the six original assistants, one was a Franciscan friar. When later Caldas established his newspaper, the *Semanario del Nuevo Reino de Granada,* at least six priests contributed articles on scientific topics. In Mexico the Jesuits had early shown an interest in science, and among Alzate's contemporaries, one secular priest left in manuscript a *Compendium of Algebra* and published a study on the major rivers of the world, while another composed the non-Euclidian geometry section for Father Gamarra's philosophy course. In the Plata area the Jesuits appear to have been the first to introduce the study of Newton and the experimental sciences. With their expulsion, scientific interests were taken up by the Franciscans, notably by Friar Cayetano Rodríguez who composed a treatise on physics in 1796. However, there appear to have been few scientific experiments or investigations carried out in the area, certainly nothing to compare with the botanical expedition of New Granada.

## Economics

The promotion of useful knowledge was largely non-academic. Private economic societies were organized to this end, usually with some official support, in eighteenth-century Spain and Spanish America. Primarily interested in agriculture, they also promoted education and the dissemination of a wide range of practical knowledge. About ten such societies were founded in Spanish America, but few were of major importance. None ever existed in Mexico City or Buenos Aires. One was founded in Mompox, New Granada, of which Father Mutis was a corresponding member, and a short-lived one was founded in Bogotá by Mutis himself. Where these organizations did exist, the clergy formed an important element of the membership, including an occasional bishop as well as curates and friars.

Outside the societies the program was pursued by individual reformers. Archbishop Caballero y Góngora of Bogotá with his plans for university reform, Alzate with his *Gaceta,* and Bishop José Antonio de San Alberto of Córdoba with his advocacy of manual training and the education of women are well known. Many others were interested, but some were ill-prepared to contribute to the spread of truth. The work of an obscure priest in New Granada contains an amusing potpourri of fact and fancy. His books, composed for the entertainment and edification of his fellow priests, show his acquaintance with Father Feijóo, the great popularizer of the Enlightenment in the Spanish world, as well as with the standard classical commentators on natural phenomena. For example, he recommends Father Feijóo's remedy for killing moths (tobacco smoke) and cites some of the latest authorities in his discussion on the length of the Spanish league. However, in his section on meteorology he repeats some of the erroneous opinions of the ancients. He classifies air as one of the elements and comets as signs of impending catastrophe.

## Politics

The political role of the clergy is far more complex than their participation in "enlightened" economic, scientific, or philosophical affairs. A contributing factor was the emergence in the eighteenth century of two distinct and divergent currents of "enlightened" political thinking. Although both advocated increased national authority, one branch supported "enlightened despotism," while the other demanded some form of constitutionalism. In the first two decades of the nineteenth century the political situation in Latin America was further complicated by a widespread drive for independence from the mother country, a drive resulting in large part from "enlightened" political ideas on rights and freedom.

Prior to 1808 there was little disloyalty to the crown among either priests or laymen. Miranda and Nariño are exceptions, and their clerical support was insignificant. True, a youthful seminarian in minor orders was involved with Nariño in Bogotá in 1794, and the Viceroy of New Granada accused other unnamed ecclesiastics of complicity. Miranda, it appears, received some help from Jesuits exiled from Latin America. However, there is no evidence of widespread disaffection, desire for independence, or advocacy of constitutional government among the clergy. The clergy obviously were loyal to Spain, but does this mean that they were out of tune with "enlightened" politics in all respects? The facts will not support such a contention.

Two important issues divided the clergy in the eighteenth century: regalism vs. ultramontanism and divine-right monarchy vs. constitutionalism. The Jesuits and the hierarchy were at odds on both. Since one of the goals of "enlightened despotism" was the extension of national authority over autonomous or semi-autonomous bodies within the state, the crown broadened its sphere of control over Church affairs beyond the limits of papal grants. With the notable exception of the Jesuits, however, the clergy of Latin America, including the bishops, acquiesced without serious protest. Furthermore, the hierarchy accepted the expulsion of the Jesuits in 1767, and some heartily approved it, banning the use of books by Jesuit authors in the schools and seminaries. In a pastoral letter of April 1769, the archbishop of Mexico bitterly attacked the Jesuits for their methods of operation, their philosophical doctrines, and their educational system. The following year the bishop of Oaxaca issued the following order when certain Jesuit papers were discovered in New Spain.

> We order under pain of greater Excommunication *latae sententiae . . . ipso facto incurrenda* and other penalties . . . that this and any other paper, printed

> or manuscript, even a private letter, which proclaims
> as unjust the expulsion of the Jesuits from any mon-
> archy throughout the world . . . [be placed in our
> hands within three hours of being discovered].

The bishop of Puebla justified the expulsion on the grounds
that the king had the right to protect himself from subversion which the Jesuits were teaching.[1]

From this résumé, it might be concluded that until 1767
the Jesuits, admitted ultramontanists, were the bulwark of
"unenlightened" politics. But not quite—the clue lies in the
accusation of subversion made against them by the bishop
of Puebla. This subversion consisted in the fact that the
Jesuits held and taught the doctrine of "probabilism" and
the constitutionalism of the Spanish Jesuit theologians
Suárez and Mariana. The bishop maintained that the Jesuits
were thereby undermining all authority, civil and ecclesiastical. It appears, therefore, that Jesuit political theories which
favored liberty over authority, advocated the right of
revolution, and insisted upon limitations to royal power
should be considered in harmony with "enlightened" political thinking. So too, the regalist views of the hierarchy should
be considered. Conversely, both Jesuits and bishops should
be classified as "unenlightened" in their respective positions
as ultramontanists and divine-right monarchists.

With the replacement of the Spanish Bourbons by the
French Bonapartes in 1808, the political climate began to
change rapidly in Latin America. Creole leaders in many
parts of Spanish America succeeded in establishing regimes
which were independent of the mother country but which
still proclaimed loyalty to the dethroned monarch, Ferdinand VII. In many areas great numbers of the lower
clergy supported these movements even after they became
frankly separatist and republican. There were loyalists, to
be sure, and many, perhaps a majority, who played no

---

[1] The three pastoral letters cited are included in *Papeles
Diversos* of the García collection of the University of Texas.

active role on either side. The bishops and the upper clergy, with some exceptions, opposed separation and independence.

Few of these clergymen can be categorized as "enlightened" or "unenlightened." Dean Gregorio Funes of the Cathedral of Córdoba was unquestionably a devotee of the Enlightenment. Interested in modern philosophy, the new science, and the spread of useful knowledge, he was also among the first to rally to the Revolution of May despite the opposition of his own bishop, and consistently supported the exercise of the civil power, whether monarchical or republican, in ecclesiastical affairs. Also "enlightened" were Father Servando de Mier of Mexico and Father Juan Azuero of New Granada who supported not only the independence movement but the new government's desire to obtain the patronate over the Church. So too, apparently, was Bishop Cuero y Calcedo of Quito who not only advocated the spread of useful knowledge but joined the fight for independence. Captured by royalist forces, he died in Lima on his way to exile. Conversely, the best example of politically "unenlightened" clergy are the bishops of Mexico who bitterly opposed the independence movement until it was taken over by the conservative Iturbide who promised to establish a Catholic conservative regime in place of the liberal Spanish monarchy of 1821. In renouncing their loyalty to the king, the Mexican bishops also renounced their regalism; although they supported a strong native monarchy, they opposed its attempts to control the Church.

Now for some complications. The Dominican friar Isidoro Guerra of Buenos Aires, an "unenlightened" scholastic and anti-Cartesian, supported the independence movement. Father Mariano Medrano of Buenos Aires, an eclectic in philosophy, an admirer of Newton, a supporter of independence, took an anti-regalist position toward ecclesiastical reform in 1822. Medrano, then vicar-general of Buenos Aires, argued that the proposals invaded the rights of the Church in threatening institutions which owed their origin to the independent power of the Church. The clergy of

Bogotá seriously differed among themselves on this same question in 1820 when the new government requested their opinions. Father Azuero, as noted above, held that the government had an absolute right to exercise the patronato, while Father Garnica, a Dominican, insisted that it could be exercised only by papal grant. The government, dissatisfied with the variety of opinions which it received, put the question to the capitular vicar, Father Nicolás Cuervo, who refused to commit himself, suggesting that the government request the opinion of the Holy See.

Similar problems arise with the opponents of independence. In Yucatán several loyalist priests advocated limited constitutional monarchy, and strongly supported the Constitution of 1812 and the liberal revolt of 1820 in Spain. To reconcile Catholic doctrine and the new political philosophy, one of these priests founded the Association of St. John. Originally established as a discussion club for priests and laymen, the association soon evolved into a political organization. Despite persecution and imprisonment, they remained loyal to Spain to the end of the colonial regime. Another loyalist, a canon of the Cathedral of Mexico, supported political absolutism, but at the same time was an advocate of education, an admirer of Humboldt, and a promoter of useful knowledge. Somewhat similar is the case of Manuel Abad y Queipo, bishop-elect of Michoacán. An advocate of social, economic, and even political reform, Abad was no democrat. Loyal to Spain and to the king, he felt that reform should come from above. When Hidalgo began his revolt, no prelate in New Spain more bitterly denounced the patriots. . . . Archbishop Fonte of Mexico presents the most interesting reactions to conflicting drives. Politically conservative, he alone among the upper clergy of Mexico remained loyal to liberal Spain in 1820 and 1821. His *Edict* of July 1820 contains a queer combination of regalism, loyalty to the mother country, and defense of liberal doctrines. Obedience to the constitution is a civil duty and a religious obligation, said the archbishop; the person of the king is sacred and inviolable, and citizens must not disturb public order. Surprisingly, he offered no criticism of the decree suppressing the Inquisition, pointing out that not by such institutions alone does the "preservation and triumph of our holy religion . . . depend." The archbishop also commented that the press law was a grant of liberty not license, significantly adding:

> But above all, let us not judge the goodness or the justness of the law by the evil use which is made of it, in the same way that it would be absurd to attribute imperfections to the divine law because of the frequent violations of its precepts.

On political liberty and equality he said:

> In the Spanish Constitution [these terms] mean civil liberty and political equality; in that these citizens are free of all arbitrary acts and unjust injury, but subordinate to the law. Therefore it would be absurd to confuse this rational and honest liberty with license to do whatever caprice or the impetus of the passions might suggest. . . . In the same way, with the grant of political equality in rights and obligations, an absolute is not established; therefore, the possessions of the rich are not to be taken from them to make them equal to the poor; however, neither the one nor the other will enjoy any preference or any advantage before the law; their conduct will receive equally, reward or punishment, for their only difference . . . will be in their own vices and virtues.[2]

It must be concluded, obviously, that the role of the clergy in the Latin American Enlightenment was a major one with differences from area to area being of degree and emphasis rather than of kind. Secondly, the evidence is clear that the clergy were seriously divided in their response to

---

[2] *Edict* of Archbishop Fonte of Mexico, July 18, 1820, in F. H. Vera, *Documentos eclesiásticos de México* (Amecameca, 1887), II, 341–347.

the movement. Books and ideas condemned in Rome and Madrid were read and absorbed by numerous clergymen in Latin America, but not all reacted similarly. The bishops excoriated the independence movement, but their anathemas went unheeded by many of the lower clergy. The Jesuits taught a doctrine of constitutionalism and ultramontanism, the bishops were regalists and absolutists. The Franciscans in Buenos Aires taught the experimental method in the sciences, the Dominicans in Bogotá adhered more to authority. Mutis advocated the observation of nature, the Bishop of Cuenca wanted to destroy the tower of his old cathedral, then being used for astronomical observations, to make way for a new cathedral. Finally, strict classification of most of the clerical participants as "enlightened" or "unenlightened" is inaccurate. Although many opposed the new philosophy, fewer objected to the use of the experimental method in science, and hardly any murmured against improved economic well-being. Various political views could be held by the same person, some of which could be considered "enlightened" and some not. Furthermore, certain clergymen could be "unenlightened" in one field, while wholeheartedly supporting "enlightened" ideas in one or more other fields. I have attempted no head count of the clergy in Latin America to determine their sentiments; it appears an almost impossible task. A careful study of the bishops, heads of religious communities, and the faculties of universities may indeed prove rewarding, and would probably turn up similar complexities. Professor Lanning's recent observation strikes me as coming close to the mark:

> Of forty-nine hardworking bishops, at any one moment, I would guess forty went about their business, while seven actively promoted the aims of the Enlightenment and two grew sour.[3]

---

[3] John T. Lanning, "The Enlightenment in Relation to the Church," *The Americas*, XIV, no. 4 (April, 1958), 493.

## 15

## Richard E. Greenleaf

# The Mexican Inquisition and the Enlightenment

*Enlightenment social and political philosophy were a major concern of the Holy Office of the Inquisition in the last century of its operation in New Spain. Archival data suggest that the Inquisition was not a moribund institution in the late eighteenth century, but rather that it was groping for ways to cope with rapid ideological change within the Spanish intellectual environment and with the shifting diplomatic and political alliances of the Spanish state. This selection won Honorable Mention in 1968 at the Conference on Latin-American History.*

Many scholars have called attention to the fact that the Holy Office of the Inquisition was a political instrument. What has not been examined in detail is the relationship that existed between heresy and treason during the three centuries of Spanish and Spanish colonial Inquisition history. The belief that heretics were traitors and traitors were heretics led to the conviction that dissenters of any kind were social revolutionaries trying to subvert the political and

From Richard E. Greenleaf, "The Mexican Inquisition and the Enlightenment 1763–1805." Reprinted by permission, from *New Mexico Historical Review*, Vol. 41, pp. 181–191. Copyright 1966 by the University of New Mexico Press.

religious stability of the community. These tenets were not later developments in the history of the Spanish Inquisition; they were inherent in the rationale of the institution from the fifteenth century onward, and were apparent in the Holy Office's dealing with the Jews, Protestants, and other heretics during the sixteenth century. The use of the Inquisition by the later eighteenth-century Bourbon kings in Spain as an instrument of regalism was not a departure from tradition. Particularly in the Viceroyalty of New Spain during the late eighteenth century do the Inquisition trials show how the Crown sought to promote political and religious orthodoxy.

The Age of Science and the Age of Reason in seventeenth- and eighteenth-century Europe had powerful reverberations in the New World colonies of Spain. The attack on Scholasticism and the campaign against divine right kingship represent a joint political-religious venture all the more significant because the papacy was also divine right institution. Regalist prelates came to dominate the Church in Spain and Spanish America, and they were just as combative in their efforts to quell the new exponents of natural laws of politics and economics as were the Spanish monarchs. The environmentalism of Montesquieu and Rousseau was as much a challenge to Spanish rule in America as were the doctrines of empiricism and methodical doubt to the supremacy of the Roman Catholic faith and dogmas. During the period 1760 to 1805, the vicissitudes of Spanish-French politics and the shifting diplomatic and military alliances of the Spanish rulers in Europe complicated the problem of stemming the tide of rationalism in Mexico. The opening decade of the century had heralded the arrival of the French Bourbons on the Spanish throne, and the Spanish royal house and the French monarchy coordinated their diplomacies by the Family Compact of 1761. This made it difficult to prevent the circulation of Francophile ideas in the empire.

The Frenchmen in New Spain openly espoused Enlightenment ideas. Before 1763 they had infiltrated the periphery of the Viceroyalty of New Spain—merchants, sailors, and even clergy who came from Louisiana or the French-held islands of the Caribbean. In addition to French Protestantism, they began to disseminate the pre-revolutionary ideas of the *philosophes* and French literary figures. Technicians at the military-naval department of San Blas on the Pacific, physicians all over the empire, royal cooks and hairdressers in the viceregal capital, regiments of soldiers—all of these added to the Francophile *ambiente* in eighteenth-century Mexico. In the two decades, 1763 to 1783, and even afterwards, the residuum of French influence in Louisiana caused New Orleans to be a center of sedition.

Before philosophe thought culminated in the bloody French uprisings of 1789–1793, the Holy Office of the Inquisition found itself hamstrung in enforcing orthodoxy because of the *afrancesado* leanings of Charles III (1759–1788) in his administrative techniques and his economic theories. For all of these reasons French literature was read in Mexico, not only for its freshness and its vitality, but as a guide for the "promotion of useful knowledge." An inherently dangerous ingredient of this milieu was the Holy Office's necessary relaxation of censorship, with the subsequent proliferation of French ideas on many levels of Mexican society. As the French Revolution gained momentum, the fear of its export to Mexico gave impetus to a resurgence of inquisitorial activity, demands for expulsion of Frenchmen and other suspicious foreigners from Mexico, and confiscation of their properties. This cycle of Francophobia gradually ended as the political alliances of Spain vis-à-vis France and England again shifted, and as the reactionary Directorate consolidated its power in revolutionary France. After 1800, it soon became apparent that Napoleon Bonaparte was unwittingly spreading libertine doctrines over Europe, and the Holy Office once again had the task of defining and enforcing Mexican orthodoxy in a confused ideological and diplomatic environment. The investigatory activities of the Mexican Inquisition and the trials of the era must be examined against this background.

Enlightenment men in France—and in New Spain—were talking of popular sovereignty and the inalienable rights of man. The men who questioned the divine right of kings and severed the royal head of Louis XVI from his divine body were also prone to question papal authority, the practice of indulgences, the Triune God, the Immaculate Conception of Mary, and the doctrine of original sin. Both Voltaire and Rousseau had unorthodox religious ideas as well as iconoclastic social and political ones. Those who analyzed orthodox Christianity and established Mexican societal patterns from the philosophe point of view often found them wanting. Fear lest the French Revolution spread to the Mexican viceroyalty was so great that after 1789 the Holy Office forbade citizens to read about the deplorable event. Late in 1794 plans were made to expel all Frenchmen and French sympathizers in the manner of the Jesuit expulsion three decades earlier.

The Inquisition's control over printed matter, including books, pamphlets, manuscripts—and even printed designs, some of which, for example, showed the Tree of Reason—extended well beyond mere censorship of questionable material. In theory, all books which entered New Spain were inspected by the Inquisition; much of the data in the Inquisition archive of Mexico consists of lengthy lists from the *aduana,* together with inventories of books being detained in the port of Veracruz. With the aid of these lists one can trace the evolving definition of orthodoxy by noting what works, once banned, were later passed. The books ordered by individual Mexicans throw light on colonial mentality through a knowledge of what men were reading.

Monelisa Lina Pérez-Marchand made an extensive study of the books prohibited in Mexico by the Inquisition, and her research determined that in the latter part of the eighteenth century, works of political philosophy predominated.

It is important to note that the majority of books proscribed by Holy Office edicts during 1763–1805 did not simply question specific policies but rather challenged the theoretical existence or *raison d'être* of the State. This indirect attack made it possible for the colonist to read and apply general theories to particular circumstances—Spanish mercantilism, monopolization of office by peninsular Spaniards, monolithic religion, etc. Because the colonists saw the French Revolution as an attempt to put these ideas into practice, accounts of it had to be zealously prohibited. Such works always carried heretical religious propositions. The banned *Lettres d'une Péruvienne* (1797) are a case in point. The Holy Office charged that they were filled with sedition and heresy and "injurious to monarchs and Catholic rules of Spain . . . and to religion itself." The same decree also prohibited *Les Ruines ou Meditation sur les revolutions des Empires* by M. Volney and others. A separate ban of the Volney tract alleged that:

> its author affirmed that there neither is nor could be revealed religion, that all (people) are daughters of curiosity, ignorance, interest, and imposture, and that the mystery of the birth of Jesus Christ, and the rest of the Christian religion are mystical allegories.[1]

The Holy Office of the Inquisition did not limit its censorship to French books; English Enlightenment works were also a matter of concern. The works of Alexander Pope were most frequently mentioned in edicts of the Inquisition, particularly his *Cartas de Abelardo y Heloisa,* a translation of *Eloise to Abelard,* telling the tale of a nun's love for Peter Abelard. Proscriptions of Pope occurred in 1792 and 1799, and by 1815 all of his works were banned. Other English books on the lists were *Gulliver's Travels* (1803), *Tom Jones* (1803), and *Pamela* (1803). The most important edict of the

---

[1] Archivo General de la Nación (México), Inquisición, Tomo 1310, fols. 262–263v.

period was the one issued on August 25, 1805, for it presents a comprehensive and alphabetical listing of all books prohibited since 1789. Several hundred works appear on the list. The edict not only reflects concern with the French Revolution, but also with the ascendancy of Napoleon.

In many cases the Inquisition not only found it necessary to prohibit political philosophy, but to deny its content and validity. An example of this was the edict of November 13, 1794 with regard to a volume published in Philadelphia by Santiago Felipe Puglia entitled *Desengaño del Hombre*:

> The author of this book, writing in their own language, blows his raucous trumpet to excite the faithful people of the Spanish nation to rebellion of the most infamous sort. . . . The pedantic writer has made of himself a bankrupt merchant in such sublime goods as politics and the universal right, and [is] equally detestable for his impiety and insolence that, for his ignorance of sacred and profane literature and for the vile and ignominious style with which he speaks of Kings divined by God, imputes the odious name of despotism and tyranny to the monarchial regime and royal authority that arises from God himself and from His divine will . . . and the universal consent of all the people who from most remote antiquity have been governed by Kings . . . [He attempts] to introduce the rebellious oligarchy of France with the presumption to propose [it] as a model of liberty and happiness of republics, while [it is] in reality the best example of desolation brought on by pestilences and anti-evangelical principles.[2]

Of course many of the polemics of the rationalists were against the Inquisition itself, and to maintain its station in colonial life the Holy Office could not tolerate them. In the ban of *Borroquia o la Victima de la Inquisición* the judge

---

[2] *Gaceta de México*, 13 de noviembre de 1794.

condemned the book as full of "ridiculous falsehoods that the enemies of religion have vomited against the Holy Office." He claimed that the purpose of the tract was to weaken and eventually destroy the Inquisition and to introduce heresy.

Such "book reviews" as these must have greatly whetted the colonists' appetite for prohibited foreign books. For those unable to read there were the French prints, and there were watches, snuffboxes, and coins bearing the figure of the goddess Liberty. But many could read, and large quantities of revolutionary literature were being assimilated into colonial thinking. Among the most avid readers were the clergy, who naturally made up a large part of the literate classes. In his letter of October 4, 1794, the Mexican Archbishop lauded the Inquisition for its zeal, and took pride in the fact that until that time he had had no knowledge of any priests being involved in foreign intrigues. His Reverence was being naive if he thought that the exciting new publications from abroad were not being read by members of the clergy. In the same month the Holy Office commenced the trial of Juan Pastor Morales, a professor at the Royal and Pontifical Seminary of Mexico who had read the prohibited French books extensively and who openly espoused seditious ideas. It was alleged that he approved of the republican system, defended the execution of Louis XVI, and claimed that the King of Spain was an oppressive "puritan rogue" who ought to be dealt with in the same way as his French counterpart. He was also accused of speaking against the Pope and the Inquisition.

Juan Ramírez, a member of the Franciscan Order, was also tried in late 1794 for appearing to be an "assemblyist" who applauded the execution of the French monarch, possessed prints of scenes from the Revolution, and called Voltaire the "holy father of the century." Anastasio Pérez de Alamillo, the priest and ecclesiastical judge of Otumba, was tried in the same year on counts of religious and political heresy. He maintained a little shop where he sold works by Voltaire and small images of the French philosopher Ferney. Copies of many revolutionary manuscripts and books were found in his possession. Perhaps French philosophy inspired Pérez de Alamillo to express disbelief in the apparition of the Virgin of Guadalupe and the miracles purported to have accompanied the event. The padre was defended in this famous trial by the later-renowned Carlos María Bustamante. Inquisition processes against the Franciscan Ramírez and the hierarchy clergyman Pérez de Alamillo are forerunners of the great trials of Hidalgo and Morelos after 1810. In each of the four cases it appeared as though the clergy had tried to remain theologically orthodox while embracing philosophical eclecticism. For the most part, however, the Mexican clergy rejected the new thought of the Age of Science and the Age of Reason and cooperated in ferreting out heretics. Priests were under orders promptly to report any evidence of French influence they might encounter in casual conversation, or in the confessional. "The people were to be taught the 'ancient and true' principles of obedience and fidelity 'to the king and to all their superiors.'" In the main, however, the Church, like the State, looked to the Holy Office of the Inquisition to deal with the men, books, and ideas which threatened both.

The best evidence of the union of heresy and treason appears in the trials of men haled before the Tribunal of the Holy Office during the 1790's. Unorthodox clergymen received special treatment and their trials and punishments were private matters. On the other hand, great pains were taken to make a public example of foreigners who were active disseminators of the dreaded libertine ideas. On Sunday, August 9, 1795, the residents of Mexico City witnessed their first major *auto de fé* in six years. The procession included five heretics convicted of Enlightenment ideas— three of them in person, and two in effigy. The latter were Don Juan María Murgier and Don Esteban Morel, both of whom had committed suicide in the Inquisition jail. The effigy of Murgier was burned with his bones, but since Morel had given signs of repentance in the last moments of his life, he was reconciled posthumously. The cases of Murgier and Morel had caused a scandal and great embarrassment to the Inquisitors.

The most interesting case of this *auto de fé*, obscured by the attention given to the sensational suicides of Murgier and Morel, was the trial of Don Juan Longouran of Bordeaux, who had lived in Cuba and Honduras as well as New Orleans before he emigrated to Mexico. In addition to having a lucrative career as a merchant, Longouran was an army doctor. His rationalistic medical view of the universe and the nature of man led him to question religious phenomena. Rash statement of his views in public led him into the halls of the Tribunal of the Holy Office. Shortly after his arrival in the viceregal capital in 1790, Longouran was invited to a dinner where he blantantly expounded heretical ideas. His host made him leave the house, and the next morning denounced Longouran to the Inquisition. He reported that Don Juan had said that fornication was not a sin, and that in taking the women they desired, men simply followed natural law, which was, after all, the guiding motivation of the world. He had claimed that Hell was nothing more than the labors and sufferings men undergo in their mortal lives. He opined that a God of Mercy would not save Christians alone, for there were only three and one half million of them in a world of thirty-three million souls. Such a situation would make for a "small Heaven and very great Hell." He also questioned the doctrine of the Incarnation, the adoration of images, and various other mysteries of the faith, saying he would not kiss the hands of bishops and popes or call for a priest at the hour of his death. He had spoken at length in favor of the French Revolution, and claimed it was legal and just to deny obedience to the Papacy.

The Holy Office of the Inquisition made a secret investigation of the Longouran affair, quietly gathering testimony and keeping the accused under surveillance as a "Protestant" and "secret spy." Perhaps he escaped immediate arrest while the Holy Office gathered more data on his background from Cuba, Honduras, and Louisiana. As the Reign of Terror in France intensified, and as the Spanish prepared to expel Frenchmen from the viceroyalty, the Holy Office arrested Longouran on July 17, 1793, and confiscated his property. After long judicial proceedings, Juan Longouran was convicted of heresy and sedition. He was reconciled in the *auto de fé* of August 9, 1795, did lengthy penance in the monastery of the Holy Cross at Querétaro, and was finally deported from Veracruz in October 1797, to serve eight years of exile in a Spanish prison. Juan Longouran was the typical example of the learned man who had separated religion and science in his thinking, and whose eclecticism undermined his orthodoxy.

The Inquisition's concern with French Enlightenment thought continued after the crowning of Napoleon Bonaparte, and as the Napoleonic soldiers spread philosophe doctrines in the areas they occupied. Don Antonio Castro y Salagado, another native of Bordeaux, was tried for Francophile sentiments in 1802. Castro, who had been in France at the time of the Revolution, was a devotee of Rousseau and, as one witness put it, "infected" with revolutionary ideas. Lic. Manuel Faboada testified that Castro could recite entire passages of *Emile* from memory, and that he spoke of Rousseau as "the greatest man of the universe," while he denounced St. Augustine as "a horse" and St. Thomas as a "beast" and spoke of theology as a "useless science." Other testimony proved that he was an agnostic, if not an atheist, and detailed his formal lack of respect for established religious principles. Castro heard his sentence in a private *auto* conducted in the chambers of the tribunal with only the Inquisitors and his family present. Apparently this procedure was necessary because he was a man of great influence in the viceregal capital. After an abjuration ceremony *de levi,* Antonio Castro y Salagado spent a year in the monastery of Santo Domingo doing penance for his sins. He was then banished from the realms of New Spain for ten years.

He was to spend six years in the service of Spain in the Philippine Islands, where his conduct would be supervised by the Inquisition Commissary in Manila.

At the same time that the Holy Office of the Inquisition was preoccupied with the impact of philosophe thought, Freemasonry made its first inroads in the Viceroyalty of New Spain. Foreshadowing the nineteenth-century Mexican Masonic movement, the thinking of the late eighteenth-century group tended to be more political than religious. First formal notice of Masonry in the Indies was taken by the Supreme Council of the Spanish Inquisition in 1751, when that body sent a letter of warning to the New World bishops requesting them to send lists of soldiers and foreigners who might have Masonic affiliations. Unfortunately, the Holy Office never made a clearly defined distinction among Masonry, Enlightenment philosophy, and Protestantism, and the term *Francomason* took on a very broad meaning.

To conclude, as some writers have, that the Holy Office of the Inquisition in Mexico declined in power and became decadent in the late eighteenth century because it developed into a political instrument is clearly fallacious. It is obvious that it had always been a political instrument from the time of its founding in New Spain. Only when the Enlightenment publicists, and the French Revolutionary activists, tried to split religion and politics did the distinction between political heresy and religious heresy become manifest in New Spain. For the most part, the Spanish monarchy and the Mexican Inquisition rejected the idea that politics and religion could be separated. The Holy Office tried heretics as traitors, and traitors as heretics. For the Mexican Inquisitors, Enlightenment social and political philosophy *was* heresy.

The seeming decadence of the Mexican Tribunal of the Inquisition after 1763 resulted from a whole complex of political and diplomatic circumstances which, in the end, led to a weakening of the institution. The shift of diplomatic and military alliances between Spain and France, and Spain and England, made it difficult for the Holy Office to punish foreign heretics within the Viceroyalty of New Spain. It was equally difficult, if not impossible, to contain foreign political ideas. From the standpoint of domestic politics and Empire policy, the activities of the Holy Office were severely hampered and began to atrophy because of the tendency of royal and ecclesiastical officialdom to embrace philosophical eclecticism. Certainly in the case of the clergy this became a dangerous trend, since, in the final analysis, the new philosophical and political ideas tended to undermine orthodoxy. Social and economic tensions in the Mexican colony, pragmatically evident, were reinforced by consideration of the new natural laws of politics and economics being expounded from abroad. On the threshold of this societal discontent, the Holy Office was often forced to make an ideological retreat, adopting an attitude of tolerance or inaction instead of its former firmness—in reality a new kind of "flexible orthodoxy."

The total documentation in the Mexican Inquisition archive for 1763 to 1805 reveals that the Holy Office cannot be indicted as loath to prosecute unorthodoxy of any kind. It only confirms the fact that the overriding political considerations of the State made the Inquisitors responsible for enforcing a rapidly changing "party-line" kind of orthodoxy, an almost hopeless task. It was impossible to police the far frontiers from California to Florida, from Colorado to Guatemala, from Havana to Manila, a problem as serious to the Inquisitors as the problem of "flexible orthodoxy." Perhaps it was a sense of frustration in coping with the larger problems that led the Holy Office to concentrate on smaller ones. The tendency to engage in hairsplitting and tedious controversies over jurisdiction and judicial competencies was one result of this frustration. Another was the preoccupation with protecting the position and dignity of the Tribunal of the Inquisition.

The interpretation that the clergy (and the Inquisition) mirrored the times and the society to which they ministered is no doubt true of the Mexican experience during the second half of the eighteenth century. Would the Inquisition and the Crown have reacted any differently had the revolutionary political themes then in vogue been circulating fifty or one hundred years earlier? Probably not. At all events, the policies of Charles III (1759–1788) and Charles IV (1788–1808) did little to strengthen the Mexican Inquisition's mission to preserve political and religious orthodoxy. Indeed the Spanish kings weakened the institution by failing to define the place of the Holy Office of the Inquisition in defining the Imperial self-interest.

## 16

Clarence Haring

# The Wealth of the Church

*Among the most controversial issues in Latin-American Church history is the question of Church wealth. Liberal attackers and conservative defenders of religious institutions alike marshall evidence to show on the one hand that the Church was an economic burden on the colonies, and on the other hand that the Roman Catholic Church and its agencies were the primary philanthropic and educational agency in the Spanish Empire. In this excerpt from the major treatise on colonial institutions Professor Clarence Haring examines both sides of the question.*

That the increase of the monasteries in wealth and numbers tended to be out of all proportion to the needs of the new American settlements, and was inconsistent with conditions of life in pioneer, New World communities, was early sensed by Spaniards both in Europe and in America. As early as 1535, the crown decreed that lands in New Spain might be bestowed on *conquistadores* and other worthy settlers only on condition that they were never alienated to an ecclesiastic, a church, or a monastery. In 1559 it was decreed that monasteries outside the cities must be at least 6 leagues apart. As many of the establishments had only

---

From *The Spanish Empire in America* by Clarence Haring, copyright, 1947, by Harcourt Brace Jovanovich, Inc., 1963, pp. 175–178. Reprinted by permission of the publisher.

a few inmates although possessing considerable revenues, and as these were increasing in number, Pope Paul V in 1611 issued a bull suppressing all not occupied by at least 8 resident friars. At this time, according to the ecclesiastical writer Gerónimo de Mendieta, the Franciscans alone in New Spain had 166 religious houses. And besides these there were the houses of the Dominicans, Augustinians, and other Orders. In Lima at the same time, a city of some 26,500 inhabitants, with 19 churches and monasteries, a census revealed that 10 per cent of the population were priests, canons, friars, or nuns. Moreover, the erection of these countless churches and monasteries, their upkeep, and the maintenance of so numerous a clergy, rested chiefly if not wholly upon the labor of the Indians. The clergy shared in the use of forced labor in the form of the *mita* or the *repartimiento* as did other Spaniards, and often only served to increase the heavy burdens upon the miserable aborigines.

The colonists themselves felt the inconveniences of this state of affairs, as when in 1578 the *cabildo* of Mexico City urged the viceroy to limit the acquisition of land by the Church. Again in 1644 the *cabildo* of the same city petitioned the king to this effect, and also requested that no more convents or monasteries be founded, that no more friars be sent to New Spain, and that the bishops be restricted in the number of clergy they might ordain.

Not until the eighteenth century, under the new Bourbon dynasty, was any real effort made by the Spanish government to remedy this situation. A decree of 15 March 1717 declared that the number of friars was a burden upon the land, hindered the cultivation of the fields and the increase of public wealth, and that thereafter no conventual establishments were to be created in the Indies. In 1734 the crown ordered, with the approval of Rome, that for ten years no one in New Spain be admitted under any pretext to a religious Order. Twenty years later, in 1754, the king expressly forbade any member of a religious Order to interfere in the drawing up of wills. The extensive domains of the monasteries were generally acquired by bequest, for, as the Chilean historian Barros Arana remarked, "a will which did not include some legacy in favor of the monasteries passed for an act against religion." But although in 1775 a decree was again issued forbidding confessors or their convents to be heirs or legatees, the policy of the crown was not always consistent, nor were its decrees enforced. When the great German scientist Baron von Humboldt visited New Spain in the opening years of the nineteenth century, he found in Mexico City 23 monasteries and 15 nunneries with over 3,300 inmates in a population of perhaps 100,000.

Whatever may have been the services of the Church in maintaining and spreading the Christian religion and in gradually weaning the Indians from barbarism, there can be little doubt that in certain respects the ecclesiastical establishment, as the royal decree of 1717 declared, was an economic burden upon the colonies. These were chiefly two: the acquisition of so much of the best agricultural land by way of benefactions, purchase, or mortgage, and the system of ecclesiastical taxation, especially the tithe. The tithe amounted to a ten per cent income tax collected at the source on agricultural and pastoral industries. While this assessment was common throughout European Christendom, its effect must have been prejudicial to the progress and prosperity of a young, frontier, agricultural society. The gross amount of tithes collected in New Spain in the decade 1769–79 was nearly thirteen and a half million pesos. In the following decade, it rose to nearly eighteen and a half million.

The engrossing of much of the best land by the Church was unfortunate for the colonies in that it aggravated the evils of the system of large estates. The Church was not responsible for the *latifundia,* nor were all the *latifundia* in the hands of the Church. But the concentration of so much land in the control of one great corporation, or group of allied corporations, intensified the drawbacks of the system in the American colonies. For in most pioneering countries relatively small landed holdings and the stimulus of private ownership by many individuals are generally needed to encourage immigration and secure the most profitable and economical use of the soil. In the case of ecclesiastical lands the outlook was the more hopeless because the "dead hand" of the Church prevented properties from changing owners or being redivided and distributed.

The amount of ecclesiastical property in the Spanish American colonies controlled by the secular Church or by the Orders, in estates and in mortgages, has been variously estimated. Humboldt wrote, in his description of New Spain at the beginning of the nineteenth century, that in some of the provinces four-fifths of the land was held in mortmain. The estimate must have included lands on which ecclesiastical societies held heavy mortgages, for the Mexican historian Alamán, a not unfriendly writer, tells us that there was scarcely an estate in New Spain that was not so encumbered, and that at least half of the landed wealth was controlled by the Church. At the end of the colonial period the aggregate value of agricultural property belonging to the Church and to pious endowments in what is now the Republic of Mexico was probably in the neighborhood of fifty million pesos. Indeed the property and wealth of the Church, and the political influence which such wealth enabled it to exercise, constituted one of the most troublesome problems bequeathed to the nascent republics of the nineteenth century.

The prevalence of ecclesiastical mortgages arose from two circumstances typical of Spanish colonial society. Agriculture was not a capitalistic enterprise that endeavored to produce a surplus of liquid capital for investment. In fact there was little opportunity for investment except in land or mines, and of land the great proprietors already had a great sufficiency. The colonies were not industrialized communities. On the other hand, the Spanish American landed aristocracy in general inherited a tradition of prodigality and extravagance that may be said to have come down to them from the feudal society of medieval times.

As there was little surplus liquid capital, there was little need of organized banking until near the close of the colonial era. In 1716 the viceroy Linares reported that there were only two banks in Mexico City, one under control of the Tagle family, the other belonging to Isidro Rodríguez. It was not until the time of Matías de Gálvez (viceroy, 1783–4) that the celebrated Bank of San Carlos was founded. Consequently, when the improvident landowner needed to borrow, he applied to the monasteries. For they alone, generally less prodigal and extravagant than the private landowners, had an accumulated surplus to invest. They were in a sense the banks of Spanish colonial America.

There is, however, another side to the picture. Virtually all of the social services of the community in colonial days were the peculiar and exclusive domain of the clergy. They created and managed the schools, hospitals, and asylums. They administered the numerous pious funds established by devout laymen or ecclesiastics. Private philanthropy was as common in Spanish colonial society as it is in these more modern times, perhaps more so than has been customary in the Spanish republics of today. But in a society so completely suffused with ecclesiasticism, in which education, science, and letters were largely dominated by the clergy, and charitable activities were entirely in their hands, private beneficence was canalized in the direction of the Church. A repentant millionaire, instead of endowing private colleges, laboratories, or museums, built a chapel or a monastery or gave money to the Church to be administered for the poor and infirm. This not only brought great wealth to the Church, but also imposed vast responsibilities upon it. Consequently its social and charitable contributions to society in the colonies were quite as important as its religious ministrations.

## 17

Asunción Lavrin

# The Church as an Economic Institution

*Documented analysis of the Church as an economic institution is rare. Professor Asunción Lavrin of Rosary College won the Robertson Prize of the Conference on Latin-American History for the best article in the* Hispanic American Historical Review *during 1966 for this selection. It provides a meticulous account of the role of the nunneries in the colonial economy of eighteenth-century New Spain.*

The Catholic Church occupied a preeminent position in the economy of colonial New Spain. It owned a substantial share of the land of the country and had large amounts of capital invested in agricultural enterprises or in loans to landowners and businessmen. Toward the end of the eighteenth century the secular branch of the Church possessed the greater portion of its riches, but according to Humboldt the monastic orders still had considerable wealth and influence. Their investments in land, industries, and urban properties played a decisive role in the shaping of the general economy of New Spain. This position declined in

From Asunción Lavrin, "The Role of the Nunneries in the Economy of New Spain in the Eighteenth Century," *Hispanic American Historical Review,* 46 (1966), 371–393 *passim.* Reprinted by permission of the Duke University Press.

the nineteenth century, however, owing to the economic limitations imposed upon the Church by Charles IV, by the wars of independence, and by subsequent expropriations during the republican period.

Less numerous than monasteries, nunneries played an interesting and important role in the economic life of the viceroyalty. In the first two centuries of colonial life convents acquired and received land and other property, which they exploited with variable success. Since the administration of this property was frequently inept, however, it did not exert as great influence upon the economy as it might have otherwise. Toward the end of the seventeenth century substantial changes had taken place in the manner of investment and administration of the nunneries' capital. Convents showed a greater inclination to buy urban property. They also started to invest their capital more frequently in loans to the producing classes of merchants, landowners, and miners. During the eighteenth century the activities of convents as property holders and lending institutions increased to such an extent that they gained considerable influence in their society as major financial centers, quite capable of affecting the economic development of the community and of the country in general.

Funds for the foundation, subsistence, and further investments of nunneries came from various sources. Donations from patrons and the dowries of nuns were the primary ones. These in turn were invested in properties or loans, thus providing another source of income. Founding patrons endowed nunneries with their initial capital, which was usually given partly in cash and partly in investments in order to allow the nuns a stable revenue for their internal expenses. Other donations came in the form of legacies, bequests of properties, or payments for the building of the convents by subsequent patrons. They ranged from modest offerings of less than one hundred pesos to large gifts of thousands of pesos. The original funds were drawn from the patrons' properties, which could be mortgaged for their total value or for a limited sum of money. Such properties included houses, pulquerías, haciendas, sugar mills, and mines. Thus much of the rural and urban property of New Spain came to be tied to the Church.

The growth in economic importance of nunneries corresponded to the establishment of a certain type of landed economy in the hands of a creole nobility and a class of hacendados, miners, and merchants. François Chevalier points out that already in the seventeenth century these classes had become the great protectors of the Church, the founders of schools, *capellanías,* and convents. This interesting correlation between the foundation and growth of convents and the established pattern of property ownership, dating back to the seventeenth century, was accentuated in the eighteenth century. The traditional hacienda continued to be the typical form of land tenure. Mining flourished again, while cattle raising and textile production enriched many persons directly or indirectly concerned with these activities. Wealthy hacendados and merchants became alcaldes, corregidores, or captains of the militia. Decorations of the Orders of Calatrava or Santiago were given to many of them, while titles of nobility were granted to the richest and most illustrious. These men were the usual patrons of the Church in general and of nunneries in particular.

The majority of the convents founded in the eighteenth century were located outside the capital of New Spain, many of them in minor towns; this fact demonstrates the willingness of rich hacendados and property owners in mining areas to patronize the Church. A typical case is the foundation of the convent of San Miguel el Grande by the Canal family. Manuel Tomás de la Canal, a knight of the Order of Calatrava, was a well-known patron of the Church, who toward the end of his life set out to found a convent of Capuchin nuns. The project started in 1740, but the death of the founder halted its progress. Only four years later, however, one of his daughters decided to continue it, and with the help of her tutor, the Conde de Casa de Loja, established a Conceptionist convent in 1756.

In Querétaro the Capuchin convent of San José de Gracia was patronized by José Caballero Ocio, a priest, the son of a militia captain, and himself a former captain in the city. In Mexico City the convent of Santa Teresa la Nueva was proposed by the daughter of Captain Esteban Molina Mosquera, who had previously repaired and endowed the convent of Santa Teresa la Antigua. All the wealth of the family passed to these two convents. Sister María Ignacia Azlor, founder of the convent of La Enseñanza, belonged to the distinguished family of the Marquis of San Miguel Aguayo, a title conferred by the crown in 1682 and possessing a very rich mayorazgo invested in land. The convent of Nuestra Señora de Guadalupe, of the Order of Mary, was founded for Indian girls through the interest of the Marquis of Castañiza.

Nuns were also among the most reliable patrons of their convents. They could donate money without breaking the vow of poverty, since the action of becoming a patroness was interpreted as one of jurisdiction and not of dominion. At profession nuns made wills of their properties which very often were bequeathed to the convents in which they professed. On those occasions when they did not make wills, any inheritance that they might receive passed automatically to the convent. This practice was already in vogue in the sixteenth century, possibly to help the newly founded nunneries to increase their revenues. It provoked certain abuses, however, which were reported in a royal cédula of November 1578. In this cédula prelates were advised not to force professing nuns to retain their properties or to forbid them to bequeath properties, thus giving the convent legal grounds to claim them later. There is no record of such coercion in the eighteenth century. Available lists of received or expected legacies in various convents show that many nuns made rather considerable contributions to their convents in this manner.

Another form of donation by nuns was the *reservas*. Convents allowed nuns to have a private income for their personal needs in order to relieve themselves from the burden of communal expenses. This income was separated by nuns at the time of profession from their personal property or was assigned to them by parents or relatives. Nuns usually made provisions in their wills bequeathing this money or its revenue to the convent. The capital of reservas ranged from several hundred pesos to as much as 20,000 pesos. In 1757 the convent of Santa Clara in Mexico City listed nine nuns enjoying reservas, the total capital amounting to 29,700 pesos. In 1760 the convent of Santa Isabel in Mexico City expected to receive 20,000 pesos of reservas willed to it.

While bequests and reservas were supposed to be voluntary, dowries were required, and these proved to be a dependable and constant source of capital. Dowries were set at 3,000 pesos during the seventeenth century and part of the eighteenth century. Eventually many convents increased the minimum to 3,500 and by the end of the eighteenth century most convents received 4,000 pesos from professing nuns as dowries. Many families who could not raise that amount would mortgage their properties temporarily or impose a lien on them. As would be expected, large and wealthy convents obtained considerable sums of money through dowries. La Concepción in Mexico City received around 275,000 pesos from 1763 to 1812. La Encarnación, also in Mexico City, received 118,000 pesos from 1791 to 1811.

Once the initial capital was acquired, the task of administering or investing it to provide the nunnery with an income was assigned to an administrator or majordomo. Majordomos were usually notaries, lawyers, or men who held responsible offices in the government, though sometimes they might be priests. The majordomo possessed legal rights to collect income from the property of those convents under his care; his payment was usually a flat rate plus a percentage of the collected sum. The vicar general of nuns or the provincial of the order supervised minor transactions, and ultimately the bishop or archbishop approved all final settlements.

The exact nature and value of much of the property of nunneries in the seventeenth century remain to be investigated. There is evidence that convents owned some land and continued to own certain rural properties throughout the eighteenth century. On the other hand, available documents indicate that toward the end of the seventeenth century nunneries were inclined to acquire more urban than rural property. The books of accounts of the convent of Jesús María in Mexico City record no other type of property but houses. These records extend throughout the entire eighteenth century and show the convent buying houses, constructing new ones, or repairing old ones. No purchase of rural land is found. This inclination to acquire urban properties was firmly established in the eighteenth century.

At the end of the colonial period it was acknowledged that nunneries and monasteries possessed a large proportion of the urban estate of Mexico City. The convent of La Encarnación, in an account of its properties in 1749, listed sixty-five houses, sixty-five rooms and multiple-tenant dwellings, and twelve shops. They were evaluated at approximately a half million pesos. In 1750 Jesús María declared that it possessed thirty-five houses, though neither the total value nor the income received from them was stated. The only type of financial transactions in which these and almost all other convents appear to have been engaged was connected with houses. In 1812 the majordomos of all convents of Mexico City had to report to the royal treasury the income of the urban properties under their control.

Though the number of houses belonging to each convent was not stated, the incomes of some of the largest nunneries were high enough to indicate ownership of a great number of houses. La Concepción estimated an income of 63,752 pesos per year, La Encarnación 41,920 pesos, Santa Catarina de Sena 34,172 pesos, and Jesús María 32,128 pesos. On the other hand, the very small annual income of some other convents indicates that they possessed the least number of houses. Examples are the convent of San Juan de la Penitencia with 7,839 pesos, Santa Brígida with 3,726 pesos, and Nuestra Señora de Guadalupe with a mere 2,900 pesos.

In 1826 a detailed report on the economic condition of nunneries, written by Juan B. de Arechederreta, listed the number of houses owned by the majority of convents of Mexico City and the income they produced. The total number of houses was estimated at 576, though those belonging to Franciscan convents were not included. The term *fincas urbanas* used in the report is vague and could refer to properties of multiple tenants. Comparing this report to that of 1812 makes clear that in most cases the income of each convent had remained very stable. Thus it is logical to assume that in the first years of the Republic much of the urban property in Mexico City still belonged to nunneries.

The ownership of urban or rural estates, however, was not the sole source of income of nunneries. Censos and depósitos contributed a substantial share of this income, and in some instances became the sole source of revenue for some convents. Censos were used by pious donors as a means to provide a regular income to convents. The convent was made a beneficiary to a mortgage on property held by the donor or his heirs, receiving a yearly income of five percent on the capital or principal. Censos were usually made in perpetuity, but in many instances the owner of the property retained the option of canceling the censo by paying the stated principal to the convent. Censos were a common method for patrons to endow a convent or for parents to provide for the dowries of their professing daughters. Most patrons of convents founded in the eighteenth century did not offer all of their money in cash but mortgaged their properties, recognizing a censo in favor of the foundations. In the late seventeenth and eighteenth centuries the censo was ingeniously modified in order to circumvent the law forbidding lending at interest. The principal could be recovered by selling the annuity to another investor. This operation became of universal use in the eighteenth century.

*Obras pías* were a more restricted type of censo or lien. These were the deeds of citizens or nuns who wished to support the expenses of a religious feast in the church of their chosen convent or other expenses of the nunnery. The pious deed usually entailed an obligation on the part of the convent to celebrate a number of masses for the soul of the donor. The *capellanía* was still another form of censo. It was a mortgage which provided funds for the support of a chaplain (monk or priest) who cared for the spiritual needs of the nuns, officiated at the service of the convent church, or said a number of masses for the soul of the patron. Capellanías and obras pías were invested in either urban or rural property, since such investments were usually not the choice of the nunnery itself but that of the owner of the property.

The term *censo* was rather loosely applied, both to the types of endowment already mentioned which did not require the exchange of capital and to financial operations in which money was involved. Such were the liens by which landowners mortgaged their properties for ready cash, paying five percent interest to the convent from then on. Another type was used to improve properties, which might be mortaged with a censo, the owner receiving a stipulated capital. After several years the capital was returned and the censo annulled. Chevalier has pointed out that the Jesuits used this type of lien very frequently, borrowing capital on many occasions from rich nunneries.

In the eighteenth century all legal disguises for the interest-bearing loan were put aside. Members of the Church became openly engaged in the business of lending money. These loans were known as *depósitos*. They were temporary loans which paid an annual interest of five percent. Unlike the censo the depósito was not tied to any property and was usually paid back in a relatively short time or at least had a deadline for its final redemption. Throughout the eighteenth century merchants, hacendados, and masculine orders increasingly used deposits as a way of acquiring capital for the development of commerce, agriculture, or the improvement of their properties. For the nunneries this type of loan was a secure way to obtain a safe income for a number of years, while guaranteeing the return of capital for further investments. In order to protect themselves from loss of capital, nunneries usually demanded the signature of two bondsmen or collateral in the form of some type of security in real estate.

The importance of deposits as a source of funds may be seen in the following examples. In 1720 the convent of San Juan de la Penitencia in Mexico City had a total of fifty-two deposits, almost all of them lent for a period of two to four years. The sum of money lent was 162,036 pesos. In 1771 the Augustinian college of San José de Gracia in Guadalajara obtained 15,000 pesos on loan from the convent of Santa Mónica to repair its buildings. During the 1780s the convent of Jesús María provided over 16,000 pesos as a deposit for the construction of the parochial church at Chalco. The convent of La Encarnación borrowed from other convents 17,125 pesos from 1791 to 1794 for the construction of a new building. These particular loans paid only 4½ percent, probably as a form of reciprocal discount rate. A loan of 100,000 pesos was solicited from the convent of Jesús María by Juan de Guadarmino, a wholesale merchant (*almacenero*), in March 1763. The sisters intended to give him 65,000 pesos, already held in the coffers, and hoped to complete the sum when the Mariscal de Castilla returned 30,000 pesos previously borrowed. Members of the nobility also borrowed heavily from nunneries. The Count of Santiago, the Marquis of Figueroa, the Count of Valenciana, and the Count of San Bartolomé de Xala are only a few among the many names of nobles found in the accounts of different convents.

.   .   .

The colonial government in Mexico City was also well aware of the lending capacities of the Church. After the middle of the seventeenth century the crown had sought to interest the Church in investing money in juros (a kind of treasury bond used in Spain since the sixteenth century). It found some response among nunneries. Similarly, in 1794 when the Real Renta del Tabaco was mortgaged in order to provide funds for the exhausted royal budget, the convents of San Juan de la Penitencia and La Enseñanza in Mexico City lent 5,000 and 10,000 pesos respectively at a nominal interest of five percent. In a society where capital was normally tied to the land or in business enterprises and was, therefore, seldom readily available, the ability to provide such immediate loans conferred upon nunneries a position of great significance in the economy.

Despite their very important role in the general economy of the viceroyalty, nunneries frequently found themselves in financial difficulties because of poor management of funds and other internal economic troubles. There were no fixed rules with regard to the administration of the convents' income, each having a different manner of allocating its funds and covering its expenses. It is important to mention, however, that there were two different forms of fulfilling religious life which resulted in differences in the administration of incomes. Discalced nuns were not meant to have any income for their meals, being completely dependent upon alms for this purpose. And because of their very modest way of life they also had fewer expenses. Most of the convents of New Spain contained *calzada* nuns, however, and these were provided with weekly money by the nunnery for the purchase of their meals. They did not live in a communal manner, and each nun was allowed a personal income from her own private sources to spend as she desired. Some convents provided nuns with basic foods, such as meat and bread and gave them a smaller allowance for the rest of their meals.

. . .

From the end of the seventeenth century, the administration of the income of many convents was frequently unsound, and their expenses considerably greater than their income. The affluent convents of La Concepción and

Jesús María in Mexico City were found in such economic trouble around 1670 by Archbishop Payo de Rivera that he approved a change in the internal administration of their income, granting nuns more freedom in the use of the weekly allowances provided by the convents, and thus relieving the nunneries of the burden of providing food and other basic necessities. The convents welcomed this measure, and it became a *modus vivendi* for most of them in the eighteenth century. Thus when the reform of religious observance known as *vida común* proposed a return to a community of expenses, the nuns vehemently opposed the measure.

.    .    .

There were several reasons for these economic troubles in the nunneries of New Spain. One of the most important was the lack of a sound and continuous administrative policy. There were few nuns with a clear idea of how to keep the accounts of their convents efficiently. Any nun in the convent could be appointed to the position of accountant, regardless of her abilities. Also, the term of service of the mother accountant (three years) was too short to straighten out such confused accounts as nunneries usually had. Once in a while an active nun put in charge of the accounting achieved some positive results. Such was the case in 1779 of Mexico City's La Concepción. The nuns decided to take into their own hands the reorganization of the old books in view of the majordomos' inefficiency. They attributed the nonpayment of several pious funds totaling 26,500 pesos to previous maladministration and told their superiors that they hoped to recover most of the sum. On the other hand, some convents, such as Jesús María, seemed to have been well administered. Its records throughout the eighteenth century are in good order and show a clear statement of all the expenses incurred.

Still another source of economic burden was the very large numbers of masses and feasts that convents had to celebrate in the memory of their patrons. Almost every donation involved an obligation of this kind, to which were added the masses and feasts instituted by nuns themselves. These religious occasions were costly. The accumulation of legacies, pious offerings, and capellanías throughout two centuries made the financial burden almost unbearable to several convents. They found that they could no longer afford the expenses involved in the fulfillment of these religious and economic obligations.

· · ·

Thus the general picture of the economic situation of nunneries in the eighteenth century was contradictory. Though there existed a number of convents circulating vast amounts of money throughout the country in the form of censos and depósitos, closer examination of the private financial situation of many nunneries often discloses a precarious internal economic balance. This situation might be explained by the fact that considerable amounts of capital had been given to nunneries as pious deeds for specified, restricted purposes, so that income from such capital could not be used by the communities to make good their deficits. In addition wealth was distributed unevenly among nunneries. Some, such as La Concepción and La Encarnación in Mexico City or Santa Clara in Querétaro, were the favorites of the richer patrons, who gave them larger and more frequent bequests. They were also more popular among those wishing to profess, receiving more nuns than those convents of more modest life and lesser financial means. This fact insured the richer convents even larger incomes from dowries ready for investment and preserved their already solid economic position. For these reasons the larger convents represented the more successful financial enterprises while the lesser ones were in many instances more of a burden than an asset to the towns in which they were located.

During the last three decades of the eighteenth century the Church in Spain and in the colonies was affected by a series of increasingly stiffer laws reflecting the regalist policies of the Bourbon Kings Charles III and Charles IV. These laws had the purpose of subordinating the Church to the state in temporal matters and of curtailing the economic power of the clergy. Restrictions were placed on the power of ecclesiastical judges in the administration of capellanías and the validation or nullification of pious testaments; bequeathing of property to confessors was forbidden; and the rights of nunneries to claim *ab intestato* properties of dead relatives of nuns were revoked.

## 18

E. Bradford Burns

# The Church and
# Economic Theory

*The most important exponents of economic develop-
ment in colonial Latin America were the clergy. Better economic conditions produced social stability and
a better environment for missionary activity. There
were many mercantile theorists and physiocrats in the
ranks of the colonial clergy. In Brazil as well as in
Mexico, these priests and bishops labored to find
solutions to practical problems of economic growth.
E. Bradford Burns, professor of history at the University of California at Los Angeles, examines the
activities of Bishop José Joaquim de Cunha de
Azeredo Coutinho in bringing ideas of the Enlightenment to Brazil.*

José Joaquim de Cunha de Azeredo Coutinho contributed
to the introduction of the Enlightenment into colonial
Brazil and, thus, unintentionally, albeit significantly, to
Brazilian independence. His role as an essayist and educator speaking for the Enlightenment, at first glance, might
seem to be in conflict with his role as royal official and

From E. Bradford Burns, "The Role of Azeredo Coutinho in
the Enlightenment of Brazil," *Hispanic American Historical Review*, 44 (1964), 145–160 *passim*. Reprinted by permission of the
Duke University Press.

General Inquisitor of the Realm. On the one hand, Azeredo Coutinho's secular, scientific, philosophic, and literary studies and pursuits were those of the eighteenth-century Enlightenment. Yet on the other hand, Azeredo Coutinho held fast to certain traditional opinions and professional orientations as exemplified by his several positions with the Portuguese Inquisition. Whatever the psychological problems resulting from the conflict of roles, this essay is concerned solely with the contributions to the Enlightenment in Brazil made by the remarkable Bishop Azeredo Coutinho.

Born on September 8, 1742, at Campos dos Goitacazes in the Captaincy of Rio de Janeiro, into a wealthy, sugar-owning family, Azeredo Coutinho spent a rustic childhood on his father's country estate. At the age of six he was taken to Rio de Janeiro to begin his formal education. He studied Latin, grammar, rhetoric, and philosophy with the best teachers of that growing colonial center. Young Azeredo Coutinho had an able mind but was of delicate health. After his graduation in 1762, his father sent him to Minas Gerais on a trip intended to improve his health. The extended journey into the interior gave the youth an opportunity to gain a firsthand familiarity with Brazil's mining industry and the conditions surrounding it. Gold extraction was near its height.

Upon the death of his father in 1768, Azeredo Coutinho became even more closely connected with another important aspect of the Brazilian economy: as the eldest son, he became director of the family sugar plantations and mills. Ably administered, the family fortunes did not suffer under his supervision. The young man, however, became disenchanted with rural life, and he inclined increasingly toward a religious and scholarly career. Information about the reforms of the University of Coimbra and about the contributions of his own relatives to those innovations reached him in Brazil, and he renounced his inherited rights and migrated to the metropolis in order to enroll in that venerable university.

At the age of thirty-three, Azeredo Coutinho began his studies in the school of canon law at the University of Coimbra, which Pombal had reformed three years earlier, in 1772. Whether that able Prime Minister of José I cared to admit it or not, there is little doubt that those reforms were influenced by the Enlightenment extant in the Europe of that period. With a new emphasis on the importance of the natural sciences, Pombal introduced Cartesian methods into the teaching of all subjects, ordering experiment and practice to take the place of dogmatic doctrine and speculation. Pombal allocated funds to build a new observatory, a medical amphitheater, a botanical garden, and physics and chemistry laboratories. He hired the most intelligent men of the kingdom as professors, and, to the extent that the resources of Portugal were sufficient, he induced a number of Italian scholars to come to Coimbra. Concurrently, the philosophy of the French physiocrats gained popularity among the faculty. In a modest way at least, Coimbra became aware of the ideas of the Enlightenment.

Azeredo Coutinho began his university studies when this reform atmosphere, reflecting as it did certain tendencies of the Enlightenment, was at its peak at Coimbra. The creole student read widely, by no means limiting himself to canon law. He became interested in natural history, physics, and chemistry, and studied them enthusiastically. Azeredo Coutinho quickly proved himself to be a true son of the new university reforms. At the end of five years of study he received his first university degree and was ordained. He returned to Coimbra five years later to complete an additional year of study and to earn his *licenciado* degree.

An appointment in 1784 as a deputy of the Holy Office in Lisbon dissuaded him from returning to Brazil and kept him in Portugal for over a decade. During his residence in Lisbon, he probably served Brazil better than he could have had he returned to his native land. It was during this period that he wrote his two most significant economic essays concerning Brazil, essays which were to have a profound repercussion in the colony.

Having become intimately acquainted with the Brazilian sugar economy through his experience in the administration of his family's sugar plantations for seven years, Azeredo Coutinho was disturbed by a law proposed in Lisbon to fix the price of sugar, which could have worked to the serious disadvantage of the Brazilian producers because of the rising price sugar was commanding in a world market temporarily deprived of Haitian sugar. Aware of the injustice to the Brazilians of this contemplated legislation and of the financial harm it would cause his own family, Azeredo Coutinho vociferously opposed the artificial stabilization of the price of sugar. In 1791, as a consequence, he wrote his first important economic essay, *A Memorial on the Price of Sugar,* as an argument against the proposed act. According to the prelate-economist, the revolutionary tumults and adverse weather in the Caribbean evidenced the hand of Divine Providence, and the Portuguese ought to take advantage of the situation to sell increasingly scarce sugar on the world market. Price rises, due to the sudden sugar shortage, encouraged production, which, in turn, could accelerate the development of Brazil. Increased production and high prices would enable the Brazilians to buy more from Portugal, and, of course, more trade would give an impetus to the Portuguese merchant navy. The chief beneficiary of rising sugar prices would be the Portuguese empire, and those benefits would offset any higher price the Portuguese would have to pay for their sugar. Azeredo Coutinho also argued that any governmental regulation of the price of sugar would thwart the natural economic order—a classical idea of capitalism of the period. The clear economic reasoning of the *Memorial* apparently convinced the Portuguese authorities that price-fixing would be unwise. At any rate, the influence of that essay has been given as the cause for the defeat of the proposed artificially fixed price of sugar.

As a result of the impact of that essay on the intellectual class of Lisbon, Azeredo Coutinho received an invitation to join the prestigious Royal Academy of Science, a high distinction for a creole. The Royal Academy in Lisbon, established in 1779, was modeled after the Royal Academy in Paris, and to a large extent it carried out within the Portuguese world the same objectives as the Parisian Academy did within the French world. The Royal Academy in Lisbon published the *Memorial,* and, thereafter, Azeredo Coutinho's name and activities were closely associated with that institution of the Portuguese Enlightenment.

Doubtless the Royal Academy of Science had a deep impact on the thinking of Azeredo Coutinho. Already introduced to the physiocrats at Coimbra, in the Academy he was exposed still further to the school of economic thought inspired by François Quesnay. Physiocrat philosophy pervaded the Lisbon Academy as it had its model, the French Academy. Thus, the Secretary-General of the Lisbon Academy, José Correia de Serra, could write in 1789, "The first step of a nation, in order to profit from its advantages, is to become acquainted perfectly with its own territories, what they contain, what they produce, and of what they are capable." This statement was but a rephrasing of the fundamental idea of the physiocrats. Azeredo Coutinho absorbed those ideas and acted accordingly.

Knowledge of the physiocrat philosophy and practical experience in and first-hand observations of the Brazilian economy formed the background for Azeredo Coutinho's second essay, *An Economic Essay on the Commerce of Portugal and Her Colonies*. The careful exercise of economic logic apparent in his second essay was destined to have a great importance in Brazil and to be one of the first notes of a hymn to Brazilian independence. In 1794 the Royal Academy in Lisbon published this essay with considerable commendation. In addition to two more Portuguese editions, 1816 and 1828, the essay had three English editions, 1801, 1807, and 1808; two German editions, 1801 and 1808; and two French editions, 1803 and

1808. The English, French, and German newspapers and magazines commented on and recommended this essay. In short, one of the effects of this essay was to elevate the Portuguese (or Brazilian) prelate to a position of prestige in the enlightened economic circles of Europe.

Although this essay suggests some far-reaching adjustments to the Brazilian economy, it does not intimate that they should be instituted by any other means than by reform within the empire. Belonging to a small group of enlightened reformers in the metropolis who sought to modernize and to improve the Portuguese empire, Azeredo Coutinho preached neither revolution nor independence. In other words, no one can or did classify the essay as a "revolutionary" tract. Its most potent effect undoubtedly was that for the first time it classified and clarified a series of economic reforms highly desired by the Brazilians. Azeredo Coutinho wanted those reforms to be carried out within the empire. When those basic economic reforms were not forthcoming from Portugal, Brazilians came to realize that only by control of their own destiny could needed economic reforms be enacted. Hence, by indicating the path to economic reform, Azeredo Coutinho's essay had the unexpected effect of increasing the Brazilians' desire to be economic masters in their own house.

This thoroughly patriotic essay discussed the rich resources and potential of Brazil and recommended policies which would permit the best utilization of them. Azeredo Coutinho emphasized and repeated frequently the physiocrat doctrine that agriculture is the true source of wealth. Gold was a false wealth which, instead of enriching the empire, had impoverished it. Sugar, wood, coffee, cacao, and a myriad of other natural products of the immense empire were the true sources of wealth. In that connection Azeredo Coutinho ably discussed the natural resources and economic possibilities of Brazil, which, if developed with a minimum of restrictions and a maximum of liberty, he claimed, would reinvigorate the entire Portuguese empire. Specifically he urged the abolition of the salt monopoly so that cheap salt would encourage a salted meat and fish industry, which Brazil was highly capable of developing. He recommended the abolition of restrictions and monopolies of forest products, so that the Brazilians could engage more easily in shipbuilding industry and in the export of lumber. Aware of the Indians' pleasure in fishing, Azeredo Coutinho encouraged the development of a large fishing industry based on Indian labor. In this way the Indians could also be trained as sailors. The essay called for the withdrawal of Portuguese restrictions on the manufacture of basic necessities in Brazil and spoke frankly in favor of expanded trade outside the empire. Azeredo Coutinho concluded his *Economic Essay* with sage advice, probably beyond the comprehension of his times, which, if followed, would have benefited Portugal considerably. He wrote:

> If Portugal, in fine, keeps up a considerable navy and large merchant fleets; if, satisfied with her vast dominions in the four quarters of the globe, she renounces all conquests; if she promotes by every means the development of the riches which her possessions are capable of producing; if she establishes manufactures only of the most indispensable necessities, and abandons those of luxury to foreigners, in order to afford them an opportunity of purchasing her superfluities:—if Portugal, I say, does all this, no enemy will molest her, or disturb her quiet: for all the nations will feel in her preservation an interest closely connected with their own.[1]

One of the direct results of his essay was the abolition of the salt monopoly in 1801. Speaking as a Brazilian who saw his native land's future hindered by unjust regulation by the metropolis, Azeredo Coutinho had written with irrefutable logic in opposition to the salt monopoly. His

---

[1] George W. Robinson, *Brazil and Portugal in 1809* (Cambridge, 1913), p. 23.

sentiment and some of his contentions are conveyed in such remarks as the following:

> On account of the vast sum of money which is thus every year drawn from Brazil for the sole purpose of enriching the individual to whom the salt trade has been farmed out, all the rest of the inhabitants of these countries are made losers; at least their gain is materially prejudiced by the monopoly. The whole commerce of Portugal, indeed, is made forfeit, by this abuse, infinite emoluments and advantages, which would otherwise accrue to it from a greater abundance of salt, fish, butcher's meat, bacon, cheese, and butter, than would be preserved and brought to market.[2]

Possibly more than any of his other writings, this essay revealed the foreign influence, the influence of the Enlightenment, present in his thought. The prologue to the *Economic Essay* demonstrated that Azeredo Coutinho possessed a wide knowledge of eighteenth-century French history. Throughout the essay, the ideas of François Quesnay and the French physiocrats were discernible. The influence of the ideas of Adam Smith were also seen, for Azeredo Coutinho was wont to cite Smith occasionally in his works.

There is no doubt that Azeredo Coutinho was acquainted with the works of Montesquieu, *L'esprit des lois* in particular, because the *Economic Essay* took special pains to combat the French philosopher's remarks on the influence of climates. In doing so Azeredo Coutinho became one of the first of a long line of Brazilians who have contended that the tropics do not breed inferior men. Arguing vigorously against Montesquieu's celebrated and universally received theory of climates, Azeredo Coutinho set out to prove that, contrary to the French philosopher's theory, the

---

[2] José Joaquim de Cunha de Azeredo Coutinho, *An Essay on the Commerce and Products of the Portuguese Colonies in South America* (London, 1807), p. 9.

people of Brazil were valiant and energetic. In chapter five of part one of the *Economic Essay,* he attacked Montesquieu in the following manner:

> Montesquieu and the partisans of his system of the climates, having laid it down as a general principle that the inhabitants of hot countries are feeble and faint-hearted from their birth, and that, by the same inference, the Indians under the torrid zone are unfit for seafaring life, particularly for the service of the navy; I find myself called upon to examine the reasons by which an opinion so general is supported— an opinion from which inferences have been drawn not only absurd of themselves, but offensive to the nations inhabiting hot countries, nay even to those of the south of Europe.[3]

A third essay, *A Discussion of the Present State of the Brazilian Mines,* published in 1804, completed the economic triptych on Brazil written by Azeredo Coutinho while he was in Portugal. In this essay the author correctly attributed Brazil's economic illness to an overemphasis on mining and an underemphasis on agriculture. He held that agriculture should be given first place in the Brazilian economy and that mining should be made more efficient through the introduction of the latest scientific mining knowledge and machinery from Europe.

The ideas expounded in the three essays found a response in the depressed Brazilian economy of that period. Sugar, unable to enter many former European markets because of the continental wars, and unable to meet the competition of Haiti and Jamaica, sold poorly abroad. Gold, because of overproduction, glutted the market and brought a low return. Not finding a ready market for her two principal products, Brazil staggered along an uncertain and rugged economic road. The future looked bleak if not

---

[3] Robinson, *op. cit.,* p. 16.

hopeless. In such a crisis it is understandable that the creoles were receptive to new economic ideas.

One significance of the three economic essays is that Azeredo Coutinho applied the ideas as well as the methods of thinking of the Enlightenment to Brazilian economic problems. Certainly physiocrat thought, with its emphasis on agriculture as the true producer of wealth, was well suited for a discussion of Brazil's economic problems. By focusing the beacon of the Enlightenment on the Brazilian economy, Azeredo Coutinho was able to clarify and to suggest remedies for many Brazilian problems. In terms of the eighteenth-century Enlightenment, he expressed to the Brazilians hitherto unformulated economic ideas and reforms. Azeredo Coutinho was the first, then, to organize and to enunciate many of the economic desires of the Brazilian creoles, such as the desire for less-confining trade and for removal of monopolies and restrictions.

As various Brazilians have pointed out, one of the important results of those essays was that they spiritually and mentally helped to prepare Brazil for independence. Azeredo Coutinho expressed a series of economic ideas which the Brazilian creoles wanted to implement. The creoles became willing to declare Brazil's independence from Portugal in order to put into practice some of those ideas. As a colonial economist formulating and expressing economic complaints and desires of the colony vis-à-vis the metropolis, Azeredo Coutinho played a role in the declaration of Brazilian independence somewhat analogous to the role played by the better-known Mariano Moreno in Argentine independence.

## 19

## Jerome V. Jacobsen, S.J.

# The Argentine
# Mission Frontier

*The missionary efforts of Jesuits in the Río de la
Plata area have received considerable attention from
scholars, but little has been written about the Abipón
missions on the western flank of the Argentine colony.
Father Jerome V. Jacobsen has studied the activities
of the greatest Jesuit preacher among the Abipón,
Father Martin Dobrizhoffer. His illuminating account of Dobrizhoffer's career in Córdoba, Rosario,
Concepción, and among the Guaraní shows some of
the problems and the achievements of eighteenth-
century mission work in South America.*

Whoever undertakes the task of writing a definitive life
of Father Martin Dobrizhoffer will enjoy an enormously
rich experience and one quite as interesting as Dr. Herbert E. Bolton found while tracing every footstep of Father
Kino in his *Rim of Christendom.* The life span of Dobrizhoffer, 1718 to 1791, covered great turning points of history. He lived during the trade-mad years, when wars for
empires and their products were taking place in the colonies of England, France, Spain, and Portugal. He was in

From Jerome V. Jacobsen, S.J., "Dobrizhoffer: Abipón Missionary," *Mid-America: An Historical Review,* 29 (1947), 139–184
*passim.* Reprinted by permission of the publisher.

Europe for the beginning and the end of the critical struggles; he was in Paraguay for one phase of the warfare. He was a contemporary of such epochal events as the Diplomatic Revolution, the Seven Years' War, the American Revolution, the French Revolution. He was one of the many Jesuit missionaries expelled from the Americas by royal edicts of the kings of Portugal and Spain, but, unlike the vast majority of his fellows, he was the exception who found an abode in Europe more cheerful than the prisons or graves that were theirs.

.        .        .

The setting for his labors among the sedentary Guarani and Mbayá east of the Paraná-Paraguay River has been amply described by many writers, but that of his efforts in four missions west of the river needs a few words of explanation.

The scene can be made clear if one conceives the Gran Chaco as a vast wilderness in the heart of South America encircled by Spanish cities and civilized Indian villages. Around the area clockwise on the east were Asunción, the Guaraní reductions, and Corrientes, marked off by the Paraguay-Paraná River. South and west were Santa Fe, Córdoba, Santiago del Estero, Tucumán, Salta, and Tarija, connected by trade roads. In the northwest were the Chiquito missions. The aborigines of the uncheerful Chaco were all of the same Guaicuran linguistic family. The principal tribes were the Mocoví who ruled the southern and western Chaco, the Abipón who infested the eastern section, and the Mbayá and Toba who roved in the north.

.        .        .

By the time Dobrizhoffer arrived on the scene scattered colonies had been established, as, for instance, the group near Santiago del Estero, and San Javier north of Santa Fe in the land of the Mocoví. Deeper in the Chaco north of San Javier lay the Abipón lands. Beginnings to extend a chain of colonies up the Paraná River had already been made with the foundations of San Jerónimo in 1748, Concepción in 1749, and San Fernándo in 1750. The Jesuits were hoping to get all the Abipón into these three colonies. Dobrizhoffer had been assigned to Concepción to replace Father Bartolomé Araoz who had assisted Father José Sánchez in founding the reduction in 1749.

. . .

His introduction to Abipón ways was frightening. Nearing the site of the colony on the Inespin River, over a hundred miles due north of San Javier, the newcomers were met by its savage horsemen who had come to scout the Mocoví. Leaving the main body of his followers in the plain Dobrizhoffer reached Concepción with a small guard. Father José Sánchez came forth to meet him. The *cura* was a pitiable figure, begrimed, tattered, and afflicted of heart. He literally fell into his rescuer's arms. But before the greetings were finished the marketplace was in an uproar. The Mocoví had entered and were exchanging threats with the Abipón. In the midst of the turmoil of galloping horses and wild shouting a lightning storm burst. A night of terror and watching was followed by several days of fear and anxiety as skirmishing continued. Then the Mocoví went elsewhere.

Still, this brought only a respite. Troubles had begun between the Abipón of Concepción and those of the colony of San Jerónimo, nearly thirty miles east, over the theft of horses, the abiding passion of Chaco tribesmen. It came to a crisis when Ychoalay, chieftain of San Jerónimo, rode into the colony of Concepción and boldly warned its leader, Alaykin, that he would destroy the place if the stolen horses and wild shouting a lightning storm burst. A night peace with the Concepción colonists as long as they consorted with his enemies. The time was roughly fifteen months after the foundation of the colony, or about the middle of 1750. When the violence would commence could not be foretold.

Then, when all seemed quiet, the Mocoví returned. At

first there were skirmishes and night raids, during which Dobrizhoffer and Sánchez had to keep watch, muskets in hand. Sometimes the Mocoví were successful in driving off horses, sometimes they were routed with losses. They decided finally to have done with this petty strife and to gather all of their Chaco allies for a mass assault on the colony. This was indeed bad news, for it signified a general uprising with the ultimate aim of united attacks upon all of the Spanish settlements and estates. Warning would have to be conveyed to the governors, hence, Sánchez told Dobrizhoffer to go to Santiago del Estero for Spanish arms to stop the insurrection in its beginning at Concepción.

Father Martin with three Abipón companions made the hazardous trip of some 300 miles westward to Santiago del Estero in sixteen days, ending it by swimming the dangerously swollen Rio Dulce. The first three days were made in rain, the remainder through marshes and flooded areas. The last three days found the messengers in a starving condition since the meat, their only food, had putrefied. Although the Indians caught a large fish in the Salado River, they refused to give even a morsel to the father. Considering the nature of the Chaco we must grant that the journey, made probably in May and June, 1750, was heroic.

The governor of Tucumán, Barreda, heard the news of the impending strife, but having troubles of his own along similar lines, could release only nine of the forty farmer-soldiers requested by Dobrizhoffer. The missionary started back with these, and the party made ninety-four leagues. Then the soldiers took fright at the sight of some Indians. They turned back toward Santiago with Dobrizhoffer in pursuit. They halted in the security of the missions of Turugón, where Dobrizhoffer waited reinforcements from the governor and, incidentally, preached a panegyric on July 16. After twelve days he got a detachment of twenty-four. What with swimming rivers, a prairie fire, a tiger, and various scares to impede them the padre and his company got back to Concepción five months after he had left it.

There affairs had grown worse. Troops had arrived from Santa Fe and had left the impression among the Indians that the fathers were on the side of the Spaniards against the Indians. Again the Abipón fled to their secret haunts, leaving an empty mission church and two empty-hearted missionaries. Under such unhappy conditions the missionaries could boast of no great harvest of souls. In fact, they record baptisms only of the aged and dying as their chief spiritual works. The Abipón were too busy with their trickery, their sallies from the colony, their carousing at home, to listen to any instruction in religion. The scene was definitely a testing ground for Dobrizhoffer's vocation to missionary work. Amid the various tumults and scares he lived in a straw-roofed hut with little protection from dust, heat, and rain which with patience might have been suffered. Combined with annoyances from the innumerable frogs, toads, mosquitoes, gnats, fleas, and ticks, they permitted no hour of comfort. His diet, apparel, and lodging were not such as would be classified as civilized. He ate the rough food of the natives and he slept in a bull's hide suspended on four poles. Daytimes he cultivated the fields and garden. The Abipón away from the stockade or near it were neither solace nor companionable. His lone amusement was found in raising a dog and two young crocodiles. Let us welcome the crocodiles to history for the light they shed on the transfer of the colony to another site.

To salvage the colony and to eliminate sources of strife the governor fell back upon an old plan. He resolved to remove Sánchez, Dobrizhoffer, and the Concepción braves elsewhere. Now Dobrizhoffer says that it was a full fifteen months from the date of its founding, 1749, when the difficulty over the stolen horses arose. His journey to Santiago del Estero took another five months, May to October, 1750. The crocodiles died after seven months, done to death by a sharp frost, during the journey of twenty-one days occupied in removing the colony westward. Frosts take place in that area in the winter months, May, June and July. The conclusion is that Dobrizhoffer moved to the new site on the Salado River during the winter, possibly June, of 1751.

The physical labor of the Jesuits on the buildings and in the fields came to naught. From the fertile lands on the Inespín River all belongings and herds were transferred to a desperately poor site eighty leagues westward on the Salado River. Here with great effort they put up new dwellings and tilled the soil fruitlessly in a pest-ridden spot. "A long drought" and the sterile ground killed the project just after they had begun to occupy the buildings. The governor and the Indian leaders had sought out another site agreeable to all on the Rio Dulce. The move to this seems to have been made in late December of 1752 or in early 1753, that is in the Chaco summer months after the long drought. The site well down the Rio Dulce toward the Mar Chiquito was more permanent than any of the other thirteen inhabited by the Concepción colonists. To this place went Father Sánchez, who, surviving a thousand perils to his life, at length died at Ravenna in 1805, the last survivor of all the Chaco Jesuit missionaries. Dobrizhoffer parted with this brave man for a new assignment at San Jerónimo.

The Abipón colony of San Jerónimo was very close to the site of the present city of Reconquista, Argentina, nearly two hundred miles north of Santa Fe and some five miles west of the Paraná River. It had been located on the northern shore of the Rio or Arroyo del Rey before the Jesuits decided to take the Indians out of the periodical flood lands to a hill on the southern shore. The land and the wide plain around it, excellent for farming and grazing, was deeded over to the Indian colonists by the Spanish officials in the presence of Father José Cardiel, who thus became the Jesuit founder, even though his place as *cura* in the same year 1748 was soon taken by Father Joseph Brigniel. The soldier-farmers, with the governor at the time of the foundation, had constructed several dwellings, such as only soldier-farmers might construct. They were of straw and mud and were a casual shelter for the missionaries, who had to replace them, since when it rained it "rained harder in the room than out of doors." The settlers across the river and in the cities had promised the customary supply of animals and grain for the support of the colony in payment for the protection it offered, but, as usual, the padres had to scurry to obtain the necessities of life.

Two sources of comfort awaited Dobrizhoffer when he arrived in San Jerónimo early in 1753 for his two-year sojourn. First of these was the pleasant companionship of Brigniel, wise in the Abipón tongue and mild in his handling of his roistering "parishioners." In Dobrizhoffer's history we find high tribute to his teacher and fellow worker, especially as the composer of a grammar, vocabulary, catechism, and group of sermons in Abipón. In imitation of his teacher Dobrizhoffer offers a fifty-page grammar on the language of the Abipón in his second volume, and enjoys some comparative linguistics. Again, Brigniel is lauded as the man who established a long peace between the Abipón and the Spaniards. Undoubtedly, much of what Father Martin later wrote about the customs of the Abipón, much of the history of their wars, was jotted down during his stay with Brigniel.

The other friend was the unforgettable Ychoalay. The missionary makes much of his story of his San Jerónimo days revolve around Ychoalay, in fact makes him loom as the complete picture of the best type of Abipón mind and habit. This leader, though not the chief of the colony, is a native subject well suited to the pen of novelist or dramatist. From his savagery Ychoalay became a ranch hand training horses in Santa Fe on a Spanish estate. He had even been a wagon driver in a caravan to and from Chile. Turning against the Spaniards because of a non-payment of his wages he brought back to the Chaco his hatred together with a very useful knowledge of their traits. Shrewd and capable he had roamed the Chaco a veritable scourge to the whites at the head of his wild raiders. Wavering between complete savagery and civilization he at length listened to the plan to organize a colony in the in-between area around San Jerónimo. His Abipón followed their leader after hearing his pursuasive address. Once Ychoalay was in San Jerónimo the periphery of the Chaco breathed more freely. Dobrizhoffer's pen expresses the wealth of thanks which the Jesuits owed to him, their great protector and defender of the peace, who finally came to outdo the Spaniards in the practice of the Christian virtues of charity and justice. His public baptism was performed before throngs in the city of Santa Fe, while his death brought universal sorrow.

Physical activity filled the daily life of the missionary. At the outset about three hundred Abipón were in the colony, but as time passed many others came to the clearing, lured more by the meat and provender than by religion. The site had to be moved, new dwellings and a chapel had to be constructed, which meant hewing trees and carrying them from distances. Ychoalay with his braves lent much help, yet, at times according to their whims the natives might stand by twitting the fathers at their work on the stockade or in the gardens. The constant excursions of the temperamental natives to no place in particular forced the fathers out either as companions or as searching parties. Whenever they donned their hideous make-up for a war the fathers were left either standing guard, gun in hand, in a distressed state of mind, or were forced out to investigate what mischief might be afoot.

Sometimes this tendency toward perpetual motion could be put to service, if not completely harnessed. Frequent trips were necessary to find both straying Indians and animals, to procure herbs for medicine, to hunt deer for food, to return stolen horses. We have a picture, too, of the padre crossing the brimful Paraná to the supply estate, paddling a skin raft amid the bobbing heads of swimming Abipón, and then returning with a herd of cattle swimming the river under the skillful guidance of the Indians. One day a week was set aside for slaughtering twenty beeves and preparing meat to satisfy the enormous capacity of the colonists for eating.

The unfavorable realities preventing the fathers from converting the Abipón to Christianity were almost as many as the natives. By agreement the natives were under no compulsion to take instruction, hence they clung to their superstitions. Drunkenness, lying, stealing, hate, and revenge ranked high among Chaco "virtues." Unhappy was the brave who did not have an enemy to stalk or to fear. Watching the tribesmen prepare for a battle by drinking brews from the skulls of slain enemies, Spanish or natives, as well as seeing other disgusting ceremonies, called for fortitude of soul and stomach on Dobrizhoffer's part. He had to study carefully all odd customs and Indian attitudes in order to assess the group mentality before attacking specific problems of leading nomads first to community life and next to Christian practices. Teaching even the children and aged was extremely difficult in view of their proximity to Chaco habitudes. The restless forays, the disorganization, were daily offenses to his sense of order.

Patience and tact were the watchwords. Example meant little to the primitive minds essentially irresponsible, and it is to their no small credit that the Jesuits remained at San Jerónimo twenty years and fashioned a Christian village of eight hundred souls out of such obstinate materials. Such spiritual and humanitarian acts as nursing their sick, clothing and feeding the poor, continency, kindness, were to the Indians mysterious odds and ends without character pattern. Morsels of gratitude rarely fell to the padres. The hours spent in healing the wounded or the snake-bitten or the fever-ridden were soon forgotten by the beneficiaries. In fact, the semblance of gratitude would put the fathers on their guard, for the Abipón were least to be feared when they were arrogantly boisterous and most to be feared when docile. Experience schooled the Jesuits in the native tendency to bluster and bluff while being fearful that some enemy might cause them to shed their blood. Among themselves they were not so chary of shedding their blood since they quarrelled with knives, or let quantities to relieve fever, or lost it in tattooing and other primitive surgery.

Dobrizhoffer made good use of his time in San Jerónimo if we are to judge by his descriptions of its vegetable, animal, and human life. Apparently, he had a vacation interlude during the two years, for he tells of receiving the gratitude of a matron of Santa Fe while he was there on a visit. He remembered the date as April 10, 1754. Possibly, this was the time when Ychoalay was baptized. Toward the end of the same year there came a new appointment to the third of the Jesuit colonies among the Abipón, San Fernando y San Francisco. We estimate the time to have been in late November, 1754, for he boarded an old boat to go north on the Paraná, but the floodwaters, which happen in November, December, and January, forced him to land at Santa Lucia across the river, whence he went by horse to Corrientes.

.     .     .

The trouble in the Chaco was caused by some rascally Abipón who one by one had been deserting the colonies of Concepción, San Fernando, and San Jerónimo. These renegades from civilization, banded together with the dregs of the Chaco, made lairs in the woods, whence they sallied forth to plunder the goods of the three colonies. They were a threat to the settlements as well as to boats carrying Paraguayan products. They devised a clever scheme to get protection from the irate Indians and at the same time insure themselves a livelihood. They would ask to have themselves established as a colony and be located at a strategic spot for their raids, and possibly for interceptions of down-river boats. In the guise of converts to a better life their wily representatives appeared before the governor of Asunción with their petition.

Everything was against such a project. The incorrigibility of these Abipón was known. The site chosen was a useless waste, sterile, pest-ridden, and the worst sector of the Chaco for man or beast. Despite the obvious ulterior motives of the renegades, Governor Fontes and Commander Fulgentio de Yegros granted the petition. If the lands and grasses would not support the colony, the settlers would, they promised. Since a padre was needed for the work, the Jesuit Provincial, Nicolás Cartucci, was ordered to supply a missionary.

Cartucci was then residing at Santa Rosa, about 150 miles south of San Joaquín. There Dobrizhoffer had journeyed on business in August, 1763. There he soon received orders to establish the colony. His account leaves it quite clear that the Jesuit superior and the Spanish officials acted in defiance of all common sense and the weighed judgment of all experienced persons. Despite his foreknowledge of failure, Father Martin obeyed his marching orders. He returned to San Joaquín, made his farewells to Guaraní land, then moved west to Asunción, arriving there on August 28, 1763. The town gave him four fine horses as a parting gift.

The little missionary had to wait four months at Asunción before going down the river to his colony. During this time the governor was collecting tithes from the settlers and surrounding farms, in the form of cattle, sheep, horses, and grain. All was given grudgingly; the beasts were few and broken-down. Worse, his four horses were stolen by some Spaniards. The grain was moldy. Three full months elapsed in preparations. On November 24 the expedition started south with a salute from the town's guns. Four hundred farmer-soldiers were divided, some on the three large ships with Dobrizhoffer, Yegros, and Fontes, and others on horseback.

The site of the colony of San Carlos y Rosario was a hundred air-line miles south of Asunción, or roughly double the distance by horse and boat. It was ten miles west of the Paraguay River, opposite the point where the Tibicuary enters the Paraguay from the east; it was on the south side of the Little Salado, in the region called Timbo from the trees there. After waiting in heavy rains for three days on the east bank of the Paraguay, the expeditionaries crossed, then marched inland to Rosario. The whole plain was inundated, the residence of the padre, previously put together of grass, palm branches, and mud, was dissolving in the rains. The soldiers constructed another while Dobrizhoffer fixed up a crude chapel, with a grass floor. The ever present mosquitoes and fear of attack swayed the governor toward a quick departure. He and all the Spaniards took to their boats, leaving Dobrizhoffer alone with the savages.

It would be foolhardy for anyone to attempt to improve on Dobrizhoffer's narrative of his heart-breaking and health-shattering stay in Rosario del Timbó, or to present in other words the vivid drama, the climax of his history of the Abipón. He was there from early December of 1763 until September or October of 1765. The climate is recognized as possibly the hottest in this hemisphere. Mosquito swarms, brackish waters, floods, jaguars, one of which he shot, reptiles, vermin, filled the woods and swamps. He became carpenter, farmer, physician, nurse, and one-man defence of the stockade. All the while he lived in deep loneliness of spirit convinced of the folly of trying to maintain the colony under such hopeless conditions. He had neither Jesuit nor other white companionship. Of two overseers sent by the officials to care for the farm across the river one proved a thief and the other was insane.

His remarkable frankness in both his *Historia* and his letters from the scene will probably prevent his ever becoming what popular opinion in Asunción proclaimed him, "a confessor of the Faith," for he is scathing in his criticism of the niggardly officials, selfish townsmen, Spanish farmer-soldiery, and, no less, of the judgment of his superiors. Moreover, passages describing his personal heroism may be deemed self-gratifying, even though his intentions were to refute charges that he was a coward. His many days without food, his many nights without sleep, his sufferings during a fever, his calloused feet, his arrow-pierced shoulder, his tireless attention to Indians infected with smallpox, his bearing of savage insolences and ingratitude—these he presents as proofs of his courage, but also of the divine help sustaining him.

Major heartaches terminating in disaster came from the proclivities of his Indians. Restless, dissolute, and untractable, they remained obdurate to civilization. The colony stockade was to them only an officially protected lair with no soldiers to exact sanctions for their misconduct. Their thefts of horses stirred up warfare with the Mocoví and Toba, and worst of all made them and Dobrizhoffer enemies of Ychoalay, his erstwhile friend. Guerrilla skirmishes, open assaults, and counter-raids became the order of the day. This raw, animal type of existence left no moment of security day or night. The one restraint, the one fear, was the father's musket and a small swivel cannon, which he presented on occasions to protect his village or had at his side during his night watches.

Accompanying these threats to the existence of the colony came the dread killer, smallpox. From May 14 to November, 1764, it had its way. Dobrizhoffer attended as physician and nurse to three hundred cases, many of them three to twelve miles away from the settlement in the jungles to which they had fled. Apparently, he did well in his role, for only twenty died. One of the deaths occasioned a crisis in Dobrizhoffer's life. A Toba chief, remaining in the colony as a spy after his men had made a raid, became infected. Before his death he had been baptized by the padre. When the Toba heard the news they painted themselves for a revenge assault, highly aroused because they believed the baptismal water brought about the death. They attacked the colony, driving off the cattle, its food supply. The wily Abipón chose the occasion suitable to rush messengers up to Asunción to ask for four hundred Spanish farmer-soldier cavalrymen who with themselves could visit a lasting punishment upon the Toba. And so it was done. After the massacre of the Toba the cavalry under Yegros returned to Asunción, the Abipón to Rosario, bloated with victory and spoils in the form of horses and forty prisoners. They were now insufferably insolent over what they considered their victory, for not a Spanish gun would fire owing to the wet powder.

Dobrizhoffer knew that the Toba and their kin of other tribes would mass for vengeance. He asked for aid in his letters, all to no effect. At regular intervals from August 9, 1764, until January 14, 1765, he despatched messages telling of his plight. Once, five Spanish guards arrived in Rosario, but these quickly found an excuse to leave. As the plague was rather widespread in the Chaco the officials and the Jesuit authorities supposed that none of the tribes would be able to attack; nor did they care to expose themselves to the contagion. At length on the verge of despair he wrote out of his desolation to Father Antonio Miranda, Rector of the Jesuit College at Asunción, as heart-touching letters as one will find in mission annals. In one dated January 6, 1765, he says in part:

> I have been gravely ill repeated times because of the rebelliousness of my Indians, the intolerable heat, and the polluted water. I pass many days without eating, many entire nights without sleeping, many mornings without Mass, and in fine, I do not know how I remain alive; I wish I had a companion who might be witness to what is suffered here . . . Until things change appearances here it is barbarous to allow a sole priest to be exposed in this mournful post.[1]

At the end of the Paraguayan mid-summer, perhaps in late February, 1765, a more violent fever stopped the missionary's pen. After twenty-seven days of this continuous fever, and a return of the tertian fever, he resembled a skeleton. He tells of hearing no words of hope, but rather the reminder from his charges monotonously repeated that he was going to die. Indians brought word of his condition to other colonies. Finally, from Asunción came a Jesuit

---

[1] Guillermo Furlong Cárdiff, *Entre los Abipones del Chaco, Segun Noticias de los Misioneros Jesuitas* (Buenos Aires, 1938), pp. 161–162.

father with twelve soldiers to take over in case Father Martin had died. We gather that this Jesuit was no hero. He arrived eight days after Easter, did everything he could to get Dobrizhoffer on his feet, was happy to leave after a week with the majority of the soldiers, and was in bed for three months on his return to the city. Why the authorities did not get the poor man out of the place is beyond comprehension. Even in October of the preceding year the Provincial, Father Juan Andreu, knew the conditions, but told Dobrizhoffer he was powerless to remedy them. Andreu on his visitation came in the evening of October 6 and did not close his eyes until he left next noon because of mosquitoes and fear of attacks. Father Martin evidently was to be spared for more work.

The long-expected return of the Toba was heralded by many signs, very similar to those used by Indians of our western plains, smoke signals, stealthy approaches by the spies, cries in the night, and horses being driven off by small bands. Four Spanish guards were sent from Asunción, whose fear and stupidity are rather immortalized by Dobrizhoffer. Their deeds in no wise illustrate the legend of Spanish cruelty, and were all soldiers of their ilk the world would forever be rid of wars. More useful in the defense measures were eight Abipón of the colony who for their own unfathomable reasons chose to fight in the stockade.

At four o'clock in the morning of August 2, 1765, when the moon was full and the colony was deep in slumber, six hundred mounted Toba and their various allies rushed the stockade. The Spanish night watchman, awakened from his sleep, and the three other soldiers began to gather their kits for a hasty departure, instead of firing the cannon and muskets. Dobrizhoffer, from this point on, tells an amazing story of his defense of the stockade. Fear or despair gave him courage. With four pistols and a musket he approached the paling of the stockade amid falling arrows. An arrow with five hooks pierced his shoulder. He went into the house where the captain of the guard was reclining and had him twist out the arrow. He returned to the yard with the musket in his left hand, since his right arm was bloody and useless. The enemy was withdrawing, awed by the sight of the weapon. A fleeing Toba was killed by an arrow shot by one of his Abipón. Although the shouting and attacks continued for some hours only himself and an Abipón had been wounded, while a number of the enemy apparently were hit. Two muskets had been fired, one by an Abipón and one at the beginning of the fray by one of the soldiers, who aimed his weapon at the moon!

The account of the battle, written after years of retellings, has the polish of a novel, but it leaves us somewhat surprised at Father Martin's lack of modesty. Definitely, we are disappointed with the Toba type of courage, if we consider that six hundred of them could not take, could not even set fire to the stockade defended by so few men and a little padre with a blunderbuss. Perhaps he and his helpers and later the citizens of Asunción were right in attributing the victory to heavenly aid. A great moral victory had indeed been won. The colony was saved, the Abipón underwent a change of heart toward the fathers. Accustomed to boasting they now had much to boast about; word of the stout defense went abroad in the Chaco. The government and the Jesuit superiors adopted new attitudes toward the desolate mission of Rosario, and there is no telling what the final success of this and the other Abipón missions would have been if the suppression of the Jesuits had not occurred.

On the night of the victory Dobrizhoffer wrote a report to the governor of Asunción. He sent with it the arrow and his bloody shirt sleeve. The Abipón messengers spared no embellishments in their verbal descriptions. Neither did the four soldiers when they arrived. And, be it said, neither did Father Martin when he talked years later to his Viennese audiences. His arm pained exceedingly for some days, but was completely cured in sixteen days with a remedy unthought of in modern pharmaceutics—melted fat of a hen! Two unique problems developed over the event. The ecclesiastics debated his status as martyr or confessor of the

Faith. They argued that the occasion for the attack was his administration of baptism to the Toba chief, therefore he had shed his blood out of hatred of the Faith. But he had not died, and hence could not be called a martyr, but might be called a confessor. The second poser developed when the governor wished to settle a pension upon him as a missionary. He retorted that the missionary's pension could not be given to him but that he could apply for the soldier's pension. He got neither.

## 20

## Eleanor B. Adams

◆◀▶◆

# Jurisdictional Conflict in the Borderlands

*In the New Mexico colony, the effective transfer of jurisdiction from regular clergy to diocesan adminis-tration prescribed in the sixteenth century never took place. Repeated hassles over jurisdiction between the bishops of Durango and the Franciscan friars of New Mexico lasted until the late eighteenth century. The slow advance of the mission program was blamed on the ineffectiveness of the Franciscans. In 1759 the last visitation to colonial New Mexico by a Durango bishop was carried out. His difficulties in asserting authority and his report on conditions among the Indians and the Spanish settlers are the subjects of a distinguished treatise on eighteenth-century New Mex-ico by Eleanor B. Adams, research associate professor of history at the University of New Mexico and editor of the* New Mexico Historical Review.

In the autumn of 1759 Dr. Pedro Tamarón y Romeral, six-teenth bishop of Durango, set forth on the first of a series of episcopal visitations, during which he covered a large part of his vast diocese. According to Bishop Tamarón's

From Eleanor B. Adams, *Bishop Tamarón's Visitation of New Mexico, 1760.* Reprinted by permission of *New Mexico Historical Review* from vol. 28 (1953), pp. 81–114 *passim.*

definition, his see included "the kingdoms of New Vizcaya and New Mexico, with part of New Galicia and the provinces of Sonora, Pimería Alta and Pimería Baja, Ostimuri, Tarahumara Alta and Tarahumara Baja, Chínipas, Sinaloa, Culiacán, the province of Topia and that of Maloya, with the district of the Real del Rosario and the villas of San Sebastián and San Xavier with many towns subordinate to them, all of which comprise what is called Tierra Caliente." [1]

.  .  .

[The bishopric] was far too extensive for effective ecclesiastical control by a single bishop. These circumstances were inevitable at a time when geographical knowledge of much of the area involved was still extremely vague. Indeed, nearly 140 years later when Bishop Tamarón was preparing to make his episcopal visitation, parts of it had not yet been fully explored.

This prelate was quite aware of certain inadequacies in the definition of his see, but he refused to admit any doubt of the validity of his claim to jurisdiction over New Mexico. In this he was following the tradition set by his predecessors, beginning with the first bishop of Durango, Fray Gonzalo de Hermosillo. Nevertheless, the Franciscan Custody of New Mexico had never been entirely willing to submit to the authority of the bishopric of Durango. For many years neither the bishops nor the Franciscans could bring themselves to accept any compromise weakening what they considered their lawful powers. The legal principles involved in this lengthy and bitter controversy over ecclesiastical jurisdiction are far too complicated for discussion here. They were of basic importance, and a final decision in the New Mexico case would necessarily have applied to similar mission areas in charge of religious Orders throughout the

---

[1] P. Tamarón Romeral, *Demostración del vastísimo obispado de la Nueva Vizcaya, 1765* (*Biblioteca histórica mexicana de obras inéditas*, vol. 7), Mexico, 1937, p. 5.

Spanish Empire in America. Undoubtedly this was one reason why the Crown avoided making a definitive interpretation of the royal cédulas, papal bulls, and decrees of the
Church Councils on which the rival ecclesiastical authorities based their claims to jurisdiction.

Missionary activity in New Mexico had been a monopoly
of the Franciscan Order from the start. The friars there
were under the authority of the Franciscan Province of the
Holy Gospel of Mexico. In 1616 or 1617, some years after
the Crown had decided to maintain the unproductive frontier province for the sake of the missions, New Mexico became a custody of the Province of the Holy Gospel and
continued subordinate to the mother province throughout
the colonial period.

To facilitate the work of evangelization in the New
World, soon after the Spanish conquest of Mexico papal
bulls had conceded a number of extraordinary privileges to
the religious Orders. Moreover, in places where there was
no bishop within a reasonable distance, the local missionary
prelates were authorized to exercise quasi-episcopal jurisdiction in certain specified cases. The friars were very jealous
of these privileges and resented any encroachment on them
by the bishops. Although the early concessions were modified by later bulls and decrees of the Councils, the tradition of independence remained strong in remote mission
areas such as New Mexico and resulted in bitter disputes
over jurisdiction.

As has been said, the New Mexico missions did not achieve
provincial status within the Franciscan organization. In the
hierarchy of the Church as a whole, petitions for the creation of a bishopric in New Mexico failed. The first attempt
was made in the 1630's. While the matter was under consideration, there was considerable difference of opinion as
to the advisability of such a step. Fray Alonso de Benavides
expended considerable effort in 1630-1635 in the hope of
attaining this end. The papers he presented in Spain included memorials by Fray Juan de Santander, Commissary General of the Indies, and Fray Francisco de Sosa,

Commissary at Court and Secretary General of the Franciscan Order, supporting the project. The Council of the Indies referred the petition to Don Juan de Solórzano, then fiscal of the Council, for an opinion in 1631. Although Solórzano favored the erection of a bishopric in New Mexico and suggested that the episcopal office should be conferred upon a member of the Franciscan Order, the Council advised the King to make no decision before receiving reports from the Viceroy and the Archbishop of Mexico.

.    .    .

In 1723 Benito Crespo, a former dean of Oaxaca who had taught at Salamanca, became bishop of Durango. He served until 1734, and during these years the controversy between the bishops and the Franciscan Order began in earnest. The case dragged on for many years, and the details are so numerous and complex that even to outline them would require a separate, and lengthy, study. Not only are the legal arguments on which the parties based their conflicting claims to jurisdiction exhaustively presented and considered, but bulky reports on conditions in New Mexico and its missions were made in the interests of the opposing groups. In general, whatever the allegiance of the particular writer, these leave us with a deplorable picture of the state of affairs there in the eighteenth century.

Bishop Crespo started the ball rolling by including the El Paso area in his episcopal visitation in 1725. He had intended to visit interior New Mexico as well, but gave up the idea, so he said, because he had been misinformed about the distance and had made insufficient preparations for the journey. Apparently he was treated with reasonable courtesy on this occasion, and in return he made some conciliatory gestures. He issued a title as vicar and ecclesiastical judge to Fray Salvador López, the vice-custos at El Paso, and his successors *ex officio,* or, failing them, to the guardian of the El Paso mission. He also sent a similar title to the custos, who had left for Santa Fe in haste to avoid meeting the bishop. Undoubtedly the New Mexico Franciscans made no strong protest at this time because the bishop did not insist upon proceeding beyond El Paso. This gave them time to consult their superiors in Mexico City. The latter immediately took up the cause, and in 1728, when Bishop Crespo announced his intention of making a second visitation, to include interior New Mexico, the Commissary General of New Spain, Fray Fernando Alonso González, politely, but very firmly, questioned his right to do so. He also sent a petition to the King, begging him to forbid the Bishop of Durango to molest the kingdom of New Mexico by making a visitation. This petition failed, for a royal cédula of December 7, 1729, gave the bishop permission to visit the New Mexican pueblos and others on the borders of his diocese. As a matter of fact Crespo did not receive this cédula until after he had returned from his visitation of 1730.

If anything, the Franciscan objections strengthened Bishop Crespo's determination to enforce what he considered his rightful episcopal authority. This time, when he arrived in El Paso in July, 1730, he found his Franciscan opponents prepared to show active resistance. The leader of the friars was their custos, Fray Andrés Varo. Both parties stubbornly refused to make any concessions, fearing to prejudice their case in future. So the bishop proceeded to Santa Fe and made the rounds of the mission pueblos, returning to El Paso in September. Father Varo, who had received orders from the Commissary General of New Spain and the Provincial of the Province of the Holy Gospel not to allow the bishop to exercise jurisdiction, did succeed in preventing Crespo from making a formal visitation of the churches, parish records, etc., or publishing edicts. The bishop performed the rite of confirmation in Santa Fe and most of the missions. He also appointed Don Santiago Roibal, a secular priest, as his vicar and ecclesiastical judge at Santa Fe. Roibal was to hold this office for many years, although the legality of his appointment was long in question.

Bishop Crespo had already instituted proceedings to

force the Order to recognize the episcopal jurisdiction of Durango over New Mexico. Although the final decision was deferred again and again, the tendency of the Crown and the viceregal authorities was to authorize the bishops of Durango to use limited episcopal powers in New Mexico pending the outcome of the suit. A viceregal decree of February 17, 1731, revoked Crespo's appointment of Roibal as vicar. By the autumn of 1732 the Crown had received a number of communications from both parties. Father Varo and Father González again protested that the Bishop of Durango had no legal right to jurisdiction in New Mexico. In addition, they renewed the petition of a century before for the erection of a separate bishopric. Bishop Crespo had also been heard from. A royal cédula of October 1, 1732, referred the dispute to the viceroy for a decision. Another of the same date requested the Audiencia of New Spain for information as to whether New Mexico was part of the diocese of Durango. And the Commissary of the Franciscans received orders to provide a sufficient number of competent priests with knowledge of the native languages to serve in the New Mexico missions.

By a decree of July 24, 1733, the viceroy upheld the right of the bishop to exercise diocesan jurisdiction over New Mexico and ordered the Franciscans to present the bulls and privileges on which they based their claim to exemption so that a final decision could be reached after both parties had been heard.

Martín de Elizacoechea, who served as bishop of Durango from 1736 to 1747, continued the suit initiated by his predecessor. He made a visitation of New Mexico in 1737, but we have no details regarding his reception. In December, 1738, the Council of the Indies upheld the viceregal decrees of 1733 permitting the Durangan prelates to make visitations of New Mexico. On the other hand, they ordered the enforcement of the decree of February 17, 1731, which forbade him to leave a vicar and ecclesiastical judge there. The Franciscan Order was to be given every opportunity to present its case to the authorities in New

Spain. The viceroy and audiencia were again ordered to report whether New Mexico was included in the demarcation of the Bishopric of Durango or that of any other dioceses in the vicinity. If not, what was their opinion on the question of erecting a new bishopric? In May, 1739, a royal cédula to the Bishop of Durango informed him that the case had been remitted to the viceroy. It gave him permission to visit New Mexico but revoked his appointment of an ecclesiastical judge.

The case against the New Mexico Franciscans had always rested partly upon derogatory opinions of their administration of the missions. Bishop Crespo had found much to deplore in this respect and made serious charges. Following the old tradition, settlers and provincial officials continued to accuse the friars whenever they found an occasion. For their part, the Franciscans covered reams of paper hotly defending themselves against these attacks.

Before the suit over ecclesiastical jurisdiction initiated by Bishop Crespo had come to any definite conclusion, the internal conflict between the Franciscans and the civil government reached another violent crisis in 1749. Early in that year Fray Andrés Varo, an old and indefatigable warrior in the Franciscan cause, had made reports concerning New Mexican affairs which were presented to the viceroy. Before coming to a decision about Varo's recommendations, the viceroy decided to send Don Juan Antonio de Ornedal y Maza to New Mexico on an official tour of inspection. His account of the conditions he found was highly unfavorable to the missionaries. His charges and the reforms he recommended drew sizzling replies from Varo and other friars, to say nothing of bitter denunciations of the civil government, whose side had been espoused by Ornedal.

.    .    .

The most important evidence that the Bishopric of Durango had continued to keep a foothold in the Custody

of New Mexico is the fact that three secular priests were
serving there when Tamarón came. There were two in
the El Paso area, one of whom held the office of vicar
and ecclesiastical judge, and Don Santiago Roibal still
maintained his precarious title to the same office in
Santa Fe.

Whatever their inner feelings about the bishop and
their dislike for one another, the secular authorities and
the Franciscans joined in receiving the prelate with due
solemnity. When he neared El Paso, Don Manuel de San
Juan, captain of the presidio and chief magistrate, the
custos, Fray Jacobo de Castro, and the vicar went out
to the Río de Santa María to meet him. They even per-
suaded him to spend an extra night in the dangerous
open country so that proper preparations for the ceremonies honoring his entrance to El Paso could be completed. The custos accompanied the bishop to the interior of New Mexico, where he was also received with
every evidence of respect and coöperation. Governor Marín
del Valle sent an escort to meet him at Sandia and came
out to greet him in person shortly before he reached
Santo Domingo. The reception at Santa Fe accorded him
full ritual honors as prelate. To establish his jurisdiction on
a firmer basis, and in the hope of avoiding future litigation, the bishop gave appointments as his vicar to three
Franciscans: to the custos for El Paso, and to the missionaries of Albuquerque and La Cañada for their respective
districts. They were pleased to accept and acknowledged
the clauses in them reserving the episcopal right to make
such appointments at will.

As his itinerary shows, Bishop Tamarón gave himself
no time to rest, but carried out his visitation with the
utmost dispatch. He reached Tomé, the first settlement of
the interior, on May 18. By July 7, when he returned to
Tomé, he had visited all the Spanish settlements and missions as far as Taos, except Zuñi and a few other pueblos
which he was unable to reach because of adverse traveling
conditions. On July 18 he was again at El Paso, ready to

continue his journey through other provinces of his diocese for yet another year.

Even in so short a time, it is improbable that the bitter feelings which were agitating all classes of society in New Mexico can have entirely escaped the notice of a man as observant as Bishop Tamarón, although he did not see fit to discuss them in his official reports of his visitation. He seems to have maintained courteous, if rather distant, relations with the Franciscans and their prelate, whom he never condescends to mention by name. There is no evidence that he was on more intimate terms with Governor Marín del Valle, who was still in office at the time. Apparently he leaned more heavily on information and opinions from Father Santiago Roibal, whom he may have considered a comparatively neutral observer, as well as one who was bound by his own interests to be sincere with the Bishop of Durango. Correspondence he quotes shows that he later kept in touch with New Mexico affairs in spite of his many other serious preoccupations. There are letters from the custos, from Don Santiago Roibal, and from the governors. The fact that he was aware of certain defects in civil administration is evident from some severe remarks he made elsewhere about the *alcaldes mayores* in many parts of his diocese, including New Mexico:

> . . . some poor men whom the governors install as alcaldes mayores, individuals who have not prospered in other office or who have been ruined in trade; or deserters from studies by which they did not profit, who become paper shufflers and swindlers. Such are usually the qualifications of these alcaldes mayores, a career aspired to by useless or ruined men. What are individuals of this kind to do except oppress and squeeze the population in order to eat and to obtain and pay the contribution agreed upon to the one who gave them employment? [2]

---

[2] Tamarón (1937), p. 219.

He devoted most of his criticism and recommendations to two major problems. The first was the fact that the Christianization of the Indians was hardly more than a superficial conformity to a few outward practices which they did not understand or have much interest in. Like other critics of earlier and later times, he believed that one of the chief reasons for the failure to indoctrinate them was the language difficulty. Only a few of the New Mexico Franciscans had ever had sufficient mastery of the native languages to minister to their flocks without the help of interpreters. And although a number of Indians knew some Spanish, their understanding of it was insufficient for them to grasp abstract religious ideas. The friars resented this criticism from outsiders and made many attempts to refute such charges, but the weight of the evidence is overwhelming that there was much truth in this point of view. Among themselves, the more objective missionaries admitted and deplored this handicap in terms as strong as those of their opponents.

Just why they had never been able to improve this situation in nearly two hundred years remains a question. Part of the answer may lie in the character and strong traditional culture of the Indians with whom they had to deal. It must be remembered how few missionaries there were in proportion to the work they were expected to accomplish, and with little or no aid from the lay Spanish population. This led to a very unnatural way of life which may well have affected the ability of many to deal successfully with their charges—the physical and psychological difficulties confronting a lonely man, cut off from normal intercourse with his equals and expected to guide and teach an alien and indifferent, if not hostile, community.

Bishop Tamarón felt that a more determined effort to solve the language problem would provide the most efficacious solution. The records do not indicate that his fervent commands and exhortations to this end succeeded to any great degree. His criticisms of the spiritual state of the Indians struck at the very foundations of the mission system in New Mexico. Certainly they were nothing new, nor do we find anything new or constructive in the inevitable rebuttals. If his recommendations for solving the linguistic problem had been heeded, perhaps they would have brought about some improvement. Little was done, and some fifteen years later a Franciscan visitor was to feel the same distress at finding the Indians still neophytes after so many years of Christian teaching.

Bishop Tamarón was rigid in his assumption of the valid right of the Diocese of Durango to jurisdiction in New Mexico. He believed that more effective control by the bishops would help to remedy matters. He therefore recommended that four Spanish parishes—El Paso, Santa Fe, Albuquerque, and La Cañada—be turned over to the bishop. The secular priests appointed would be vicars and would have sufficient income from obventions and firstfruits to support assistants. This was not the first time such a suggestion had been made, and as always it was resented by the Franciscans. Although the bishops now and again succeeded in introducing secular clergy in a few New Mexico parishes, this innovation seldom lasted long or brought about any real change.

The second major problem which alarmed and disturbed Bishop Tamarón was the ineffective defence against the incursions of hostile Indians. This was a danger which threatened the very life of the frontier provinces as a whole. The bishop had definite ideas about a more successful method of coping with this menace, and in particular he advised greater use of infantry. . . .

A Franciscan copy of the part of Bishop Tamarón's report to the Crown of 1765 pertaining to the Franciscan missions in his diocese is followed by a few remarks worth noting. They are as good an indication as any of what the friars thought of it.

I reflect that in the discourse and comparisons of this report the Lord [Bishop] Tamarón makes specific statements with regard to the missions where the

King gives something to the Province; but where he gives nothing, he makes no note of it, perhaps so that the King may not know of our services. And even when he finds great need of aid, he does not ask for it as he does for the curacies of his secular priests, and even perhaps where there is no need, or at least not the greatest.[3]

---

[3] Biblioteca Nacional de México (Mexico City), leg. 9, no. 59.

# IV

## Arts and Letters

## 21

Pál Kelemen

Colonial Religious Architecture

*Cathedral building during the 300 years of Spanish and Portuguese domination in America was a fascinating dimension of the Church's activities. The intellectual climate was reflected in architecture. Plateresque, Gothic, Baroque, and Rococo describe social characteristics as well as architectural styles. Culture, both religious and secular, was preserved in towering edifices erected as tangible evidence of the spiritual conquest of America as well as of the piety and devotion of the Spanish colonists. Style and construction varied over the continent according to the craftsmen and regional origins of the priest-architects. Pál Kelemen, the Hungarian-born scholar, has written a learned survey of Latin-American colonial art history, providing a description of colonial cathedrals.*

The story of the cathedrals in Latin America reflects the rise and decline of the colonial empires there. The seat of the bishop was established in those towns to which the king's officials attached considerable hope. Often the expectation was fulfilled, and today the cathedral dominates the main plaza of a bustling city. But it also happened that the reasons for choosing the location—geographical,

From *Baroque and Rococo in Latin America* by Pál Kelemen, Dover Publications, Inc., 1967, pp. 24–28, 43–47. Reprinted through the permission of the publisher.

military, or perhaps economic—lost pertinency with the passing of time, and the cathedral now stands on some sleepy square in a shrinking out-of-the-way town.

In sixteenth-century Europe the cathedral was a well-established institution, with both direction and continuity to its program. It had developed out of the Christian civilization of Western Europe and reflected the character of its age; the bishops and their functionaries were integrated into the pattern of the administrative, economic, and social life which made up the complex picture there. But for the bishop who was sent from Spain into the New World in those early decades the situation was without precedent. He came into the primitive beginnings of colonial city life, where he found little of the resplendent ceremony to which he was accustomed in the homeland. When he celebrated Mass, there were no rows of elegant gentlemen—and still fewer noble ladies—before him; splendid vestments were rare, priestly assistants were few, and the music and ecclesiastical vessels were far from later standards.

The community centered about the main plaza; beyond lay dusty plots with, for the most part, a few shacks scattered here and there. Horses and cattle grazed about, and in some places the howling of monkeys and the cry of tropical birds mingled with the ringing of the church bells. In most cases the early church in the New World was a barnlike structure of wood and reeds, with a peaked roof built of timber and thatched. Descriptions and sketches which remain from those days show little that is spectacular, either in magnitude or in design; the notable exceptions include the cathedral of Santo Domingo in the republic of the same name and the "fortress churches" in Mexico.

Yet before the Conquest was a century old, ambitious and spacious buildings had been erected. Sometimes only a handful of ecclesiastics carried through projects the grandeur of which amazes us even today. A bishop's church was an expression of his own eminence, an acclamation of his own renown, and its construction, enlargement, and embellishment were in his power; here he could exercise his authority in making his New World cathedral worthy of comparison with those in the motherland. Where a document connected with the construction of a church survives, the name of the prelate always is mentioned, that of the donor more rarely, and still less frequently—unless the paper be a contract—the names of the artists and craftsmen who actually carried out the work.

For the erection or re-edification of an important building in the Spanish colonies plans were sometimes sent from Spain at the instigation of high ecclesiastical authorities or as a part of the king's contribution; more often, however, they were drawn up in the colonies and were then, theoretically at least, submitted to Spain for approval. Of the nearly four hundred plans of buildings in the Americas and the Philippines which have been published from the material in the Archive of the Indies, in Seville, less than 6 per cent date before 1610. In some instances an architect or sculptor of renown in Spain designed a small-scale model of a church or an altar which could be sent over (Brazil even received dressed stone from Portugal for some of its coastal buildings). More rarely a famous architect or artist came over himself to supervise the erection of some important work. But even then, as was also the case in Europe, the original plan was usually modified considerably in the course of realization. Furthermore, even when a project was laid out by a Spaniard or other European in the colonies, the actual execution lay in the hands of the workmen of the New World. And almost incredible is the number—tens of thousands—of regional churches produced exclusively by local labor in Latin America.

The people of the countryside soon learned their crafts from the traveling carpenters, the *maestro canteros* (master masons), sculptors, painters, and the *ensambladores,* who might best be translated as the co-ordinators or foremen of the project and who might belong to any of the builders' guilds. Books, drawings, etchings, woodcuts, and other reproductions of European art and architecture as well as treatises on the techniques of construction and painting were a continuous source of information and inspiration. Printing, a new craft in Europe, was introduced into the New World as early as 1539, and engravings were reproduced and widely circulated. The market was insatiable.

Labor and building material were available in abundance in the New World. Nearly always some type of stone suitable for the project was close at hand, and the natives in many districts were skilled in the manufacture of adobe bricks and blocks even before the Conquest. Some regions furnished a soft stone, easy to quarry and to carve, which hardened upon exposure to the air, and the magnificent virgin forests provided extremely durable lumber for beams, rafters, and columns. The problem of transporting the material was secondary, for the Indian was accustomed to carrying or, if necessary, rolling incredible weights over incredible distances.

The colonial cathedral is imposing and substantial, built of stone or, more rarely, of brick and nearly always employing masonry vaults. Often it was set on a stepped platform above the level of the plaza and boasted a broad atrium, or open court, before it. This provided a stage, a dramatic setting with the façade of the building as backdrop, for the various ceremonies and colorful processions that enlivened the religious life of the age. Decoration was lavished on this façade, with columns, pilasters, niches, and statues a part of the embellishment. Three entrances were usual and, in the early structures, one tower. In later centuries two towers became customary. These towers not only served as belfries but also buttressed the façade and helped anchor the side walls.

As a rule the interior of the colonial cathedral, like the European, was laid out in three aisles—corresponding to the three doorways in the façade—separated by the pillars or clustered columns which supported the vaulted ceilings. All three might be of the same height, as in the hall-type church, or the center one might be given greater importance by higher vaulting. In certain regions domes were favored, although they were not always placed over the main body of the structure, perhaps because of the ever-present danger from earthquakes. For side chapels, either bays or niche-like recesses were provided.

In the grander buildings, following the scheme common in Spanish cathedrals, the choir occupied part of the central area of the nave; it was enclosed on three sides and faced the main altar, with a relatively narrow space between. The choir stalls, the organs, retables, and pulpit all lent themselves to lavish ornamentation. The side chapels also were ornate, many of them being dedicated by individual families or brotherhoods, who vied with one another in this expression of their devotion.

By the first quarter of the seventeenth century ecclesiastical edifices were adorning the land, a justifiable source of pride to the inhabitants and, for posterity, documents of the artistic and technical ability of colonial craftsmanship. Only a few cathedrals exist today, however, which have not seen major renovations. Earthquakes, lightning, fires, and, later, revolutions took their toll of colonial beauty; finally, the execrable taste of mid-nineteenth century and later, which added little of artistic value, demolished numberless old buildings or "modernized" them in the atrocious French bourgeois style of Napoleon III and the Victorian fashion.

The cathedral of Santo Domingo, on account of its historical priority in the Conquest of the New World, must be given first place among the noteworthy façades there. Not two months after Columbus first set foot on the territory of the New World—the island which he named San Salvador—he discovered a neighboring island which in his correspondence he called Hispaniola, the Spanish Island. Its early capital, Santo Domingo, has seen much turbulence during the centuries.

This was the spot from which the conquest of the American mainland was directed. Here Hernán Cortés arrived at the age of twenty and, as a public scribe, learned the manners and customs of colonial life. From here Velázquez sailed to become the governor of Cuba, intrigant and antagonist of Cortés in the conquest of Mexico. Figures both great and small in the most spectacular drama of the Americas passed through this port: Ojeda to the Tierra Firme of South America (1509), Ponce de León—later famous for his exploration of Florida—to Puerto Rico in the same year, Balboa to the Pacific (1513), and Pizarro to Peru (1522). For about a half-century Santo Domingo was the capital of "all the Indies" known at that time, but its importance waned after the conquest of Mexico, when Havana was made the port of reunion for the fleets, homeward bound with their valuable cargo.

In the first years of occupation the religious needs of the new colony grew so rapidly that Diego Colón, son of the great admiral and governor of the island, complained in a letter to the Spanish king that the very small straw-covered church then being used could not accommodate half the crowd. It was not long before plans for a new structure were taking form.

The cathedral as it stands today was projected as early as 1514, but seemingly the first stone was not laid until 1521 or 1523. In 1541 the building was dedicated, and the tower was begun soon after. The main façade has been attributed to the Spanish architect Rodrigo Gil de Liendo and, more recently, to his successor, Luis de Moya. This façade is clearly Plateresque in style. The double entrance, formed by two arches, is divided by a central column—a scheme that recalls the Gothic, as do also the gable and the round window above the cornice; but in the Gothic the dividing column is generally part of the recessed doorway whereas here it is on a plane with the outer wall. It is of the slim Corinthian type favored in the early Renaissance, and the form is repeated in the fluted columns which flank the two niches in the upper order. The two arches are splayed in a curious manner so that the recessed windows are brought close together, suggesting the eyes of an owl. Bands with typically Plater- esque motifs outline the arches, and smaller patterns of the same type are ingeniously adapted to fit the curved soffits. The frieze, surmounted by a powerful cornice, and the medallions of allegorical figures applied to the face of the abutments, also in the spirit of the Plateresque, ef- fectively frame the portal.

In the lower order, highly fanciful tempietti, each dif- ferent, serve as baldachins for the niches; the figures painted on the wall beneath them replace earlier statuary. In this façade can be observed two characteristics that are peculiar to colonial architecture: components of various styles are blended, and architectural elements which were originally functional are turned to purely decorative uses. The side walls are plain and the few windows compara- tively small. Castellation along the roof is the only orna- mentation. The vaults in the interior rest on round pillars and are of equal height, as in the medieval hall churches.

In this venerable edifice is said to be the tomb of Christopher Columbus. In 1586 the English corsair Francis Drake ransacked the colony and burned its archive; thus with the first building discussed here we encounter that ever-recurring shadow which beclouds colonial art history in Latin America—the lack of archival material.

In South America the region around Tunja, Colombia, likewise attained its greatest importance early in the period of occupation; in 1539 Jiménez de Quesada and his captains subdued this portion of the New World. Be- fore the Conquest the site was the residence of Hunza, chief of the Chibcha people, whose many gold objects, cast in a characteristic wire technique, awakened Spanish greed; here an annual ceremony took place in which gold dust was blown over the glue-covered body of the chief— hence the name El Dorado (the gilded man). But the mineral wealth of gold and opals proved not so great as had been anticipated, and the region was later eclipsed by the richer gold and emerald mines to the west as well as by the fertile agricultural lands of the Cauca Valley further southwest, which had the additional advantage of direct connections with Ecuador and Peru. Tunja's colonial houses, with their adobe walls and stone corners and door-ways, their balconies, their colonnaded patios, and their proud coats of arms, retain today the atmosphere of the sixteenth and seventeenth centuries.

The Tunja cathedral, contracted for in 1569 and erected as the "principal church" of the town, was not raised to its present status until 1880. Fortunately, despite several alterations, it preserves the main features of the façade originally designed in 1598–1600 by the Castilian Bar-tolomé Carrión. The building, constructed of a smooth, reddish stone, is set off from the plaza by a raised atrium. Great restraint was observed by the designer. The heavy entablature serves as a base for the central niche and its accompanying ornamentation. A classical pediment crowns the whole, resting on pilasters which frame the entire central section. Above the entrance is placed in Plateresque tradition a cherub head with spread wings. A great single tower, its square bulk built of a different stone, contrasts with the façade (its upper sections, as well as the balustrade and the central dome, are relatively late additions).

The house . . . called the Atarazana, was a depend-ency of the church, and from its second-story balcony ecclesiastical pronouncements were read to the community.

The interior of Tunja cathedral is on the basilica plan, with a cruciform shape suggested by chapels at the sides. The nave is separated into three aisles by arcades and originally had a wooden ceiling of Mudéjar design. . . .

This cathedral as it stands today, under Tunja's for-bidding skies, between the early colonial mansion and the modern residence of the bishop, is a tangible expression of the frozen Renaissance which characterizes this part of Colombia.

The cathedral of Mexico dominates a vast square which, together with some of the adjoining blocks, was the site of the main Aztec temple and its annexes. After all the pagan edifices had been razed on the order of Cortés, the stones were used to fill in canals to form streets and as building material, usually in foundations and ground walls. The cathedral of Mexico, until recently the largest church building in the Western Hemisphere, is one of the most complex in the stylistic richness of its architecture and art.

But it, too, had its modest predecessor. This early building was started in 1525, and in 1584 it was thoroughly repaired. Usually this structure is referred to disparagingly as small and poor. . . . Its portal is described as in classical style with fluted pilasters. The entrance had a central window and two round ones containing *encerados,* or paintings on waxed cloth, of the Virgin, St. Peter, and St. Paul. In the interior the grillework was gilded, and a beamed ceiling was executed in the Mudéjar manner. Among the artists and craftsmen who carved the plastic decoration, painted the canvases, and worked on the interior, such European names as the Flemish Simon Pereyns and Adrian Suster appear, as well as a number of Spaniards. Mention is repeatedly made also of Indian carpenters, painters, and gilders from Tlatelolco and Texcoco, to whom orders had to be given through interpreters. In the rich inventory of this cathedral, taken in 1588, chalices, ciboriums, monstrances, censers, and communion vessels of fine quality are listed, with vestments of exquisite workmanship and tapestries representing King Saul, Judith and Holofernes, and the history of Solomon among the other valuables. This early structure was in use until 1626, by which time all of its functions and many of its treasures had been transferred to the new building.

The present cathedral was begun close by in 1563. Originally a pretentious plan was proposed, one befitting an archbishop's seat in a capital of great promise. But a realistic view of the situation showed that first consideration must be given to the problem of laying firm foundations on the soft ground of a dry lake bed in an earthquake region. In 1558 a canal was constructed for transporting the materials and five years later the first stone was laid. By 1615 the walls were up only to about half their projected height and eight vaults had been completed. It is recorded that Alonso Pérez de Castañeda (1563–1615) proffered a design, taking into consideration the state of the building as it then was, and that the king had his own architect, Juan Gómez de Mora, look it over and contribute his advice. After considering these suggestions, the authorities in Mexico decided that the work should proceed according to the plans of Claudio de Arciniega and the model made by Juan Miguel de Agüero. Thus Arciniega is considered the "father" of the cathedral of Mexico. In 1656, almost a century after the work was begun, the cathedral was dedicated to the Assumption of the Virgin Mary; the interior was completed in 1667. The towers, however, were not finished until 1791; their huge bell-shaped tops (1786–1793) are the work of José Damián Ortiz de Castro, a native of Coatepec, Veracruz. To Manuel Tolsa are attributed some of the statues on the façade, as well as the design of the lanterned dome, which was completed in 1813.

Standing today at the very heart of a modern city, this cathedral presents a truly majestic appearance. It is a gigantic structure of basalt and gray sandstone, and in it diverse styles of several centuries are blended with a harmony that defies analysis and demonstrates the mellowing effect of time. Although certain details may suggest architectural masterpieces of Europe, in its total effect the building, consisting of divergent components, does not resemble any of them.

.     .     .

Nobler in design, more distinguished in execution, but also suggestive of a palace is the cathedral in Salvador, the capital of Bahia, Brazil. . . . This structure was built by the jesuits between 1652 and 1672 and at one time housed the most important church and college in Brazil; not until the demolition of the old cathedral in 1935 was it elevated to its present rank.

Prior to 1763 Salvador was the capital of the entire Portuguese viceroyalty, but the removal of the seat of government to Rio de Janeiro in that year had little effect on the affluence of the town. It had already grown immensely rich because of its proximity to large sugar plantations and its advantageous commercial situation on a fine harbor. The Jesuits, the first missionaries in Brazil, are closely connected with the development of its colonial art. Their threefold program aimed at the conversion of the natives, general education, and the training of the oncoming priesthood. But they were expelled from Brazil in 1759—eight years earlier than from the Spanish colonies —and their institutions disintegrated rapidly.

The cathedral of Salvador, which stands close to the sidewalk, shows a façade that is far more cosmopolitan than any presented thus far. The lines of the pilasters, with their unobtrusive paneling and subtle emphasis at the corners, extend from the ground to the upper cornice and even beyond into the belfries and the center gable. Here the belfries form an integral part of the façade in an arrangement met frequently also in Central America. The pediments above the openings are broken, but the insertion of a classicizing niche or an obelisk keeps them within the spirit of the late Renaissance. Baroque volutes fill in the space between the gable and the belfries, but they are so untemperamental that they pass almost unnoticed. A coolness of spirit pervades the whole building, in marked contrast to the tropical environment; this is partly explained by the fact that its design leaned heavily for inspiration on Jesuit buildings in Portugal. Eighteenth-century travelers describe the interior as magnificent; its imposing sacristy displayed a painted ceiling, altars and floors of colored marbles, furnishings inlaid with tortoise shell, and walls brilliant with tile pictures.

In Europe no valid claim can be made for a definite Jesuit style, its canons precisely laid down in Rome, and in the Americas there is even less justification for such a statement. The various regions adopted certain stylistic features, according to the exigencies of the time and place and the abilities of the builders, and out of them they created something original. A comparison of the cathedral in Havana, Cuba, with that of Bahia, just discussed, will illuminate that fact. This also was a Jesuit church, begun, as was the other, in the seventeenth century and completed in the eighteenth. It was not elevated to the rank of a cathedral until 1789, more than twenty years after the expulsion of the order from the Spanish colonies, and work on the interior continued into the nineteenth century. Although dedicated to the Virgin of the Immaculate Conception, it is today better known as the church of San Cristóbal, the patron saint of Havana. It was built of native limestone, which has darkened in the damp salty air of tropical hurricanes. Its façade, dating from 1777, shows a decided individuality in design and texture. The columnar sections on either side of the main portal are brought forward obliquely as if hinged near the door. Single, doubled, and even tripled columns are used in effective variety. The niches, pediments, and capitals suggest the late Renaissance, whereas the balustrades and volutes at the sides, the temperamental lines of the cornices, and, above all, the foliated windows, so felicitously placed, are all Baroque. The towers, similar in general design but unlike in proportion, are successfully integrated into the composition.

No two places in the Spanish world could be more different in climate and background than Havana and Potosí, in Bolivia: the one, a major harbor, the gathering place for the fleets of the Indies, prey to the attacks of corsairs, tropical in climate, and with a numerically strong Negro population; the other, remote behind snow-blown passes of the Andes, high on a treeless plateau at an altitude of 13,600 feet, with an overwhelming majority of mestizos and Indians. Yet the cathedral of Potosí shows a certain kinship to that of Havana. But what was rugged and contrasty in Havana appears here in an aerified version; the columns are more slender and the decorative scheme is confined to the portal. The plain expanse of the upper section is enriched with three windows, of which only the center one has the suggestion of a star shape in its framing. The vibrant line of the overhanging scalloped cornice connects the two towers. Their pepperpot shape is set off by the lines of the pilasters, which are carried through to the dome. In contrast to the niches in the Havana church, these are small, and the plastic decoration lies close to the wall.

Potosí reached its apex in 1611, at which time, as one of the most important mining centers of the world, it had 150,000 inhabitants. Its cathedral was erected at the very end of the colonial period, long after the city's most glorious epoch. The first stone was laid in 1809 on the site of an old church, dating from 1573. The Franciscan Manuel Sanauja prepared the plans, the most outstanding figure in Bolivian architecture in this period. It is reported that, disturbed by the rising revolutionary atmosphere about him, he requested permission to return to his home in Arequipa, but the prefect insisted that he remain to complete his work; it was not finished until 1836. For an architect so closely associated with the neoclassic as was Sanauja, the cathedral façade manifests a rare blend of stylistic elements.

At this point the term "espadaña" [will be explained]. It is a Spanish word often used to denote a belfry or a bell-wall in the upper façade. Apparently it is derived from the verb *espadañar*, "to spread the tail feathers," and [here] it is used in a broad sense to define the ornamental extension of the façade above the roof line, a feature that found a most interesting application in Latin America. This architectural member is related to the ornamental gable that masked the peaked roofs of medieval buildings. Later, even in roofs constructed at less steep angles it was retained as a decorative screen—frequently a free-standing wall—and added greatly to the impressiveness of a building.

. . .

These New World cathedrals which outrode the earth-quakes—whether seismic or political—stood at the fulcrum point of the white man's authority. It was intended that they should embody not only the power and dignity of the church but also the might of the mother country. But even in these administrative centers, where the inclination to turn toward or imitate the homeland would be strongest, regional differences sprouted from the beginning.

Numerous factors were responsible for this condition. There was the matter of distance, with the attendant difficulties of sending plans back and forth. In many cases construction was supervised by friars, carpenters, masons, and others who were not professional architects; and labor was recruited from the mestizos and the Indians of the district. Moreover, a building always had to be adapted to local conditions; the possibility of earthquakes, the problem of ground water, the presence or lack of certain materials all led from the very start to modifications of European types. Wethey demonstrates that in Lima and Cuzco the Gothic type of vaulting, with brick, was resorted to early in the seventeenth century not as a matter of style but as a practical solution, for brick construction appeared to withstand the earthquakes most successfully; from there this method spread at even later dates throughout Peru. Proportions of line and bulk were changed of necessity, and towers often had to serve for buttresses as well as for belfries.

It is apparent that different regions solved similar problems differently. Local preferences asserted themselves; for instance, Mexico has a great number of ingeniously constructed domes while Central America, where domes are less frequent, achieved superb lighting in their churches by other means. Out of an immense artistic vocabulary various regions selected their favorite motifs and by applying them with different techniques created new effects.

## 22

## Filoteo Samaniego Salazar

# Colonial Art of Ecuador

*Latin-American art, especially Church art, was en-*
*riched by a fusion of Christian and Indian styles. Na-*
*tive craftsmen often portrayed religion within an in-*
*digenous frame of reference. Painting, statuary, and*
*architecture became "American" because of this mix-*
*ture. A prime example of the delightful hybrid style is*
*seen in Quito in the art of the colonial era. Mr.*
*Filoteo Samaniego Salazar gives a perceptive descrip-*
*tion of the distinctive features of* quiteño *style, its ori-*
*gins and its florescence.*

Only a combination of exceptional circumstances can explain the rapid, spontaneous, and prolific flowering of art that began in Quito early in the sixteenth century, immediately after the Spanish conquest.

Those circumstances came, in a certain sense, to temper the adverse conditions born of the Conquest and of the subsequent violence. It is difficult to conceive of the magnitude of the clash between two totally different civilizations and to foresee the outcome of that clash, since in such encounters one side is bound to lose its men, its traditions and its heritage.

It happened thus in a great part of Hispano-America:

From Filoteo Samaniego Salazar, "Colonial Art of Ecuador,"
*Americas,* vol. 20, no. 6 (1968), pp. 2–8 *passim.* Reprinted by
permission of the Pan American Union.

Cortez in Mexico, Benalcázar and Pizarro in Colombia and Peru, had to pit their tiny forces against thousands of Indians. And when that was not possible, they had to use all kinds of tricks to obtain by astuteness what was otherwise unobtainable.

The result was not always a happy one. Ruin, death and domination were often the residue left by that formidable adventure—and, unfortunately, the extinction of cultures, of customs, of lives as well. Thousands of years of Aztec, Maya, Chibcha, Cara, Inca efforts, whose testaments were the fortresses, the cities and temples, the pre-Columbian ceramics and sculpture, yielded to the conquistadors and their new ideal.

But all was not violence. With the soldier came the friar, absorbed in his missionary passion, and he brought with him the artisan, the master builder, the teacher of singing and writing. And there the great phenomenon of assimilation came about: an artistic people, with millennial traditions behind it, was able in a few years to absorb the teachings of that handful of Flemish, Spanish, and Italian *maestros* who came with the monks. Quito began to build churches and monasteries, to expand an admirable sculpture tradition, to cover retables with paintings and reliefs, to provide private homes with pieces of popular art and, finally, to export art to all Hispano-America, from the Antilles to Buenos Aires, and to Spain itself.

For two hundred and fifty years, from 1550 to 1800, and on into the nineteenth century, the Quito School continued to amaze the world with the constant appearance of painters, carvers, and sculptors who created new temples, new retables, new marvels. Each century proudly exhibited its own artists, its own creators, and its own styles. Quito, for the critics, became the Florence of the New World. And today, in spite of the clandestine and open export of works of art, in spite of the destruction of civil buildings, the ill-advised remodeling of monumental structures, the disoriented growth of the city, Quito is perhaps the largest and most privileged architectural and artistic ensemble in Hispanic America.

There are certain characteristics that must be noted in order to understand *quiteño* art. Above all, it is eminently religious. The first conquistadors—the city's first settlers—devoted themselves to discovery and conquest. For them the cities were, perhaps, only places for brief stays, since they divided their efforts among the founding of the cities, excursions for adventure, and the consolidation of power. On the other hand, the priests stayed in the cities and established there the centers of missionary and educational activity. A true process of technical assistance in all the fields of art, of culture, and of practical crafts grew up around the monasteries, which were located in the cities but had a very extensive area of action. The first New World school of arts and crafts was founded in Quito in 1552, under the direction of two Flemish friars, Jodoko Ricke and Pedro Gosseal. And the second generation of their disciplines, almost all Indians, became the teachers of the arts, music, handicrafts, trades, and Spanish and Quechua grammar. It is not strange, therefore, that throughout this period one important list of illustrious names—the principal artists of the Colony—contains a majority of Indians and mestizos: José Olmos, called Pampite, creator of dramatic Christs; the great retable maker Menacho; Andrés Sánchez Gallque, author of the curious painting called *The Black Ambassadors,* now in Madrid's Museum of the Americas; Manuel Chili, the most famous sculptor of the eighteenth century, known as Caspicara; Gaspar Zangurima, magnificent woodcarver of the nineteenth century.

Colonial *quiteño* art is therefore essentially mestizo. That is, a mixture of Spanish and Indian, out of which comes the essence of New World baroque. Art without shackles or rules, fantastic, abundant, varied, joyful; but also, at times, dramatic; severe, in spite of the gold, and serene, in spite of the passionate concurrence of styles. In the art of Hispanic America converged Flanders and Spain, Italy and Vienna.

In it we meet the Middle Ages, still alive in the spirit of the conquistadors, and the Renaissance, seeking new forms. There are influences from the Orient, left on our shores by the commerce between Spain and China and the Philippines. With them, also, we recognize Mozarabic influences, which were still fresh on the Iberian Peninsula. Here all encountered the old American cultures, with which the baroque spirit was crossed and mingled.

To this unparalleled artistic event the native artisans brought their ancestral skills; most of them left not even the imprint of their names. Passionately they took up the new faith, in part because of a domination that left them no other choice but desperation and defeat. They discovered in the Christian Divinity the sign of an imprecise promise, and to it they gave their efforts, their sweat. Colonial *quiteño* art is of a popular nature. There was no construction of colossal palaces and administrative buildings—in this respect we are unlike Lima and Mexico City; instead, the monumental collective effort was directed toward the temples and religious worship. Some would attribute this phenomenon to a preponderant missionary domination, but that domination—even if it may have been noticeable at times, after 1650—was not present in the preceding century, that is, the first century after the founding of Quito in 1535. The missionary was nourished by his own faith, and his labor was directed exclusively toward the exaltation of that faith. And the people followed, understood, and aided in the impressive artistic work of the Colony, with the new faith as their sole inspiration.

.     .     .

The artists often drew their inspiration from prints, engravings, and paintings from Europe. Composition consequently showed little originality. But the artist was accustomed to apply his own technique, a new landscape, an original color, and of course an admirable ingenuity, especially in the area of popular art. How can the brilliance of the coloring of the paintings by Manuel de Samaniego and Bernardo Rodríguez be argued? How can one deny the misty atmosphere that lingers in Miguel de Santiago's paintings? How can one help being amazed at the Byzantine rigidity of Sánchez Gallque? And in sculpture, is not the movement surprising in Legarda's statues, whose veils are fluttered by an invisible wind? Do not those images of the Indian Caspicara alone justify the existence of the colonial Quito School—with their serene faces and their mantles that transplant the gold and varicolor of chasubles to the surface of the wood? What should one say, finally, of the architectural monuments? Only masterful hands could have planned, constructed and decorated the eight blocks of buildings that make up the Monastery of San Francisco, that Escorial of the Andes, with its enormous plaza, its broad terrace, its church shining like a golden ember, its four cloisters and its orchards and gardens. Only born artists could have allowed the Italians Guerra and Gandolfi and the German Deubler to design the Church of La Compañía and its retables and to adorn its façade with sculpture— covering its monumental naves, its choir, and its altars completely with gold leaf. Only a numerous and select personnel could have been capable of erecting—in a mere two hundred years—churches and cloisters such as Santa Domingo, San Agustín, La Merced, Los Cármenes, and ten other temples and monasteries of great importance.

The Quito School of colonial art, fully justified by its well-known masters and by its anonymous ones, is in both quantity and quality the most important example of Hispano-American baroque art.

## 23

France V. Scholes

# Missionary Scholars in Central America

*Often the scholarly contributions of colonial church-
men to anthropology, linguistics, and history are overshadowed by the mission program and the Church's
philanthropic activities. However, without the missionary chronicles and the ethnohistories of Diego de
Landa, Bernardino de Sahagún, Francisco Clavijero,
Florian Paucke, and others, modern anthropologists
would be helpless in studying cultural change during
the colonial period. Grammars and dictionaries of
the native languages were the result of painstaking
research by competent linguists. Today these manuals
stand up as scholarly contributions to knowledge. In
this selection Professor Scholes assesses the scholarship
of Franciscans in Central America.*

The introduction of Christianity in Central America was a
long and difficult task. From the earliest days of the Spanish
conquest Franciscan missionaries bore their full share of
the burden. In the lands of the Maya from the Gulf of

From France V. Scholes, "Franciscan Missionary Scholars in
Colonial Central America," *The Americas: A Quarterly Review
of Inter-American Cultural History*, 8 (1952), 391–416 *passim*.
Reprinted by permission of the Academy of American Franciscan
History.

Mexico to Honduras, Franciscan activity was centered in two areas, northern Yucatan and the highlands of Guatemala. For many years the Franciscan missions in these areas were united for administrative purposes, until the great distance separating them and the success of the evangelizing program in both the northern and southern districts prompted the creation of separate provinces in 1565: the Province of St. Joseph of Yucatan and the Province of the Most Holy Name of Jesus of Guatemala. Yet the ties that had earlier united them—the ties of history and common effort—were never completely severed. Indeed, the vast expanse of jungle which separated the Franciscan missions in Yucatan from those in Guatemala actually served as a continuing bond of union, a constant challenge, beckoning friars from north and south to complete the spiritual conquest of the Maya country. It was this challenge which first called Fray Antonio Margil de Jesús in his long career as teacher and traveler; from Yucatan came others, who followed the jungle trails to Lake Peten in search of souls to save—and of martyrdom.

While engaged in active and often very arduous missionary work, the Franciscans in Central America also made outstanding contributions to learning. In my opinion, their scholarly activities, especially in linguistic and ethnological studies, constitute in many respects their greatest achievement. The colonial chroniclers of Yucatan and Guatemala record the names of scores of Franciscans who enjoyed local fame for their learning. Many were renowned as Latinists, theologians and canonists. Others, although not so numerous, cultivated the natural sciences, especially mathematics, practical astronomy, botany and medicine. Many of these colonial scholars served as teachers in the Franciscan colleges, or houses of study, in Mérida and Antigua, where they gave instruction to members of the Order preparing for the priesthood; some held the chair of Scotistic theology in the University of San Carlos, established in Guatemala in the last quarter of the seventeenth century.

Many of the sixteenth-century teachers had been educated in Salamanca or in Alcalá de Henares and had abandoned promising careers in Spain to enlist as missionaries in the New World. The thorough instruction in arts and theology provided by these Spanish friars laid the foundation of Franciscan education in America. The fruits of their teaching were harvested in the seventeenth and eighteenth centuries, when Americans won recognition for their learning and achieved high rank in the Church. Scholarly Franciscans, well versed in theology, literature, philosophy and the natural sciences, exerted profound influence on the religious and intellectual life of Central America in colonial times and helped to form the character of culture in the area. Much of their most original and valuable work, however, was in the field of Americanist studies—ethnobotany, history, linguistics and ethnology.

Long ago Samuel Johnson remarked that the voyages of Columbus "gave a new world to European curiosity." From the sixteenth century to the present, all kinds of men have sought to describe and interpret this new world, this new field of experience called America. Colonial and modern writers have made the presses sweat in turning out books on New World themes. In colonial times important contributions to the corpus of Americanist literature were made by leaders of armies, by soldiers in the ranks, by merchants, jurists, frontiersmen, physicians and scientists. A rapid survey of the standard bibliographies will reveal, however, that in Hispanic America the missionary clergy wrote or compiled the greater part of the books now considered to have permanent merit.

The New World was as much of an adventure for the missionary friar as for the soldier at arms. The men in monastic garb who followed the roads and trails in search of spiritual conquest had the same intense curiosity as their lay associates concerning things new and strange, and they were impelled by the same eager desire to describe the scenes, characters and manner of life in the exotic lands where they were sent to labor. From their pens we have many of the classic accounts of discovery and exploration,

aboriginal life and customs, and the history of Spanish enterprise in America.

Some of the Franciscans of Yucatan and Guatemala who
wrote on Americanist themes devoted themselves to describing the luxuriant flora which gave color and variety to their
surroundings. The Indians of Yucatan possessed a rich
botanical lore, especially with reference to the use of native
plants for the treatment of disease, and it is not surprising
that several missionaries in this area compiled extensive dictionaries of Maya names for trees and plants and wrote
treatises on medicinal flora.

History was another field of Americanist studies which
claimed the attention of Franciscan scholars in Central
America. Neither of the two major chroniclers, Fray Diego
López de Cogolludo, of Yucatan, and Fray Francisco Vázquez, of Guatemala, meets modern standards of taste,
method and critical analysis in historical scholarship. Their
works were products of their time and reflect its outlook
and scholarly methods, as well as the particular interests of
the authors. The panegyric character of Vázquez's chapters
on the famous men of his province may be attributed perhaps to the pride of a native son. Cogolludo, an adopted
son of Yucatan and a fairly recent arrival when he first began to write his history, apparently took more interest in
native custom and church-state relations. The important
thing is that both men evidently found their greatest satisfaction in describing New World scenes and events. That is
why their writings still command our interest and why they
are still read and cited.

The linguistic and ethnological studies of the missionary
friars are usually more objective and have greater scholarly
merit in the modern sense. They were prompted by the
realization that the evangelizing program involved very serious problems. Both the missionary prelate and the lonely
friar stationed in an isolated Indian village were conscious
of the difficulties created by new surroundings, new languages and the character of native life, in which religious
belief and ceremonial were all-pervading elements. They

very soon discovered that the movement to introduce a new faith and to extirpate old religious customs led to a grave conflict of loyalties and great searching of heart—that many elements of native religion could not easily be uprooted. If the missionary program was to succeed, it was necessary for the friars to master the Indian tongues and to gain considerable knowledge of native life and psychology. As a result of their efforts to learn, their extraordinary skill in learning, we possess today some of the best works in linguistics and anthropology produced in the New World.

The most important step in the early study of the native tongues in Central America was the writing of these languages phonetically in European script. By doing this the missionary friars enormously simplified their own task and at the same time destroyed the monopoly of learning formerly enjoyed by the native priesthood and nobility. They were responsible for the first great advance in making the Indians of Central America a more literate people, for the new system of writing was taught in the mission schools, where an increasing number of native youths learned to read and write both Spanish and their own language. This made possible the preservation of a vast body of knowledge concerning native history that otherwise would have been lost, for all that we know about pre-conquest history in the Maya area is found in Spanish accounts based on information given by Indians or in the native literature written in European script after the conquest.

The practical purpose of the linguistic studies of the missionary friars is clearly indicated by the character of the first Indian language imprints issued in Mexico. They were chiefly doctrinal tracts designed to provide instruction in the elements of Christian faith and ceremonial practice. With increasing knowledge of the native tongues the friars began to compose collections of sermons which, together with prayers, catechisms and other forms of doctrinal material, came to be known as *Theologiae Indorum*. Modern students of these languages usually pay little attention to these, but the colonial lexicographers found them extremely valuable and drew from them many illustrations. They deserve more serious study today, for here as in the dictionaries are revealed the difficulties encountered by the friars in transferring into native languages the concepts of European thought.

Many problems of this nature were gradually resolved as the friars gained increasing knowledge of the grammatical structure of the Indian languages. For Yucatec Maya three grammars by Franciscans were printed in the colonial period. Their colleagues in Guatemala were not so fortunate, for although we possess more than a dozen grammars in Kiche and Cakchiquel written by or attributed to Franciscans, only one was printed in colonial times.

Because of their academic training and the nature of their profession, the missionary grammarians naturally used a Latin framework for their study of the Indian tongues. This approach has been rather severely criticized by modern linguistic scholars on the ground that the aboriginal languages contain many features which do not follow Latin patterns. The colonial linguists were quite aware of the fundamental differences in structure, but their principal aim was not the scientific study of Indian languages. Their task, in which they were highly successful, was to provide adequate working tools for members of their Orders engaged in the work of evangelization. Yet few modern grammars of the Maya languages are comparable in scope, and they all lean heavily on the colonial texts even when they follow modern analytical methods.

The grammars were supplemented by very extensive dictionaries in which the inexperienced friar could find a wealth of illustrative material for whatever duty he was called upon to perform. From Yucatan we now have four vocabularies compiled by Franciscans in colonial times. For the Guatemala area there are available in this country in original manuscripts or in photographic reproduction at least six dictionaries of Cakchiquel or Kiche, whose authors can be positively identified as Franciscans.

Dr. Johnson has described the lexicographer as "a harmless necessary drudge." If the learned eighteenth-century writer, who had a vast written literature to call upon, in which were recorded centuries of English usage, regarded dictionary-making as drudgery, how much more burdensome and difficult must have been the task of the Franciscan lexicographers of Central America who had no written literature to work with, at least in the beginning.

Nevertheless, as Daniel Brinton pointed out many years ago, the dictionaries of Yucatecan Maya and of the Guatemalan languages bear comparison with European dictionaries of the same period and even surpass them in scope. For example, the Maya-Spanish section of the Motul dictionary of Yucatecan Maya, usually attributed to Fray Antonio de Ciudad Real, who came to Yucatan in 1573, contains at least 17,000 separate entries with hundreds of illustrative phrases.

These Indian language dictionaries also measure up well in terms of modern theories of lexicography. Dr. Johnson's avowed purpose was to establish standards of excellence in English style, and his method was frankly selective:

> I could not visit caverns to learn the miner's language, nor take a voyage to perfect my skill in the dialect of navigation, nor visit the warehouses of merchants, and shops of artificers, to gain the names of wares, tools and operations, of which no mention is found in books; what favorable accident or easy inquiry brought within my reach, has not been neglected; but it had been a hopeless labour to glean up words, by courting living information, and contesting with the sullenness of one, and the roughness of another.[1]

Unlike Johnson, the friars were obliged to court living information if they were to make their dictionaries at all; and their inquiries no doubt were sometimes answered by

---

[1] Samuel Johnson, *A Dictionary of the English Language* (London, 1755), Preface.

sullenness and evasion. Modern students must be extremely grateful that hard-working and conscientious missionaries were willing to glean up words from "the laborious and mercantile part of the people."

A century after Johnson, Archbishop Trench set forth an entirely different theory of what a general dictionary should be and gave the impulse that resulted in the great Oxford New English Dictionary. "A dictionary," he said, "is an inventory of the language"—not merely a selective guide to good usage—and this became the guiding principle of the editors of the Oxford dictionary.[2] In the light of this theory, the work of the colonial lexicographers is very modern, indeed, almost prophetic.

The colonial linguistic studies are of great value to the present-day ethnologist as well as to the linguist, but fortunately our knowledge of Maya ethnology need not depend entirely upon inferences drawn from language. The native literature and extensive treatises by Spaniards constitute the principal colonial sources; and again works by monastic writers have greatest merit.

The friars' accounts were inspired in part by a practical missionary purpose, in part by antiquarian interest. The missionary purpose was set forth by Sahagún in the prologue to his classic account of ancient Mexican life: "The physician cannot successfully apply the proper remedies to the sick without first knowing the humor or cause from which the illness comes."[3] Although Sahagún's thesis was not viewed with sympathy by many of his colleagues, who feared that intensive study of native religion might do more to preserve the memory of pagan customs than to serve a useful missionary purpose, decrees forbidding anyone to write on this subject were never consistently enforced. The study of aboriginal life in all its aspects continued to claim

---

[2] R. C. Trench, "On Some Deficiencies in Our English Dictionaries." A paper read before the Philological Society in 1857.

[3] Bernardino de Sahagún, *Historia General de las cosas de Nueva España* (Mexico, 1938), I, 5.

the attention of missionary scholars and inspired such indispensable ethnological treatises as Fray Diego de Landa's *Relación de las cosas de Yucatán*.

Many of the Franciscan missions in Central America have long been abandoned. Some have fallen into ruin, the victims of earthquake, the ravages of time or neglect. Others have been swallowed up in the jungle forests. But the learning of the men who labored in these missions lives on and commands our admiration today.

# Selected Bibliography

The historical literature on the Roman Catholic Church in colonial Latin America is extensive, but it is generally lacking in depth and balance. The words of Father Antonine Tibesar in *The Americas: A Quarterly Review of Inter-American Cultural History*, Vol. 23 (1967), p. 317, are appropriate:

> Only a person who has tried to write a history of the church in colonial Spanish America can realize the immensity of the task. The pertinent literature is not only enormous in volume but also frequently very difficult to procure because it so often appears in books privately printed and distributed largely among personal friends or in more or less obscure journals of purely local circulation. Once the frustrating task of collecting the material has been satisfactorily completed, the author faces the much more difficult one of evaluation. For, only too often, the pertinent studies are based more on emotion than documents and are frequently so impregnated with nationalistic or even local rivalries that the mythical Gordian knot would at times be a relief for the serious historian of the church in Spanish America.

There was no overall survey of the field until recently when a two-volume work was issued by La Editorial Católica in Madrid: León Lopetegui, S.J., and Félix Zubillaga, S.J., *Historia de la Iglesia en la América Española desde el Descubrimiento hasta comienzos del siglo XIX: México, América Central, Antillas* (1965) and Antonio de Egaña, S.J., *Historia de la Iglesia en la América Española desde el Descubrimiento hasta comienzos del siglo XIX: Hemisferio Sur* (1966). Tibesar's review of these volumes in *The Amer-*

*icas,* Vol. 23 (1967), pp. 317–318, and the review by Troy Floyd in the *Hispanic American Historical Review,* Vol. 47 (1967), pp. 403–404, should be consulted for varying evaluations of the two volumes.

Three excellent short syntheses of the institutional structure and operation of the colonial Church are Clarence Haring, "The Church in America" in *The Spanish Empire in America* (New York, 1952), pp. 179–208; Charles Gibson, "Church" in *Spain in America* (New York, 1966), pp. 68–89; and Bailey W. Diffie, "Religion and Church" in *Latin American Civilization: Colonial Period* (Harrisburg, Pa., 1945), pp. 233–269. Friar Antonine Tibesar, O.F.M., as editor of and contributor to the section on Latin-American Church history in *The New Catholic Encyclopedia,* Vol. VIII, pp. 448–469, has made the most recent and fundamental attempt to present an overview of the colonial Church.

Many fine accounts of royal patronage in America have been published in Spanish, but few have appeared in English. Fortunately, the volume by W. Eugene Shiels, S.J., entitled *King and Church: The Rise and Fall of the Patronato Real* (Chicago, 1961) is one of the best studies of the subject in either language. A study of the organization of bishoprics is provided by Elizabeth W. Loughran in "The First Episcopal Sees in Spanish America," *Hispanic American Historical Review,* Vol. 10 (1930), pp. 167–187. Constantino Bayle's examination of the work of the hierarchy missionary in *El Clero Secular y la evangelización de América* (Madrid, 1950) places priests and bishops in proper perspective in the spiritual conquest. Pedro Leturia's *Relaciones entre la Santa Sede e Hispanoamérica,* 3 vols. (Caracas, 1959–1960), has data on the role of the papacy in the American Church, and the volume by Rafael Gomez Hoyos entitled *La Iglesia de América en las Leyes de Indias* (Madrid, 1961) provides a look at political supervision of the clergy. The history of the Church in the Peruvian viceroyalty can be followed in Rubén Vargas Ugarte's important *Concilios Limenses (1551–*

*1722*), 3 vols. (Lima, 1951–1954). Rómulo D. Carbia's *Historia eclesiástica del Río de la Plata*, 2 vols. (Buenos Aires, 1935), deals fairly with the Argentine Church. As a study of the Church in Brazil, the monumental work of Serafim Leite, *Historia da Companhia de Jesus no Brasil*, 10 vols. (Lisbon and Rio de Janeiro, 1938–1960), is indispensable. Rubén Vargas Ugarte's *Historia de la Iglesia en el Perú*, 3 vols. (Lima, 1953–1961), is more judicious than Mariano Cuevas' *Historia de la Iglesia en México*, 5 vols. (Mexico, 1946–1947), but both are quite valuable.

The missionary clergy and their methods have been studied in more detail than the secular clergy. A sophisticated treatment of some missionary problems is given in Ursula Lamb's "Religious Conflicts in the Conquest of Mexico," *Journal of the History of Ideas*, Vol. 17 (1956), pp. 526–539. All of Lewis Hanke's works bear to some extent on the Church and the Indian; especially valuable are *The First Social Experiments in America: A Study in the Development of Spanish Indian Policy in the Sixteenth Century* (Cambridge, Mass., 1935); *The Spanish Struggle for Justice in the Conquest of America* (Philadelphia, 1949, and in a paperback edition, Boston, 1965); and *Aristotle and the American Indians: A Study of Race Prejudice in the Modern World* (London, 1959). Herbert Eugene Bolton's classic "The Mission as a Frontier Institution in the Spanish Colonies," *American Historical Review*, Vol. 23 (1917–1918), pp. 42–61, tells how missiology was applied in the borderlands of New Spain. Constantino Bayle's "Las misiones, defensa de las fronteras," *Missionalia hispánica*, Vol. 8 (1951), pp. 417–503, deals with the Spanish-Portuguese frontier in South America. Studies of the order clergy and their missionary work abound; the following merit particular mention here: Fernando de Armas Medina, *Cristianización del Perú (1532–1600)* (Seville, 1953); Luis Olivares Molina, *La Provincia Franciscana de Chile de 1553 a 1700 y la Defensa que hizo de los Indios* (Santiago de Chile, 1961); Rubén Vargas Ugarte, *Los Jesuitas del Perú* (Lima,

1941); and Magnus Mörner, *The Political and Economic Activities of the Jesuits in the La Plata Region: The Hapsburg Era* (Stockholm, 1953).

The special privileges allowed the regular clergy during the spiritual conquest are best examined in Pedro Torres, *La Bula Omnimoda de Adriano VI* (Madrid, 1948), and the subsequent conflict between the regular and secular clergy as these privileges were limited or withdrawn can be studied in Robert Ricard, *The Spiritual Conquest of Mexico*, Lesley B. Simpson (tr.) (Berkeley and Los Angeles, 1966); in Arthur Ennis, O.S.A., *Fray Alonso de la Vera Cruz, O.S.A.* (Louvain, Belgium, 1957); and in Robert C. Padden, "The Ordenanza del Patronazgo, 1574: An Interpretative Essay," *The Americas*, Vol. 12 (1956), pp. 333–354. A particularly fine view of the intellectual side of missionary endeavor is presented by John Leddy Phelan in *The Millennial Kingdom of the Franciscans in the New World: A Study of the Writings of Gerónimo de Mendieta* (Berkeley and Los Angeles, 1956). Two studies on the role of foreign clergy in the New World deserve mention: Mary Angela Blankenburg, "German Missionary Writers in Paraguay," *Mid-America: An Historical Review*, Vol. 29 (1947), pp. 122–131, and Otakar Odlazilik, "Czech Missionaries in New Spain," *Hispanic American Historical Review*, Vol. 25 (1945), pp. 428–454.

The Brazilian Church has attracted less attention than its Spanish counterpart in the colonies. Bailey W. Diffie's "The Church in Brazil" in *Latin American Civilization: Colonial Period* (Harrisburg, Pa., 1946), pp. 718–738, is a good survey. For the sixteenth century, a brief work is Alexander Marchant, *From Barter to Slavery: The Economic Relations of Portuguese and Indians in the Settlement of Brazil 1500–1580* (Baltimore, 1942). Three studies by J. Manuel Espinosa are valuable: "Luis de Grã, Mission Builder and Educator of Brazil," *Mid-America*, Vol. 24 (1942), pp. 188–216; "Gouvéia, Jesuit Lawgiver in Brazil," *Mid-America*, Vol. 24 (1942), pp. 26–60; "Fernão Cardim, Jesuit Humanist of Colonial Brazil," *Mid-America*, Vol. 24

(1942), pp. 252–271. Arnold Wiznitzer, *Jews in Colonial Brazil* (New York, 1960), has interesting data on the Brazilian Inquisition, and Charles R. Boxer, *A Great Luso-Brazilian Figure: Padre António Vieira, S.J., 1608–1697* (London, 1957), details the life of this Jesuit who was a friend to Indian and Jew alike. Mathias C. Kiemen, O.F.M., in *The Indian Policy of Portugal in the Amazon Region 1614–1693* (Washington, D.C., 1954) has a good selection of Church material. A convenient source for Vieira and seventeenth-century Brazil is Lewis Hanke, "Vieira and the Crises of Seventeenth-Century Brazil," in *History of Latin American Civilization, Sources and Interpretations: The Colonial Experience* (Boston, 1967), pp. 233–275.

Data on the ecclesiastical history of Peru in the seventeenth and eighteenth centuries can be found in the volumes on municipal government by John Preston Moore, *The Cabildo in Peru Under the Hapsburgs* (Durham, N.C., 1954), and *The Cabildo in Peru Under the Bourbons* (Durham, N.C., 1966). France V. Scholes examines religious-political conflicts in seventeenth-century New Mexico in *Church and State in New Mexico*, 2 vols. (Albuquerque, N.M., 1937–1942). The most quoted source on Church conditions in the late Peruvian viceroyalty is Jorge Juan and Antonio de Ulloa, *Noticias Secretas de América* (London, 1826). The Juan and Ulloa account is taken to task as rhetorical exaggeration by Luis Merino in *Estudio Crítico Sobre las "Noticias Secretas de América" y el Clero Colonial (1720–1765)* (Madrid, 1965). Merino points to the need for serious study of the late colonial Church, its wealth, and its alleged immorality. Mexican data on the eighteenth-century Church comes from Alexander Von Humboldt's *Political Essay on the Kingdom of New Spain*, 4 vols. (London, 1811). Modern studies that investigate Church property are François Chevalier, *Land and Society in Colonial Mexico: The Great Hacienda*, Lesley B. Simpson (tr.) (Berkeley and Los Angeles, 1963), and the introductory sections of Michael B. Costeloe, *Church Wealth in Mexico: 1800–1856* (Cambridge, Mass., 1968). An interesting view of the Mexican Jesuits is provided by Theodore E. Treutlein in "The Economic Regime of the Jesuit Missions in Eighteenth Century Sonora," *Pacific Historical Review*, Vol. 8 (1939), pp. 289–300.

The Bourbon reforms vis-à-vis the Church are examined by Troy S. Floyd in *The Bourbon Reformers and Spanish Civilization* (Boston, 1966). On pages 48–84 Floyd asks whether faith was strengthened or weakened. Perhaps the best short treatment of the expulsion of the Jesuits is that by Magnus Mörner, "The Expulsion of the Jesuits from Spain and Spanish America in 1767 in Light of Eighteenth Century Regalism," *The Americas*, Vol. 23 (1966), pp. 156–164, but the detailed story, along with the most complete bibliography on the expulsion, is to be found in his *The Expulsion of the Jesuits from Latin America* (New York, 1965). Efforts to effect reform in the late colonial era are superbly described by Asunción Lavrín in "Ecclesiastical Reform of Nunneries in New Spain in the Eighteenth Century," *The Americas*, Vol. 22 (1965), pp. 182–203. The techniques for training missionary clergy are studied by Michael B. McCloskey, O.F.M., in *The Formative Years of the Missionary College of Santa Cruz of Querétaro 1683–1733* (Washington, D.C., 1955). Bernard E. Bobb's "The Church in New Spain" in *The Viceregency of Antonio María Bucareli in New Spain 1771–1779* (Austin, Tex., 1962), pp. 33–62, contains similar data. The most illuminating study on the late colonial Church to appear recently is N. M. Farriss, *Crown and Clergy in Colonial Mexico 1759–1821: The Crisis of Ecclesiastical Privilege* (London, 1968). G. Desdevises du Dezert, "L'Eglise espagnole des Indes à la fin du XVIIIe siècle, *Revue hispanique*, Vol. 39 (1917), pp. 112–293, is still a valuable work.

The subject of the Holy Office of the Inquisition in the Spanish Empire is as controversial as that of Church wealth and clerical immorality. Detailed treatment is found in José Toribio Medina's earlier works, *Historia del Tribunal del Santo Oficio de la Inquisición en México* (Mexico, 1954); *Historia del Tribunal de la Inquisición de Lima*

(*1569–1820*), 2 vols. (Santiago de Chile, 1956); and in Henry C. Lea, *The Inquisition in the Spanish Dependencies* (New York, 1922). My own two volumes entitled *Zumárraga and the Mexican Inquisition 1536–1543* (Washington, D.C., 1962) and *The Mexican Inquisition of the Sixteenth Century* (Albuquerque, N.M., 1969) are modern studies stressing social and intellectual history.

Much remains to be written on the intellectual fiber of individual churchmen and ideological continuity and change during three centuries of the colony. Best to study are colonial religious art and architecture. The complete work of George Kubler and Martin Soria, *Art and Architecture in Spain and Portugal and Their American Dominions 1500 to 1800* (Baltimore and London, 1959), is an excellent reference book. Pál Kelemen, *Baroque and Rococo in Latin America*, 2 vols. (New York, 1967), is a good paperback. The definitive work on early Mexico is George Kubler's *Mexican Architecture of the Sixteenth Century*, 2 vols. (New Haven, Conn., 1952), and *The Churches of Mexico 1530–1810* (Berkeley, Calif., 1962) by Joseph Armstrong Baird, Jr., is an indispensable guide. For Peruvian religious art, Harold E. Wethey's *Colonial Architecture and Sculpture in Peru* (Cambridge, Mass., 1949) is the best study. In Spanish a fundamental work is that by Diego Angulo Iñiguez, *Arte Hispanoamericano*, 2 vols. (Barcelona, 1945–1950). An idea of colonial musicology can be obtained from Lota M. Spell, "Music in the Cathedral of Mexico in the Sixteenth Century," *Hispanic American Historical Review*, Vol. 26 (1946), pp. 293–319, and from the sections on church organs in Pál Kelemen's book. The outstanding authority on colonial music is Robert Stevenson; see his *The Music of Peru: Aboriginal and Viceregal Epochs* (Washington, D.C., 1960) and *Music in Aztec and Inca Territory* (Berkeley and Los Angeles, 1968); and "The Bogotá Music Archive," *Journal of the American Musicological Society*, Vol. XV (1962), pp. 292–315.

The foremost authority on colonial education and the universities is John Tate Lanning. His major works include *Academic Culture in the Spanish Colonies* (London and New York, 1940); *The University in the Kingdom of Guatemala* (Ithaca, N.Y., 1955); *The Eighteenth Century Enlightenment in the University of San Carlos de Guatemala* (Ithaca, N.Y., 1956); and "The Church and the Enlightenment in the Universities," *The Americas*, Vol. 15 (1959), pp. 333–350. Two studies on the clergy and anthropological research complement the selections in this Borzoi volume: Ralph L. Roys, "The Franciscan Contribution to Maya Linguistic Research in Yucatan," *The Americas*, Vol. 8 (1952), pp. 417–429, and Elman R. Service, "Indian-European Relations in Colonial Latin America," *American Anthropologist*, Vol. 57 (1957), pp. 411–425.

Readers who wish to go beyond this selected bibliography should consult the *Handbook of Latin American Studies*, 28 vols. (Cambridge, Mass., and Gainesville, Fla., 1936–1968), and four scholarly journals that often include ecclesiastical history: *The Americas: A Quarterly Review of Inter-American Cultural History; Hispanic American Historical Review; Mid-America: An Historical Review; and Revista de la Historia de América.*

# A Note on the Type

The text of this book was set on the Linotype in a type face called Baskerville. The face is a facsimile reproduction of types cast from molds made for John Baskerville (1706–75) from his designs. The punches for the revived Linotype Baskerville were cut under the supervision of the English printer George W. Jones. John Baskerville's original face was one of the forerunners of the type style known as "modern face" to printers—a "modern" of the period A.D. 1800.

Composed, printed, and bound by
The Colonial Press Inc., Clinton, Mass.

# BORZOI BOOKS ON LATIN AMERICA

*Under the General Editorship of Lewis Hanke,*
UNIVERSITY OF MASSACHUSETTS, AMHERST

THE CONFLICT BETWEEN CHURCH AND
STATE IN LATIN AMERICA*
*Edited by* Frederick B. Pike

THE MASTERS AND THE SLAVES (ABRIDGED)*
A STUDY IN THE DEVELOPMENT OF BRAZILIAN CIVILIZATION
By Gilberto Freyre

DO THE AMERICAS HAVE A COMMON HISTORY? *
A CRITIQUE OF THE BOLTON THEORY
*Edited by* Lewis Hanke

AMAZON TOWN
A STUDY OF MAN IN THE TROPICS
*(With a New Epilogue by the Author)*
By Charles Wagley

A VOYAGE TO SOUTH AMERICA (ABRIDGED)*
By Jorge Juan *and* Antonio de Ulloa
*(With an Introduction by Irving A. Leonard)*

AGRARIAN REFORM IN LATIN AMERICA
*Edited by* T. Lynn Smith

THE BANDEIRANTES
THE HISTORICAL ROLE OF THE BRAZILIAN PATHFINDERS
*Edited by* Richard M. Morse

DICTATORSHIP IN SPANISH AMERICA*
*Edited by* Hugh M. Hamill, Jr.

THE ORIGINS OF THE LATIN AMERICAN
REVOLUTIONS, 1808–1826 *
*Edited by* R. A. Humphreys *and* John Lynch

THE EXPULSION OF THE JESUITS FROM
LATIN AMERICA
*Edited by* Magnus Mörner

THE MONROE DOCTRINE *
ITS MODERN SIGNIFICANCE
*Edited by* Donald Marquand Dozer

* *Also available in a hardbound edition*

A DOCUMENTARY HISTORY OF BRAZIL*
*Edited by* E. Bradford Burns

BACKGROUND TO REVOLUTION *
THE DEVELOPMENT OF MODERN CUBA
*Edited by* Robert Freeman Smith

IS THE MEXICAN REVOLUTION DEAD? *
*Edited by* Stanley R. Ross

FOREIGN INVESTMENT IN LATIN AMERICA*
*Edited by* Marvin Bernstein

WHY PERON CAME TO POWER *
*Edited by* Joseph R. Barager

MARXISM IN LATIN AMERICA*
*Edited by* Luis E. Aguilar

A CENTURY OF BRAZILIAN HISTORY SINCE 1865 *
*Edited by* Richard Graham

REVOLUTION IN MEXICO:
YEARS OF UPHEAVAL, 1910–1940 *
*Edited by* James W. Wilkie *and* Albert L. Michaels

INTERVENTION IN LATIN AMERICA*
*Edited by* C. Neale Ronning

THE INDIAN BACKGROUND
OF LATIN AMERICAN HISTORY *
THE MAYA, AZTEC, INCA, AND THEIR PREDECESSORS
*Edited by* Robert Wauchope

NATIONALISM IN LATIN AMERICA*
*Edited by* Samuel L. Baily

FROM RECONQUEST TO EMPIRE *
THE IBERIAN BACKGROUND TO LATIN AMERICAN HISTORY
*Edited by* H. B. Johnson, Jr.

*Also available in a hardbound edition*